NOLLEKENS AND HIS TIMES

Joseph Nollekens, the fashionable and infamous sculptor who worked in London between 1770 and 1823, produced 'bustos' of almost everyone of consequence in his day. Despite his eccentricity and bad manners, sordid appearance and notorious stinginess he numbered people as highly-respected as Johnson, Garrick and Reynolds among his many admirers and friends.

John Thomas Smith, keeper of prints and drawings at the British Museum, distinguished art critic and former pupil of Nollekens, first produced this 'rambling memoir' in 1828, five years after his subject's death. It not only gives a unique portrait of Nollekens himself, but is a mine of information about the topography, sights and sounds of London in its Georgian heyday.

Inviting inevitable comparison with Boswell's *Life of Johnson*, this is a memoir that will delight anyone interested in either our historic or our artistic heritage, or the characters of the past.

John Thomas Smith

Born, in a hackney coach, London	23 June 1766
Died, 22 University Street, London	8 March 1833

Joseph Nollekens

Born, in Dean Street, Soho	11 August 1737
Died, No. 9 Mortimer Street, London, W.C.	23 April 1823

The cover shows 'A Group of Connoisseurs' by Richard Cosway, by courtesy of Townley Hall Art Gallery and Museums, Burnley.

NOLLEKENS AND HIS TIMES

BY JOHN THOMAS SMITH

Introduction by Walter Sichel

CENTURY HUTCHINSON LTD
LONDON MELBOURNE AUCKLAND JOHANNESBURG

First published in 1828

This edition first published in 1986 by Century Hutchinson Ltd Brookmount House, 62–65 Chandos Place, London, WC2N 4NW

Century Hutchinson Publishing Group (Australia) Pty Ltd
PO Box 496, 16–22 Church Street, Hawthorn, Melbourne, Victoria 3122

Century Hutchinson Group (NZ) Ltd
PO Box 40–086, 32–34 View Road, Glenfield, Auckland 10

Century Hutchinson Group (SA) Pty Ltd
PO Box 337, Berglvei 2012, South Africa

ISBN 0 7126 9465 X

Printed in Great Britain by
Richard Clay (The Chaucer Press) Ltd,
Bungay, Suffolk

INTRODUCTION

Nollekens and his Times, by John Thomas Smith, the early pupil and assistant of the great sculptor, and eventually Keeper of the British Museum Prints and Drawings, was published only a few years after the death of the veteran 'little Nolly'. Its interest is at least a triple one. As a portrait it shows a character perhaps the most eccentric of the host which distinguished a century full of such exceptions from its regular surface. As a rambling memoir it stands unrivalled in queer side-lights and side-tracks concerning a large circle of eminent men and women, with as large an orbit of vanished or vanishing places, fashions, and habits. And above all it illustrates even more than Boswell's apotheosis of Dr. Johnson, the countless points of contact which brought all classes to rub shoulders together in an age of an altruism far less paraded than our own. A single instance may sound the keynote. In Covent Garden market, Tom Twigg, an old herbseller of no education, had known and appreciated almost all the wits and celebrities encountered during a long life. With infinite good humour he would retail his poignant recollections. And, further, there was not a house extant or demolished in that region of art, learning, and adventure, in the lore of which he was not versed. Experience had been his schoolmaster and may be said to have taught him more of human beings than all the hand-books of modern enlightenment. Roughly speaking (in both senses of the word), the man's outlook ruled the eighteenth century: the woman's is dominating the twentieth.

One further consideration before we proceed. Without question the author of these two volumes has tinged their pages with an acquired and thinly veiled prejudice against his 'old friend'. If possible, he does exaggerate the mean miserliness of the sculptor and his wife, while, in his later pictures, he often relies on the tattle of servants. The main cause is obvious. Nollekens, who began as a penniless boy, left the greatest fortune ever accumulated by an artist, and Smith, who was one of his executors, with reason expected a substantial legacy. When the will was read a paltry one hundred pounds was all that Smith received out of a total amounting to two hundred thousand pounds —equal, I suppose, to nearly a million in to-day's figures. It was enough to sour a saint.

Joseph Nollekens was born in Dean Street, Soho, on the 11th of August 1737, the second son of Joseph Francis Nollekens, a native of Antwerp, a disciple and copyist of Watteau, who had settled in England. His father was a devout, and the son a nominal, Roman Catholic. In his extreme youth his widowed mother married a Mr. Williams and settled in Wales. The boy was left without any settled education and forced to pick up his living as best he might. No wonder that in later life he retained the vernacular of the commoner people among whom he moved. He was placed with Peter Scheemakers, in Vine Street, a sculptor of repute, and had to rely on his native resources. From his father he derived a money-loving thrift and a talent for art, from his mother next to nothing. The one pursuit outside modelling that engaged him in his earliest youth was bell-ringing in all its departments. His will to succeed was inflexible and it persevered. In 1759—his aim being to visit Rome—the Society of Arts adjudged him a prize of fifteen guineas for the clay model of a figure, in the following year one of £31 10*s*. for a clay bas-relief and ten guineas for a dancing Faun. This was the moment of the exciting discoveries at Pompeii, and classical England was being stirred into a sort of renaissance. Taste and patrons abounded. By 1760 the precocious youth, isolated and brooding, had saved enough to visit Rome. Outside his art, as throughout his career, he was ignorant, perverse, and obstinate. But as an artist—though for him art from the first was a means to fortune—he was a genius. In 1760 at last he repaired to Rome with twenty-one guineas left in his pocket on arrival. This pittance, however, he soon increased by sending over fresh models to the Society of Arts, one, a 'Timocles', being rewarded by as much as fifty guineas. Garrick and Sterne were both visitors at this time, and through the former, who paid him handsomely for a bust-portrait, he obtained a commission from the super-sentimentalist. A cast for this lucky bust was the very one in which, on his return home a decade later, he concealed the lace ruffles which were to bedeck him on his wedding-day. His sojourn in the capital of Art not only enriched him but widened both his clientele and his horizon. Patrons flocked to him, the agents for art-collectors yielded a market for his restorations and even fabrications of antiques—though while he had toiled at Peter Scheemakers, Madame found him so honest that she could trust him to stone the raisins. Yet all this time he lived and worked in semi-squalor, professing to relish the 'cuttings' and scourings on which he subsisted. Much of his time, however, was spent in the open air.

So much had this industrious save-all acquired that in 1770, when his exile ended, he was able to buy and inhabit with unabated parsimony the Mortimer Street corner-house which had belonged to Newton the painter. This house he never exchanged for another, even in prosperity. For over half a century it proved a martyr to his dirt and a witness of his vagaries. Yet the mere dirt was not so rare in those days, even when disguised by finery. Boswell was conspicuous for it, and Nollekens gave him a well-earned snub at the opera when Dr. Johnson's familiar spirit addressed the sculptor with 'How dirty you go!'.

Garrick had given him his 'open-sesame' to distinction, and he soon became what the *Dictionary of National Biography* so well entitles him, The Sir Joshua Reynolds of Sculpture. All Sir Joshua Reynolds' society accepted him—noblemen, as well as authors, artists, and actors. The great Cham himself declared that he could 'chop a head out as well as any of them', continued to pay him visits, and ultimately sat for his bust both in bronze and marble. He never ceased to rally the great sculptor but little man, although Mrs. Thrale assured him 'You'll get nothing by blunting your arrows on such a block'. But there was another reason for Johnson's favour. The lady who bestowed her beauty and fellow-thrift on 'Molly-Nolly', only two years after London saw him again, was one whom the dictating widower had himself wished to marry (or was it her sister, 'Nancy'?) the auburn-haired Mary Welch. One of Dr. Johnson's calls on the married couple casts more light on the real Dr. Johnson than volumes of verbiage. He had conversed for a long time with the sculptor and the dinner hour approached—that hour, as Johnson well knew, was sacred and stinted. Nollekens, who attended 'the great "Cham" to the door', had perforce begged him to stay and share their meal. But Johnson only looked at him with a twinkle in his eye, and then he guffawed 'Bow-wow!' and ambled away. Is not this first-rate?

Despite all the unsavouriness of his open oddities, despite his common accent—he said 'arter' instead of 'after'—and uncommonly common ways, there must have been some human spell which did not repel either Garrick or Goldsmith or Reynolds, or even that fastidious connoisseur and wine merchant, Caleb Whitefoord. The last took him under his wing, and in 1772 the prodigy became a royal academician, and in his own line attained a fame as well as a name second to none. Civic as well as social homage was paid to him, but what are we to think of a man who at those feasts would abstract the very nutmegs from their dish, and then, when the lack of them was noticed as the rack-punch was handed, actually affected to grope for them under the table!

Willy nilly he was led to spend something over his wedding. He was gorgeously attired in purple velvet and wore an elaborately curled wig, over which he must have watched in an era when wigs were ingeniously snatched. His bride outdid his splendour, being robed in an 'expensively brocaded white silk resembling net-work, enriched with small flowers which displayed in the variation of the folds a most delicate shade of pink. . . . The pointed stomacher was exquisitely gimped . . . and at the lower part was a large pin consisting of several diamonds confining an elegant point-lace apron. . . . Her beautiful auburn hair, which she never disguised by the use of powder . . . was, upon this occasion, arranged over a cushion made to fit the head to a considerable height. . . .' A lace-handkerchief 'partly concealed the beauty of her bosom; wherein, confined by a large bow, was a bouquet of rosebuds, the delicate tints of which were imperceptibly blended with the transparency of her complexion, and not a little increased the beauty of a triple row of pearls, tied behind with a narrow white ribbon'. The *coiffure* above described must have been a sort of 'Fontange', which the caricaturists used to parody by sketching a smart fop ascending a short ladder in order to touch the summit. But fashions are as fickle as our climate, and the artistic Mary Moser, afterwards Mrs. Lloyd, in a letter to her predecessor some ten years later, writes: 'Come to London and admire our plumes; we sweep the sky! A Duchess wears six feathers, a lady four, and every milkmaid one at the corner of her cap. . . . Fashion is grown a monster. Pray tell your operator that your hair must measure just three-quarters of a yard from the extremity of one wing to another.' Mary Moser was a close friend of Mrs. Nollekens, as also was the learned Mrs. Carter, Angelica Kauffmann (of whom some scandal is related), and many another contemporary woman of distinction. How is it possible that one so charming as outwardly she was, could have haggled and pared and pinched at home as by common consent she constantly did. She and her husband had two slates hung up in their room on which each scored their daily disbursements, and over them, if this book is to be believed, they stormed like cat and dog, only to be reconciled in a rainbow of caresses. Her cheapenings and chafferings seem to have exceeded even those of her spouse without the excuse which he could plead of boyhood's poverty and inherited instinct. For her father, Mr. Saunders

Welch, the friend of Dr. Johnson and of Henry Fielding, to whose magistracy he succeeded, was a figure of the period. Though educated at the Aylesbury Workhouse he carved out a career and amassed a fortune. Handsome, popular, and courageous, he had tamed the notorious Wilkes and was honoured as an example both of justice and amenity. It is even said that Mary Nollekens was the model of Fielding in some of the touches bestowed on his 'Sophia Western', just as he certainly remembered the mantua-maker, Mrs. Hussey, in *Tom Jones*. One thing, however, should be borne in mind in balancing the many contrasts and incongruities of this extraordinary couple. She had stood for her husband's famous statue of Venus, which made her all the more jealous of the other Venuses of all classes that stepped his way. Indeed the sculptor was most susceptible to feminine beauty, whether that of the May-day milkmaid or of Miss Coleman, who declared that she had posed for Aphrodite's legs when she revisited him in grandeur after a long lapse of years. Many were the hurricanes aroused by his attentions to such saucy wretches. And yet the indignant wife, over whom he watched so tenderly during her last and long-lingering illness, named him in her will 'the sun of my life'. Beauty had not married the Beast in vain.

Nollekens was a master of technique and always emphasized the requisite of so modelling faces as to impart the modulations of fleshiness. I need not here pursue the enormous list of his works. Among his monuments two at least are pre-eminent. The one, that of Goldsmith in Westminster Abbey, the other, that of Pitt at Cambridge. Pitt was the one famous man who refused to sit for him, yet this statue is a masterpiece, and out of it and the many clay casts and other reproductions that he sold in this connexion he made thousands of pounds. He stood on no ceremony with his sitters. He told a lady of title that he wished she was not 'so shy in one eye'. And when George the Third granted him some sittings he is said to have pinched the royal nose with his callipers, and instead of squirting water into the clay to have used a more natural emollient. The king, however, was most good-humoured, and on one occasion when the artist missed an appointment only observed that he had not remembered that the day was a saint's-day—though Nollekens was a lax Roman and actually dismissed his Confessor because he had finished a bottle of wine (a present) and left none for his host. He could seem callous, moreover, when professionally summoned to houses of mourning, and is reported to have said that he liked 'to catch 'em with a tear in the eye', and, notwithstanding, there are marked traces of generous good feeling, as is evidenced by his open-handed kindness to the broken-down artist, old Richardson, which rivals Paul Sandby's to that unfortunate genius Richard Wilson. Also, being childless, he loved children and was liked by them, and he would tell mothers pushing their 'go-carts' how to doctor them. The amusements that he relished most were pantomimes and street-shows, especially Punch and Judy. He had a droll taste, too, for the rougher popular ditties and especially for a curious 'Rat-song'. And he revelled in those popular gardens, which have long since vanished from the scene, such as the two which enlivened Marylebone. With respect to one of these a story is told by Mr. Smith of Handel walking with a Mr. Fountain, when the latter observed of the music, 'This is d—d stuff.' 'It may be d—d stuff, but it is mine', was the rejoinder.

As queer as their master and mistress were the maid-servants, especially the dark, humorous, and faithful Elizabeth Rosina Clements, nicknamed 'Bronze', who remained, and the imperious, alluring 'Mary Fairy', who eventually received warning, maybe for Pepysian reasons. If the household régime was quite so disgusting as it has been painted is it likely that they would have stayed so long in bondage? In truth these and their like must have been the elves, as Nollekens was the Puck rather than the Caliban, of that desert-island or Witches' Kitchen, whichever you choose to call it.

Space compels me to omit much that is salient, and it has been wisely decided to excide the lives of artists, such as Hogarth and Roubilliac, that have no direct bearing on Nollekens. But this volume contains a charming glimpse of the romantic Gainsborough raptly listening, while Nollekens waited, to Colonel Hamilton's music, and requiting each piece played with gifts of his own drawings. Furthermore, the reader must be left to enjoy the many and most interesting curiosities of topography to be found throughout the meanderings of these memories—the ghosts of haunted dwellings. I wonder how many know that old Westminster Bridge was a whispering gallery; how many remember that the wailings of the condemned were audible not only outside Newgate but outside the prison of Westminster? And not every one, perhaps, is aware of the myth that George the Third—a premature child—was born in St. James' Square.

'Read no history', Disraeli, himself an historian, writes in *Contarini Fleming*, 'nothing but biography, for that is life without theory'. Certainly this Life of Nollekens boasts no theory, save, perchance, for the psychologist. Perhaps, after all, he was only the child that hoards pieces of string, for there was something of the child about him. At any rate he is the sole great artist known to me whose genius was wholly confined to his art, and to whom his art was mainly a means and not a medium. Inspiration and ambition were alike strangers to his unfinished organization.

The sole parallel to Nollekens in fiction is the character of the 'bonhomme' Grandet in Balzac's ruthless novel. Yet there is one keen difference between them. Nollekens worshipped the golden calf in his wilderness for its own sake. Grandet secreted wealth that his daughter might inherit it. And he was blessed, too, with a saintly wife and a romantic daughter. But in essentials they tally. It is a mistake to suppose that a miser is necessarily miserable. Nollekens was the reverse, and, if Grandet became unhappy, it was only because Fate baffled him. Unenviable as misers must always be, their name is often a misnomer.

WALTER SICHEL.
1929

CONTENTS

CHAPTER I

CHAPTER II

CHAPTER VI

CHAPTER VII

CHAPTER VIII

CHAPTER IX

CHAPTER XII

CHAPTER XIII

CHAPTER XIV

PREFACE

Mr. Roscoe, who wrote the anonymous Preface to Daulby's Catalogue of Rembrandt's Etchings, says, 'The history of a man of genius is, in general, that of his productions.' In the following memoir, I trust to do more than this; and to delineate the life, not only of a 'man of genius', but of a most eccentric character.

To dispense with the old custom of presenting a letter of introduction, or sending in my card to those to whom I am unknown, would be irregular; the reader, therefore, is informed, that I believe there can be no one better acquainted with the very extraordinary compound habits of the man of whom the following anecdotes are related, than myself; having been his pupil for the space of three years, and intimately known to him for nearly sixty. When I was an infant, he frequently danced me upon his knee.

With regard to pecuniary and domestic habits, I am convinced that England has not produced such a character since the death of Elwes.

The biographer will find, in the second volume of the following work, numerous original anecdotes, and also several valuable letters of contemporary Painters, Sculptors, and Architects of talent, particularly of Fuseli, Flaxman, and Blake, three of the greatest geniuses modern times have produced in this or any other country. Interspersed through the work, are likewise several others not less interesting, but not generally known, of personages of rank and notoriety, who have flourished from the birth of Mr. Nollekens down to the date of this preface.

In the course of these pages, I have acknowledged my obligations to several friends for their kind communications, and here hope for their pardon, for having reserved this place for my best thanks to my friend Mr. Richard Thomson, the well-known author and editor of numerous most interesting works, for his kindness in many instances.

John Thomas Smith,
Keeper of the Prints and Drawings
in the British Museum.

October, 1828.

NOLLEKENS

AND

HIS TIMES

CHAPTER I

Nollekens's pedigree.—His Father frightened by the Rebels in 1745.—Nollekens placed with Scheemakers the Sculptor.—His juvenile passion for tolling bells.—He gains premiums in the Society of Arts.—Leaves England for Rome.—Patronized there by Garrick and Sterne. He gains the Pope's gold medal.—Exposed to assassination by Barry the Painter.—Barry's rude and brutal conduct.—Nollekens a dealer in antiques.—Athenian Stuart.—Nollekens a botcher up of ancient fragments.—A lucky hit.—Successful smuggling by Nollekens.—His filthy mode of living in Rome.—He returns to London, and is chosen a Member of the Royal Academy.—He falls in love and marries.—Figure and wedding-dress of his bride.—Fan-painting.—London antiquities.

THE grandfather of Mr. Nollekens was baptized at Antwerp on the 24th of March 1665; he was a Painter, and made a long residence in England; but subsequently settled at Roanne in France. His son, who is recorded by the various names of Joseph Franciscus, or Cornelius Franciscus, or *Old* Nollekens, as he is called by Walpole,—the father of Joseph, the subject of these Memoirs, was born at Antwerp, in the parish of St. André, on June 10th, 1702; and came to England on May 3rd, 1733, where he married Mary Anne Le Sacq. As he had studied under Watteau, his pictures, in point of subject and scenery, were somewhat similar to those of his master, though in other respects they were far short of that tasteful artist's feeling; however, he supported his family with respectability, and was even enabled to make some provision for the future.

The following anecdote of Nollekens's father was communicated to me by James Northcote, Esq. R.A. who received it from our mutual friend the late eminent Sculptor, Thomas Banks, Esq. R.A. 'Old Nollekens,' observed he, 'was a miserably avaricious man, and during the Rebellion in 1745, his house was marked as belonging to a Roman Catholic, and one in which the mob thought themselves sure of finding money: however, they did not visit him; but the idea had seized him so seriously, that he lingered in a state of alarm until his death, which took place in Dean-street, Soho.' He was buried at Paddington, in 1747, under the names of *Joseph Francis* Nollekens, leaving a wife, by whom he had five children, viz. *John Joseph*, baptized January 29th, 1735; JOSEPH, the subject of the present volume, born and baptized August 11th, 1737, at the Roman Catholic Chapel, in Duke-street, Lincoln's-Inn-fields; *Maria Joanna Sophia*, baptized May 3rd, 1739; *Jacobus*, baptized April 10th, 1741; and *Thomas Charles*, baptized May 31st, 1745.

My late father, Nathaniel Smith, and Joseph Nollekens, were playfellows, and both learned drawing together at Shipley's school, then kept in the Strand, at the eastern corner of Castle-court: the house, now No. 229, is at present occupied by Mr. Helps. What renders the building the more interesting, is, that it was not only in this house that the Society of Arts had its *first* meetings, but it was subsequently inhabited by Rawle the antiquary, and friend of Captain Grose. On the 7th of August, 1755, my father was placed with L. F. Roubiliac; and Joseph, in 1750, being then in his thirteenth year, under the care and instruction of Peter Scheemakers, an eminent Sculptor, at that time residing in Vine-street, Piccadilly, on the site of the present Court of Requests. Joseph's mother subsequently married a Welshman, named Williams, who, some years before her death, conducted her to his native place.

Joseph Nollekens was considered by all the neighbours of Vine-street, as a civil inoffensive lad, but not particularly bright; however, Mrs. Scheemakers used to give this character of him, that 'Joey was so honest, that she could always trust him to stone the raisins.' His love for modelling was the greatest pleasure he possessed, though it is true that he had an idle propensity for bell-tolling, and in that art, for which many allowed him to have a superior talent, he would frequently indulge by running down George-court to St. James's Church, to know how funerals went on. He was well known both to the Sexton and his man, who generally accosted him with the joyous exclamation of 'What, my little Joey, are you come? well, you must toll to-day!' Whenever his master missed him, and the dead-bell was tolling, he knew perfectly well what Joey was at. He had so little pride, that he himself has stated he was often met slowly and steadily creeping along to save the head of a pot of porter, which the maids had sent him for on a washing-day; but, notwithstanding all his childish inclinations, he was, as he grew up, not unmindful of his art, rose early, practised carefully, and, being a true son of his father, passionately fond of money, started for the prizes offered by the Society of Arts; and it gives me infinite pleasure to state, that Joseph Nollekens and Nathaniel Smith, my father, carried off some of the first and best of its premiums, as will appear by the following extracts from the Registrar's books.

'In 1759, to Joseph Nollekens was adjudged the sum of 15*l.* 15*s.* for a model in clay of figures. In 1760, for a model in clay, a bas-relief, 31*l.* 10*s.*; and in the same year, for a model in clay of a dancing Faun, 10*l.* 10*s.*'

As Mr. Nollekens's mother had married a Welshman, who was partial to his native air, he easily persuaded her to accompany him into Wales; and the brothers and sisters of Nollekens being all abroad, he had no motive to induce him to give up an inclination he had long entertained of travelling to see the works of Michel Angelo, and of other great men. He therefore, after having served his friendly master full ten years without the exchange of one unpleasant word, left England for Rome in the year 1760, with all the little property he had acquired. Taking Paris in his way, he called upon his uncle, who, from his questions and cool manner of half opening the street door, appeared to doubt the veracity of his visitor. However, upon his seeing him in possession of a gold watch, he was tempted to ask him in, and slightly pressed him to stay dinner, but this invitation Nollekens, who had felt a chill, proudly declined.

On his arrival at Rome, he found his purse reduced to twenty-one guineas; and, from a dread of want of money, he soon executed a basso-relievo in stone, which he consigned to England, and for which, in 1760, he had the honour of receiving a prize of 10*l.* 10*s.*; but his spirits were exhilarated to a much higher degree in 1762, by the vote of a prize of 52*l.* 10*s.* for a basso-relievo in marble, which is thus clumsily noticed in 'The Public Advertiser', of Tuesday, May 25, 1762.

'At a meeting of the Society of Polite Arts, on Friday last, for a marble basso-relievo, the subject Timocles conducted before Alexander, the premium of fifty guineas was given to Mr. Joseph Nollekens, pupil of Mr. Scheemakers.'

Whilst Mr. Nollekens was at Rome, he was recognized by Mr. Garrick with the familiar exclamation of 'What! let me look at you! are you the little fellow to whom we gave the prizes at the Society of Arts?' 'Yes, Sir,' being the answer, Mr. Garrick invited him to breakfast the next morning, and kindly sat to him for his bust, for which he paid him 12*l*. 12*s*.; and I have not only often heard Mr. Nollekens affirm that the payment was made in 'gold', but that this was the first busto he ever modelled.

Sterne also sat to him when at Rome, and that bust brought him into great notice. With this performance, Nollekens continued to be pleased even to his second childhood, and often mentioned a picture which Dance had made of him leaning upon Sterne's head. During his residence in Italy, he gained the Pope's gold medal for a basso-relievo, which will be noticed in the second volume.

Barry, the Historical-painter, who was extremely intimate with Nollekens at Rome, took the liberty one night, when they were about to leave the English coffee-house, to exchange hats with him; Barry's was edged with lace, and Nollekens's was a very shabby plain one. Upon his returning the hat the next morning, he was requested by Nollekens to let him know why he left him his gold-laced hat, 'Why, to tell you the truth, my dear Joey,' answered Barry, 'I fully expected assassination last night, and I was to have been known by my laced hat.' This villainous transaction, which might have proved fatal to Nollekens, I have often heard him relate; and he generally added, 'It's what the Old Bailey people would call a true bill against Jem.' Although Barry was of an irritable and vindictive spirit, yet, after ridiculing Nollekens upon almost every subject, he would not scruple to accept little acts of kindness at his hand, and then with the greatest brutality insult him. I remember an instance of this kind of conduct, which took place soon after Barry had completed the etchings from his pictures in the Adelphi. Nollekens, who was quite delighted in procuring him subscribers, once called out to him as he entered the studio, 'Well, Jem, I have been very successful for you this week: do you know, I have procured you three more subscribers to your prints from the 'Delphi pictures?' Barry, instead of even returning a smile for his kindness, or thanking him by a nod, flew into a most violent passion; and uttering the coarsest imprecations, of which he possessed a boundless variety, bade him to attend in future to his own business, and not to solicit subscriptions to his works, adding, after the utterance of a most wretched oath, that 'if the nobility wanted his works, they knew where he was to be found, and they might come to him—he wanted no little jack-a-napes to go between him and those who ought to apply at once to the principal'. And all this bombast was because Nollekens had declared his success in the presence of his workmen in the studio. Had he received the information in his parlour, all would have been well, and he would have pocketed the money as he had done frequently before; for to my own knowledge Mr. Nollekens procured him several names of personages of the highest rank.

During Mr. Nollekens's residence at Rome, he purchased among other articles by which he made considerable sums of money, numerous pieces of ancient Roman terracottas, some of exquisite taste, from the labourers who were employed in digging gravel at Porta Latina: they were mostly discovered at the bottom of a dry well, and must evidently have been placed there for security. Nollekens, who bought them for a mere trifle, sold them, upon his arrival in England, to Mr. Townley, and, together with that gentleman's marbles, they have since been purchased by Government for a considerable sum, and are now let into the walls of the first room of the Gallery of Antiquities in the British Museum. In this collection there are many duplicates, which are so precisely like each other, that in all probability, they were pressed from the same mould. Independently of the graceful figures which are introduced in several of these compositions, the foliated ornaments are extremely light and beautiful.

Mr. Nollekens, from the year 1761 to the time he left Rome, consigned several of his productions to his friend *Athenian* Stuart, who had undertaken, in consequence of an early intimacy, to see them placed in the best of the exhibitions in London, which he certainly did until the establishment of the Royal Academy; and then, being inimical to the interests of that respectable body, he departed from his confidential trust, by suffering the works of Nollekens to be exhibited with those of the rejected artists, who were certainly of the most inferior class.

Mr. Nollekens upon his return to England discovered the treachery, and was so highly exasperated with his pretended friend's conduct that he never entirely forgave him, though he certainly now and then visited him.

The patrons of Nollekens, being characters professing taste and possessing wealth, employed him as a very shrewd collector of antique fragments; some of which he bought on his own account; and, after he had dexterously restored them with heads and limbs, he stained them with tobacco-water, and sold them, sometimes by way of favour, for enormous sums.

My old friend, Mr. George Arnald, A.R.A., favoured me with the following anecdote, which he received immediately from Mr. Nollekens, concerning some of these fragments. Jenkins, a notorious dealer in antiques and old pictures, who resided at Rome for that purpose, had been commissioned by Mr. Locke of Norbury Park, to send him any piece of sculpture which he thought might suit him, at a price not exceeding one hundred guineas; but Mr. Locke, immediately upon the receipt of a head of Minerva, which he did not like, sent it back again, paying the carriage and all other expenses.

Nollekens, who was then also a resident in Rome, having purchased a trunk of a Minerva, for fifty pounds, found, upon the return of this head, that its proportion and character accorded with his torso. This discovery induced him to accept an offer made by Jenkins of the head itself; and two hundred and twenty guineas to share the profits. After Nollekens had made it up into a figure, or, what is called by the venders of botched antiques, 'restored it', which he did at the expense of about twenty guineas more for stone and labour, it proved a most fortunate hit, for they sold it for the enormous sum of *one thousand guineas!* and it is now at Newby in Yorkshire. The late celebrated Charles Townley and the late Henry Blundell, Esqrs. were two of his principal customers for antiques. Mr. Nollekens was likewise an indefatigable enquirer after terracottas, executed by the most celebrated Sculptors, Michel Angelo, John di Bologna, Fiamingo, &c. The best of these he reserved for himself until the day of his death. The late Earl of Besborough and the late Lord Selsey were much attached to Mr. Nollekens at this time,—but his greatest friend was the late Lord Yarborough. For that nobleman, he executed many very considerable works in marble, for which he received most liberal and immediate payment. Nollekens, who wished upon all occasions to save every shilling he possibly could, was successful in another manœuvre. He actually succeeded as a smuggler of silk stockings, gloves, and lace; his contrivance was truly ingenious, and perhaps it was the first time that the Custom-house officers had ever been so taken in. His method was this: All his plaster busts being hollow, he stuffed them full of the above articles, and then spread an outside coating of plaster at the back across the shoulders of each, so that the busts appeared like solid casts.[1]

[1] I recollect his pointing to the cast of Sterne, and observing to the late Lord Mansfield, 'There, do you know, that busto, my Lord, held my lace ruffles that I went to Court in when I came from Rome?'

His mode of living when at Rome was most filthy: he had an old woman, who, as he stated, 'did for him', and she was so good a cook, that she would often give him a dish for dinner, which cost him no more than threepence. 'Nearly opposite to my lodgings,' he said, 'there lived a pork-butcher, who put out at his door at the end of the week a plateful of what he called cuttings, bits of skin, bits of gristle, and bits of fat, which he sold for two-pence, and my old lady dished them up with a little pepper, and a little salt; and, with a slice of bread and sometimes a bit of vegetable, I made a very nice dinner.' Whenever good dinners were mentioned, he was sure to say, 'Ay, I never tasted a better dish than my Roman cuttings.'

By this time, the name of Nollekens was pretty well known on the Stock Exchange of London, as a holder to a considerable amount; and he arrived in England time enough to take a lease of the premises, No. 9, Mortimer-street, Cavendish-square, then the property of Francis Milner Newton, Esq. R.A. a very indifferent portrait-painter, who had been a pupil of Marcus Teuscher, an artist of no great talent, but a very good man. Mr. Newton was Muster-Master of England, and generally wore the Windsor uniform, and had also been Secretary to the Royal Academy ever since its establishment.[1]

Mr. Nollekens soon turned the Muster-Master's painting-room into a studio for sculpture, and was honoured with orders from some of the first personages in this country, who sat to him at all hours for their busts; and so fashionable was he in that department of his art, that I have known him to have four sitters in a day! Our Sculptor now exhibited in Pall-Mall with the Royal Academy, to which he presented a fine cast of the Torso, having brought it from Rome for

[1] This office he resigned in 1788, and died at his house at Barton, near Taunton, in August 1794.

that purpose. In 1771[1] the Academicians chose him an Associate, and in the following year elected him R.A. With this election, our late gracious King, when he signed his diploma, declared himself pleased in the most flattering terms of approbation; and immediately honoured him still more by sitting for his bust.

Mr. Nollekens now, for the first time, fell desperately in love. The lady was Mary, the second daughter of Saunders Welch, Esq. the successor, in the magistracy, of his friend Henry Fielding, on his departure for Lisbon. This lady, the pink of precision, bestowed her hand upon him; and they were married at the altar of Mary-le-bone Church, in the presence of her father and sister Anne.[2]

In what style of language their courtship was carried on, how Miss Mary became better acquainted with Master Joseph, or how far he was speech-gifted in Love's soft lispings, I am totally ignorant; but it has been seen that Joseph was a 'thriving wooer'.

Mary's figure was rather too tall, but yet graceful; her eyes were good, and she knew how to play with them; her blooming complexion stood in no need of milk of roses; her nose, I must own, and it was the opinion of Nollekens too, was rather of the shortest; her teeth were small, bespeaking a selfish disposition: indeed the whole of her features were what her husband would sometimes call *scorney*, particularly in

[1] Mr. Nollekens was invited to the funeral of Jonathan Richardson, Jun. son of the author of the work on Painting, and the collector of many fine drawings. He died at his house in Queen-square, and was buried in the ground belonging to the parish, behind the Foundling Hospital, where it is recorded that he departed this life on the 6th of June 1771, aged seventy-seven.

[2] This lady, who will be mentioned hereafter, was mistress of seven languages. She was a Protestant when she attended her sister's marriage, but became a Roman Catholic shortly after her arrival at Rome.

their latter days during their little *fracas:* for be it known, she had no small sprinkling of pride in consequence of a compliment paid her by Dr. Johnson. Her light hair shone in natural and beautiful ringlets down her back to the lower part of her tightly-laced waist; such a shaped waist as her father's friend, Fielding, has given Sophia Western, in his 'Tom Jones'.

This lady's interesting figure, on her wedding-day, was attired in a sacque and petticoat of the most expensive brocaded white silk, resembling net-work, enriched with small flowers; which displayed, in the variation of the folds, a most delicate shade of pink, the uncommon beauty of which was greatly admired. The deep and pointed stomacher was exquisitely gimped and pinked, and at the lower part was a large pin, consisting of several diamonds, confining an elegant point-lace apron; certainly, at that period, rather unfashionable, but, on this happy event, affectionately worn by the lady in memory of her dear mother, who had presented it to her: indeed, Mrs. Nollekens was frequently heard to declare, that she was above 'the fleeting whimsies of depraved elegance'. The sleeves of this dress closely fitted the arm to a little below the elbow, from which hung three point-lace ruffles of great depth: a handkerchief of the same costly texture partly concealed the beauty of her bosom; wherein, confined by a large bow, was a bouquet of rose-buds, the delicate tints of which were imperceptibly blended with the transparency of her complexion, and not a little increased the beauty of a triple row of pearls, tied behind with a narrow white satin ribbon. Her beautiful auburn hair, which she never disguised by the use of powder, according to the fashion of the day, was, upon this occasion, arranged over a cushion made to fit the head to a considerable height, with large round curls on either side; the whole being surmounted by a small cap of point-lace, with plaited flaps, to correspond with the apron and ruffles.[1] Her shoes were composed of the same material as her dress, ornamented with silver spangles and square Bristol buckles, with heels three inches and a half in height; as if she meant to exult in out-topping her little husband, whose head, even when he had his hat on, reached no higher than her shoulder.

Mrs. Nollekens's father was at the expense of her marriage wardrobe, which cost about two hundred pounds: among her dresses, was one of a fashionable Carmelite, a rich purple brown, and another consisted of a lavender-silk, brocaded with white, and enriched with bouquets of carnations, auriculas, and jessamines the size of nature. The bridegroom's dress was a suit of '*Pourpre du Pape*', silk-stockings with broad blue and white stripes, and lace ruffles and frill, the whole of which articles he had brought from Rome. His hair was dressed in curls on either side, with an immense toupée, and finished with a small bag tied as closely as possible to his neck. Mrs. Holt, who was Mrs. Nollekens's domestic companion for many years, and who attended Mr. Nollekens in his last illness, has enabled me to be thus minute in my description of the dresses worn by the bride and bridegroom.

Mrs. Nollekens had a tolerable stock of reading and a pretty good memory, but no sound knowledge of any

[1] In looking at the dresses of former days, it is curious to see in what a short time fashions rise and fall from one extreme to another. In 1760, when the lace apron was declining in favour, a lady wore her hair short and thin, and quite close to her head, with a small flower or ornament on the top of her forehead, nor was it until 1769, that the head-dress was much increased; but in 1772 it became preposterously high, under the most fashionable leader of the day, D. Ritchie, hair-dresser and dentist, then living in Rupert-street, two doors from Coventry-street. In 1777, sacques disappeared, and the large bell-hoops came into fashion.

of the superior accomplishments of her sex, as her youthful studies went very little beyond delicate needle-work and translating French. She never knew the pleasures of a mother, for, in her opinion, 'children were serious responsibilities'; and her matrimonial amusements were not like those of the good Vicar of Wakefield's wife, for I never heard of her making gooseberry wine: a game at cribbage, or a rubber at whist, was her delight; but then she made it a rule never to risk more than sixpence the rub, for which resolution most well-thinking persons will give her credit; but then, when primly seated, she would insist upon the nice precision of the game, as her mother played it, 'according to Hoyle, Mr. *Edward* Hoyle'.[1] In this way of passing time, for she knew nothing of drawing or painting, she would now and then, when at home, coax her *Nolly* to join her; but rarely suffered him to touch a card when they were visiting, on account of his playing so ill, that he was sure to lose.

It gives me the highest gratification to observe, that painting is now considered so essential a branch of polite education, that many persons who are distinguished both for elegance and fashion, are never more delighted than when they are engaged in its interesting pursuits. When Mrs. Nollekens was a girl, Goupy, her father's intimate friend, was considered the most eminent of the fan-painters; and so fashionable was fan-painting at that time, that the family of Athenian Stuart placed him as a pupil to that artist, conceiving that by so doing they had made his fortune. Stuart's genius, however, in a short time soared to the pinnacle of fame by flying to Athens for those inestimable treasures which will immortalize his name, notwith standing Hogarth's satire upon the publication of his

[1] Mrs. Nollekens recollected that Hoyle, the author of a treatise on the game of Whist, was buried at Mary-le-bone, August 23d, 1769, and that he was ninety years old when he died.

first volume; for indeed we have not now a student who speaks of Stuart without the honourable surname of 'Athenian'.

Some years before I had any connexion with Mr. Nollekens as an instructor, my intercourse with him was frequent, notwithstanding the disparity of our ages; and he has often taken me to walk with him in various parts of London, when he seemed to feel a pleasure in pointing out curious vestiges and alterations to my notice, as well as in showing me some remarkable sights of the time. Perhaps these communications gave the first impetus to that love for metropolitan antiquities, which I entertained so early, and which, even now, continues unabated. His recollections of many of the places we visited, often furnished me with curious and interesting pictures of London as it appeared in his own youth; and several of the most singular of them I have ventured to introduce into these anecdotes.

CHAPTER II

Execution of Sixteen-string Jack.—Model of the King's state-coach.—Sir Nathaniel Dance Holland.—Tradesmen's signs sometimes painted by eminent Artists.—Costly one of Shakespeare exposed for sale.—Ignatius Sancho.—Mortimer the Painter and Mr. Payne Knight.—Duke of Monmouth's house in Soho.—Mary-le-bone basin and gardens, and Cockney-ladle.—Fruit-gardens in Gower-street.—Commencement of my own acquaintance with Nollekens.—His servant Bronze.—Hudson's sale of Prints, and anecdote of Sir J. Reynolds.—Nollekens's recollections of London.—Athenian Stuart.—Col. King.—Residents of rank in Soho.—Streets visible at one point.—Nollekens's first Print and subsequent collection.—Recollections of his mother.—Farthing-posts and early newspapers.—Characteristics of Mrs. Nollekens.—Dr. Johnson's bust by Nollekens.—His odd conduct to his sisters.—His parsimonious habits.—His monument for Dr. Goldsmith.

I REMEMBER well, when I was in my eighth year, Mr. Nollekens calling at my father's house in Great Portland-street, and taking me to Oxford-road to see the notorious Jack Rann, commonly called 'Sixteen-string Jack', go to Tyburn to be hanged for robbing Dr. William Bell, in Gunnersbury-lane, of his watch and eighteen-pence in money; for which he received sentence of death on Tuesday the 26th of October 1774. The criminal was dressed in a pea-green coat, with an immense nosegay in the button-holes, which had been presented to him at St. Sepulchre's steps; and his nankin small-clothes, we were told, were tied at each knee with sixteen strings. After he had passed, and Mr. Nollekens was leading me home by the hand, I recollect his stooping down to me, and observing, in a low tone of voice, 'Tom, now, my little man, if my father-in-law, Mr. Justice Welch, had been High-constable, we could have walked by the side of the cart all the way to Tyburn.' I also remember, one Sunday morning, going with my father and Mr. Nollekens to see the studio and workshop of the late Joseph Wilton, Esq. R.A. father of the present Lady Chambers, and friend of Barretti. Wilton, on his return from his travels, brought Capitsoldi and Cipriani to this country. Mr. Wilton's studio stood on the south side of Queen Anne-street East, now called Foley-place, upon the site of five houses, Nos. 22, 23,[1] 24, 25, and 26; in the house, No. 27, at the corner of Portland-street, Mr. Wilton resided for many years. We viewed his works, and the model of King George the Third's state-coach, a most beautiful little toy, exquisitely adorned with ornaments, modelled in wax by Capitsoldi and Voyers, the panels being painted in water-colours by Cipriani. The designs consisted of figures and historical emblems, and Cipriani also painted the same subjects upon the coach itself; but he was not the first eminent artist who had thus adorned a carriage, or even painted a sign. The old royal state-coach was purchased by the City of London; the panels of which were repainted by Dance, afterwards Sir Nathaniel Dance Holland, Bart. who was the painter of that most admirable whole-length picture of Garrick in Richard III. now in the front drawing-room of Sir Watkin Williams Wynn, Bart. in his town mansion, St. James's-square.

Mr. Smirke, the celebrated artist, also served his time under a Herald-painter, of the name of Bromley, who died lately in Queen-street, Lincoln's-Inn-fields.

George Morland painted a sign of a White Lion, for a public-house at Paddington.

Monamy, the famous Marine-painter, decorated a carriage for the gallant and unfortunate Admiral Byng, with ships and naval trophies; and he also painted a portrait of Admiral Vernon's ship, for a famous public-house of the day, well-known by the

[1] No. 23 was the residence of Edmund Malone, Esq. the well-known Editor of Shakspeare.

sign of the 'Porto Bello', remaining until recently, within a few doors north of the church in St. Martin's-lane. After the battle of Culloden, most of the old signs of military and naval victors gave way to the head of Duke William: and Horace Walpole has noticed this change in his thirteenth letter to Mr. Conway, dated April the 16th, 1747.

'I was,' says that elegant author, 'yesterday out of town, and the very signs, as I passed through the villages, made me make very quaint reflections on the mortality of fame and popularity. I observed how the Duke's head had succeeded almost universally to Admiral Vernon's, as his had left but few traces of the Duke of Ormond's. I pondered these things in my heart, and said unto myself, surely all glory is but as a sign!'

Clarkson, the Portrait-painter, was originally a coach-panel and sign-painter; and he executed that most elaborate one of Shakspeare,[1] which formerly hung across the street at the north-east corner of Little Russel-street, in Drury-lane: the late Mr. Thomas Grignon informed me, that he had often heard his father say, that this sign cost five hundred pounds! In my boyish days it was for many years exposed for sale for a very trifling sum, at a broker's-shop, in Lower Brook-street, Grosvenor-square. The late Mr. Crace, of Great Queen-street, assured me that it was in his early days a thing that country people would stand and gaze at, and that that corner of the street was hardly passable.

Charles Catton, Esq. R.A. was also, in early life, a coach and sign-painter: he painted a lion as a sign for his friend Wright, a famous coach-maker, at that time living in Long Acre. This picture, though it has weathered many a storm, is still visible at the coach-maker's, on the west side of Well-street, Oxford-street.

[1] Edwards has erroneously given Wale the credit of this sign.

Baker, a famous Flower-painter, decorated coach-panels with borders and wreaths of flowers; and he made a most splendid display of his taste on the panels of the coach of the famous Doctor Ward, who enjoyed almost the whole practice of his profession, after he had so successfully set the sprained thumb of King George the Second. Richard Wilson, the landscape-painter, once condescended to paint a sign of the 'Three Logger Heads', for the house so called, near the spot where he died.

In June 1780, Mr. Nollekens took me to the house of Ignatius Sancho,[1] who kept a grocer's, or rather chandler's shop, at No. 20, Charles-street, Westminster: a house still standing at the south-west corner of Crown Court. Mr. Nollekens having recollected that he had promised him a cast of his friend Sterne's bust, I had the honour of carrying it; and as we pushed the wicket door, a little tinkling bell, the usual appendage to such shops, announced its opening: we drank tea with Sancho and his black lady, who was seated, when we entered, in the corner of the shop, chopping sugar, surrounded by her little 'Sanchonets'. Sancho, knowing Mr. Nollekens to be a loyal man, said to him, 'I am sure you will be pleased to hear that Lord George Gordon is taken, and that a party of the guards is now escorting him in an old ramshackled coach to the Tower.' Nollekens said not a word, and poor Sancho either did not know, or not

[1] An extraordinary literary character, a negro, who was born on board a slave-ship in 1729. He was patronized by the Duke of Montague, who made him his butler, and left him a legacy and an annuity at his death, when he took the shop above-mentioned. In his leisure hours he indulged his taste for music, painting, and literature; which procured him the acquaintance of several persons of distinction. He was the author of some pieces of poetry, and a tract on the Theory of Music; and his letters, with his life, by Jekyll, were published after his death, for the benefit of his family.

recollect, that he was addressing a Papist. I can also remember Sancho's visiting Mr. Nollekens's studio; he spake well of art, and gave the following anecdote of the late Richard Payne Knight and Mortimer the Painter, with the latter of whom he was extremely intimate. Mr. Knight happening to call upon Mortimer at his house in Church-court, Covent Garden, expressed his uneasiness at the melancholy mood in which he found him. 'Why, Sir,' observed Mortimer, 'I have many noble and generous friends, it is true; but of all my patrons, I don't know one whom I could now ask to purchase an hundred guineas' worth of drawings of me, and I am at this moment seriously in want of that sum.' 'Well, then,' observed Mr. Knight, 'bring as many sketches as you would part with for that sum to me to-morrow, and dine with me.' This he did, and enjoyed his bottle. Mr. Knight gave him two hundred guineas, which he insisted the drawings were worth; and on this splendid reception, Mortimer, who was no starter, took so much wine, that the next morning he knew not how he got home. About twelve o'clock at noon, his bedside was visited by the late 'Memory Cooke', who, after hearing him curse his stupidity in losing his two hundred guineas, produced the bag! 'Here, my good fellow!' cried Cooke, 'here is your money. Fortunately you knocked me up, and emptied your pockets on my table, after which I procured a coach and sent you home.'

Ignatius Sancho died December 14th, 1780, at his house already mentioned, and was buried in the Broadway, Westminster.

Mr. Nollekens, on his way to the Roman Catholic chapel in Duke-street, Lincoln's Inn-fields, where he was christened, stopped to show me the dilapidations of the Duke of Monmouth's house in Soho Square. It was on the south side, and occupied the site of the houses which now stand in Bateman's buildings; and though the workmen were employed in pulling it down, we ventured to go in. The gate entrance was of massive iron work supported by stone piers, surmounted by the crest of the owner of the house; and within the gates there was a spacious court-yard for carriages. The hall was ascended by steps. There were eight rooms on the ground floor: the principal one was a dining-room towards the south, the carved and gilt panels of which had contained whole-length pictures. At the corners of the ornamented ceiling, which was of plaster, and over the chimney-piece, the Duke of Monmouth's arms were displayed.

From a window, we descended into a paved yard, surrounded by a red brick wall with heavy stone copings, which was, to the best of my recollection, full twenty-five feet in height. The staircase was of oak, the steps very low, and the landing-places were tesselated with woods of light and dark colours, similar to those now remaining on the staircase of Lord Russell's house, late Lowe's Hotel, Covent Garden, and in several rooms of the British Museum.

As we ascended, I remember Mr. Nollekens noticing the busts of Seneca, Caracalla, Trajan, Adrian, and several others, upon ornamented brackets. The principal room on the first floor, which had not been disturbed by the workmen, was lined with blue satin, superbly decorated with pheasants and other birds in gold. The chimney-piece was richly ornamented with fruit and foliage, similar to the carvings which surround the altar of St. James's Church, Piccadilly, so beautifully executed by Grinling Gibbons. In the centre over this chimney-piece, within a wreath of oak leaves, there was a circular recess which evidently had been designed for the reception of a bust. The beads of the panels of the brown window shutters, which were very lofty, were gilt; and the piers between the windows, from stains upon the silk, had probably been filled with looking-glasses. The scaffolding, ladders, and numerous workmen, rendered it too dangerous for us to go higher, or see more of this most interesting house.

My father had, however, made a drawing of the external front of it, which I engraved for my first work, entitled *Antiquities of London*, which has been noticed by Mr. Pennant in his valuable and entertaining anecdotes of the metropolis.

One Sunday morning Mr. Nollekens took me to see the boys bathe in Mary-le-bone basin. As we were going, our attention was engaged by the beadles of the parish seizing the clothes of the lads who had gone into the small pond called 'Cockney-ladle', supplied with water by an arm which looked like a ladle from the basin: this Cockney-ladle stood on the north of Portland Chapel, very near the spot now occupied by Mr. Booth, the Bookseller in Duke-street. The basin,—which was a very large, circular, and deep pond, fatal to many an inexperienced youth,—was farther in the fields on the site of part of Portland-Place and Mansfield-street.[1] The Orchestra of Mary-le-bone Gardens,

[1] A small portion of the pond denominated 'The-Six-and Thirty' still remains on the west side of the once-intended Carmarthen-square, at the end of Upper Gower-street, nearly opposite to the house in which I now reside. A part of the town, until very lately, so perfectly healthy and free from the London smoke, that at No. 33, in Gower-street,—a house till within these few years inhabited by the late Col. Sutherland, well known at print-auctions, as well as to portrait-collectors, as a most extensive embellisher of Clarendon's History of his Own Times,—grapes were ripened by the sun in the open air at the back-parlour window.

Lord Eldon often speaks of the fine fruit of Gower-street, which his Lordship enjoyed when he lived in the house now No. 42; indeed, he has also spoken in open Court of the sad effect the smoke of London had upon his garden in Gower-street. A still more extraordinary fact is, that even so late as the year 1800, William Bentham, Esq. of No. 6, Upper Gower-street, (a gentleman whose well-before which I have listened with my grandmother to hear Tommy Lowe sing, stood upon the site of the house now No. 17, in Devonshire-place, and very near where Mr. Fountain's Boarding-school[1] stood, nearly opposite to the old Church, still standing in High-street.

Upon the death of my Mother, in 1779, Mr. Nollekens, upon seeing some of my attempts in wax-modelling, kindly invited me into his studio. At that time my Father was his principal assistant, and there I was employed in making drawings from his models of monuments, assisting in casting, and finally, though in a very unimportant degree, and with the humblest talent, in carving; but I must state, that I was entirely supported by my father, and I do now *most solemnly* declare, that, from the hour of my first seeing Mr. Nollekens, till the time of his death, I never received, either directly or indirectly, the slightest remuneration from him, though whilst I was with him I have often stood to him as a model. Indeed, the only present he ever made me, was three boxes of what *had been* black chalk, which he brought from Florence; but it was so grey and rotten, that it would not bear cutting, and was therefore worth nothing. This he knew, upon asking me how I liked it; and his answer was, 'Well, never mind, I shall give you cause

chosen collection of English Topography is unquestionably the most select and perfect of any formed within my memory,) had nearly twenty-five dozen of the finest-looking and most delicious nectarines, all fit for the table, gathered from three completely exposed trees; and even since that time, the same garden, of the same gentleman, has produced the richest-flavoured celery in the greatest abundance.

[1] Mr. Fountain, who succeeded Mr. De la Place in this school, was once walking with Handel round Mary-le-bone Gardens, and, upon hearing music which he could not understand, observed to Handel, 'This is d—d stuff!'—'It may be d—d stuff, but it is mine,' rejoined Handel.

to remember me in a better way.' My being often closeted with him as his model, assisting him in casting, &c. gave me frequent opportunities of seeing and hearing much, particularly of his domestic habits, and the observations made by his sitters and visitors, who were persons of learning, rank, or beauty. As I have sometimes diverted my friends with a good-humoured imitation of Mr. and Mrs. Nollekens, I shall occasionally insert a few of their dialogues, which have either fallen under my own notice, or were related to me by their old servant, Elizabeth Rosina Clements. She was a woman possessing a considerable share of drollery; and from her complexion being of a chesnut-brown colour, somewhat tinctured with olive, she acquired from the shopkeepers, particularly those of Oxford-market, the nickname of '*Black Bet*'; but from the artists the more classical appellation of '*Bronze*', under which she will hereafter be mentioned. Indeed, she might very well call to mind the expression of Petrarch, who describes his female servant as being 'brown as a Libyan desert, and dry as a mummy'.

Langford, who was the most fashionable auctioneer of his day, occupied the rooms in Covent Garden, now held by Messrs. Robins; in the largest of which he sold that truly valuable collection of prints and drawings, accumulated by Thomas Hudson,[1] the master of Sir Joshua Reynolds, and the most celebrated Portrait-painter of his time. Though no very great artist, Hudson showed considerable ambition and taste in his selection of the best specimens of art for his portfolios, particularly in the productions of the Dutch Schools. The choice impressions which he had accumulated from the plates of Rembrandt, and his various and numerous drawings also from the hand of that wonderful master, would lead us to conclude him to have been his greatest favourite; indeed, so extensive

[1] Thomas Hudson died in 1779, aged seventy-eight.

and precious were they, that, I am informed, any ten collections united would not have equalled his either in merit or in number.

At this sale, Mr. Nollekens was a constant attendant, and he generally took me with him. I recollect Sir Joshua Reynolds,—who was present one evening, when a drawing was knocked down to his pupil and agent, Mr. Score,—after he had expatiated upon the extraordinary powers of Rembrandt, assuring a gentleman with whom he was conversing, that the effect which pleased him most in all his own pictures, was that displayed in the one of Lord Ligonier on horseback, of which there is an engraving by Fisher; the chiaro-'scuro of which he conceived from a rude wood-cut upon a halfpenny ballad, which he purchased from the wall of St. Anne's Church in Princes-street.

Another time, as we were going to view the same curious collection, Mr. Nollekens stopped at the corner of Rathbone-place, and observed that, when he was a little boy, his mother often took him to the top of that street to walk by the side of a long pond, near a windmill, which then stood on the site of the chapel in Charlotte-street; and that a halfpenny was paid by every person at a hatch belonging to the miller, for the privilege of walking in his grounds. He also told me, that his mother took him through another halfpenny-hatch in the fields between Oxford-road and Grosvenor-square, the north side of which was then building. When we got to the brewhouse between Rathbone-place and the end of Tottenham-court-road, he said, he recollected thirteen large and fine walnut-trees, standing on the north side of the highway, between what was then vulgarly called Hanover-yard, afterwards Hanway-yard, and now Hanway-street, and the Castle Inn beyond the Star Brewery.

I remember going with Mr. Nollekens to see his *old*

friend Athenian Stuart, though he had treated him so scurvily. Stuart lived on the south side of Leicester-fields; he had built a large room at the back of his house, in which were several of his drawings, particularly those he had made for a continuation of his work; they were in body colours, and in style resembled those of Marco Ricci. His parlour, where we remained until a shower of rain was over, was decorated with some of Hogarth's most popular prints; and upon a fire-screen he had pasted an impression of the plate called the 'Periwigs'; a print which Mr. Stuart always showed his visitors, as Hogarth's satire upon his first volume of *Athenian Antiquities*. Mr. Stuart, though short, was not a fat, but rather a heavy-looking, man, and his face declared him to be fond of what is called friendly society. In his later days he regularly frequented a public-house on the north side of Leicester-fields, of the sign of the Feathers, which then stood upon the site of part of the ground of Mr. Burford's Panorama; and of these friendly meetings he would frequently endeavour to persuade Nollekens to become a member.

When we had left Mr. Stuart's house, Mr. Nollekens pointed out the one in St. Martin's-street that had been inhabited by Sir Isaac Newton, which he said was then occupied by his friend Doctor Burney, who was visited by all the learned personages of the day. I have been favoured with a curious anecdote of Doctor Burney and Mr. Nollekens, by my friend Lieut.-Col. Phillips, one of the two surviving gentlemen who went round the world with Captain Cook, which the reader will find in a subsequent page.

Whilst we were once standing at the end of Rathbone-place waiting for a coach—for Mr. Nollekens now and then indulged in a *shilling* fare, particularly when he was going into the city to purchase stock, or to the Royal Academy, when he was chosen Visitor, —he said, pointing to the house east of the Undertaker's, now No. 23,—'There lived Colonel King,[1] one of my father's oldest friends; he was a very great collector of all sorts of singular things; and had a very curious old shield which belonged to the famous Dr. Woodward,[2] who was intimately acquainted with the great Sir Christopher Wren. Colonel King was very good-natured to me and my brothers, and whenever my father used to take us to drink coffee with him, we had our three-cornered-silver-laced hats on; so we had on Sundays, when we used to go into St. James's Park, with our ruffles and canes; I remember it very well.' When we had entered Soho-square, among many other remarks, he said, that when he was a little boy, and lived in Dean-street, where he was born, at the house now No. 28, there were no fewer than four Ambassadors lived in that Square; and that at that time it was the most fashionable place for the nobility.[3] He also told me that Baptiste, the famous Flower-painter, with whom he said his father was extremely intimate, lived and died in the corner house, pointing

[1] Colonel Richard King died in 1767, in his eighty-fourth year. He was visited by Pope and other celebrated men, and was executor to Doctor Woodward.

[2] This shield, which is now in the British Museum, has been erroneously attributed to Benvenuto Cellini. It is certainly of the time of Henry the Eighth, but of very coarse and inferior workmanship. I find by a letter, in the fourth volume of Biographical Adversaria, in the British Museum, that the Doctor's shield sold at the sale of Col. King, to whom he had bequeathed it, for the sum of forty pounds.

[3] It appears from the books of the Parish of St. Anne, which I have frequently searched, that between the years 1708 and 1772, the following persons of rank had inhabited Soho-square; viz. Lord Berkley, Lord Byron, Lord Carlisle, Lord Grimstone, Lord Howard, Lord Leicester, Sir Thomas Mansel, Lord Macclesfield, Lord Morpeth, Lord Nottingham, Lord Onslow, Lord Peterborough, Lord Pierrepoint, Lord Pigot, Sir Cloudesley Shovel, and several Ambassadors.

to the one now No. 18. 'And do you know,' added he, 'that I have often stood for hours together, to see the water run out of the jugs of the old river-gods, into the basin in the middle of the Square; but,' he continued, 'the water never would run out of their jugs, but when the windmill was going round at the top of Rathbone-place.'[1]

When we arrived at the French 'Change, Nollekens exclaimed, 'There, Tom, stand here, and you will see the entrances of nine streets; my mother showed them to me. There, stand just there, and don't turn your head, only your eyes;' placing me, with both his hands upon my shoulders, at about fifteen feet from Grafton-street, nearly in the centre of Moor-street. 'There, now look to the left, is not there Monmouth-street? now let your eye run along over the way to the first opening, that's Great White Lion-street; well, now bring your eye back to the opposite street in front of you, that's Little Earl-street. Throw your eye over the Seven Dials, and you'll see Queen-street, and Earl-street; well, now look on the right of Little Earl-street, and you will see Tower-street: well, now stand still, mind, don't move, bring your eye back towards you, and turn it a little to the right, and you will see West-street; bring it nearer to the right, and there's Grafton-street; and then, look down at your toes, and you'll find yourself standing in Moor-street.'

He also made me his companion in his Sunday-evening walks, as he of later years did Joseph Bonomi; a truly deserving youth, to whom it was generally supposed that he would have left a considerable part of his immense property, from his long-continued attachment to him from his birth; but he, however, as well as many other real friends, was disappointed.

[1] This windmill stood upon the site of Percy Chapel, in Charlotte-street, and the spring, which supplied the long pond before it, now remains in the cellar of Elisha, a Brick-layer, behind the Chapel.

In one of our amusing perambulations, he stopped opposite to a public-house in Vine-street, Piccadilly, very near the house formerly occupied by his master, Scheemakers, and said, 'There, Tom, stand just there; now, mind what I am going to tell, and listen to it; it was in that very house, over the way, I got the first print I ever possessed in my life.'

This was an impression of Pesné's engraving of the Death of Eudamidas, after a picture painted by Nicholas Poussin; and the way in which Nollekens became possessed of this print was both cunning and curious. He knew that the landlord of the public-house, with whom he frequently held conversations as to bell-tolling, had sailed and fought with Admiral Vernon, and knowing, also, that he could purchase of another bell-tolling friend a large engraving of the Siege of Porto Bello, for the small sum of one shilling, as it was the size of Poussin's print, he ventured to propose an exchange. To this proposition, the landlord made no objection, nor did his wife; so away little Joey posted to his friend, who was a broker, living in Great Brewer-street, parted with his shilling, and, on the next washing-day, when Mrs. Scheemakers requested him, as the maids were busy, to go for the porter, he took Porto Bello under his arm, with as much joy as the old Admiral received the enemy's colours, and obtained the print which he had so often looked at with so longing an eye; afterwards, when he became possessed of wealth, he formed a very capital collection of Poussin's works;[1] from which it has been

[1] This interesting and truly valuable collection of Poussin's prints, to which Mr. Nollekens had added even in his most feeble and childish state, was sold, after his death, by Mr. Evans, of Pall Mall; together with many other fine engravings, which Mr. Nollekens had indulged in from several of Langford's and Christie's sales, to the latter of which rooms he was a constant visitor for nearly half a century.

asserted that he borrowed many attitudes for his monumental figures. Poussin's draperies were likewise so highly esteemed by him, that he frequently adopted them; as this Painter's drapery falls well, mostly in grand and broad folds, and is unquestionably the easiest for carving, having no flutter; which is a style not only troublesome to execute in marble, but extremely expensive to cut, and bad in effect when accomplished.

At another time, when he took me with him to his Stock-broker's, as we were going up Ludgate-hill, he said that he recollected his mother taking him, when he was only four years old, to see St. Paul's; and that, in going up that street, he observed a man running backwards and forwards shaking a box, into which many of the passengers put money, and that she told him it was for the poor prisoners in the Fleet, being called 'The Running Box'.[1] Nollekens always spoke well of his mother, observing, that she was a very curious woman; and in his recollections of her stated, that she possessed an ivory model of the Holy Sepulchre; that she remembered seeing the Rebels, in 1745, brought into London, confined at the backs of the horse-soldiers; that they were brought from Scotland through Tottenham-court-road, along Hog-lane, now called Crown-street, on their way to the Horse Guards; and that she used to take in a newspaper, entitled 'All Alive and Merry; or, the London Daily Post', which was published at a *farthing*, and printed by '*A Merry Man*'.[2]

[1] In Marcellus Lauron's 'Cries of London', published about the year 1710, there is a representation of such a person, with his cry of 'Remember the poor prisoners!' inscribed beneath him. At his back a capacious covered basket is suspended by leathern straps round his arms for broken victuals; and he carries in one hand a staff, and in the other a small round deep box, with an aperture in the lid for receiving of alms in money.

[2] The full title and imprint of this curious paper are, 'All-Alive and Merry; or, the London Daily Post'. 'Lon-

But to return now from Mr. Nollekens's reminiscences to his own memoirs. The parsimonious disposition of his partner seemed to take no delight in

don: Printed for A. Merryman, and sold by the Hawkers.' It consisted of a small folio half-sheet, having three columns of letter-press on each side; and several specimens of it may be seen in the late Dr. Burney's Collection of Newspapers in the British Museum, vol. III, for 1741. It is probable, that the 'London Gazette' may be considered as the origin of most of the cheap and popular News-journals of the last century, since the name of that paper was derived from one first published at Venice, the price of which was a coin called a *Gazet;* which, says Coryat in his 'Crudities', Lond. 1776, 8vo. vol. II, page 15, 'is almost a penny, whereof ten do make a *liver*, that is ninepence'. The first of this paper printed in England, superseded the 'Intelligence and News', conducted by Roger L'Estrange, Esq. and appeared in 1665; No. 1, containing the public events from Nov. 7–14th, under the title of the 'Oxford Gazette'; it being published in that city every Tuesday, since the Court was assembled there on account of the plague being in London. It was, however, also reprinted in the metropolis, and, upon the removal of the Court, the name was altered to that of the 'London Gazette'; the first of which, No. 24, Feb. 1st–5th, 1665–66, was published on a Monday. Those papers, however, the names of which were expressive of their price, do not seem to have been published until half a century afterwards: but on July 19, 1715, appeared No. 1 of 'The Penny Post'; on March 13th following, No. 1 of 'The Penny Post; or, Tradesman's Select Pacquet'; on October 19th, 1720, No. 1 of 'The Penny Weekly Journal; or, Saturday Evening's Entertainment'; and in 1724–25, a yet cheaper publication was printed, called, 'The Halfpenny London Journal; or, The British Oracle'; whilst three other Halfpenny Posts were published three times every week. Nichols's 'Literary Anecdotes of the Eighteenth Century', London, 1812, 8vo. vol. I, page 312; vol. IV, pages 58, 86, 89, 90, 92, 94. The Farthing Posts, however, appear chiefly to have been in circulation during the years 1740–43; and in the 'Gentleman's Magazine' for November 1740, vol. X, pages 557, 558, the 'Craftsman' of November 22nd, complains, that the revenue was greatly alleviating the sorrows of the widow or assisting the endeavours of the fatherless; at least, I never heard of her trespassing on her purse that way: on the contrary, she would, like Penny's picture of a Quack-doctor,[1] look about for the bit of bacon to take from the distressed family, as will appear by the following trait of character. At the corner of her house there was a small part of the street railed in, on which she gave a poor woman leave to place a table with a few apples for sale upon a bit of an old napkin. To this miserably-hooded widow she was seen to go, when she intended to treat the family with a dumpling, with the question of, 'Pray, Goody, how many apples can you let me have for a penny?' 'Bless your kindness! you shall have three.' 'Three!' exclaimed the lady, smiling, 'no, you must let *me* have four;' and touching her left thumb with the forefinger of her right hand, she continued, 'for there's my husband, myself, and two servants, and we must have one a piece!' 'Well!' observed the miserable dependent, '*you* must take them!' Whilst eighteen-pence was the price of half a

defrauded by the printers and publishers of Halfpenny and Farthing Posts, which were publicly vended about the streets, without stamps, in equal defiance both of the law and the penalty. It is added, that though they had been frequently informed against, yet that the persons concerned in them were supposed to be such 'poor, low wretches', living in obscure parts of the town, or in the Rules of the Fleet, and other prisons, that their discovery would be very difficult; whilst a suspicion is also hinted, that they were supported by persons in power against the opposition papers and publishers. In plate iv of the 'Rake's Progress', Hogarth has introduced a boy intently occupied in reading a paper, on which is inscribed, 'The Farthing Post'. The stamping of newspapers on single sheets or half-sheets first took place on August 2nd, 1712.

[1] From this picture by Penny, who was Professor of Painting in the Royal Academy, there is an engraving entitled 'The Rapacious Quack'.

calf's head, it was a dish of which she was 'passionately fond'; but when it exceeded that amount, something else was thought of 'by way of a change': indeed, she would observe, that 'those people who live aloof from the blandishments of a Court, have little occasion for a superfluity at their tables'.[1] She took a particular pleasure in assisting her friends with 'economical' recipes, of which, at card-parties, she accumulated a tolerable stock; and the following was one she much recommended to the mammas of very delicate young ladies, for whom the physician had prescribed asses-milk. 'To make mock asses-milk. Three parts barley-water, and one part milk, to be boiled together, and sweetened with fine sugar; half an ounce of barley to a pint, the first water to be thrown away.' There was one recipe which Mr. Nollekens always wrote himself on little ragged strips of paper, which he cut off the margins of his prints, and of which he kept several in his pocket-book, to give to any persons he met afflicted with the jaundice, and now and then a pert jack-a-napes, by way of a quiz, would apply for one. 'For jaundice, take every morning a new-laid egg; let it be broke into a cup, and swallow it, the white and the yoke.'

During the time I was with him, he now and then gave a dinner, particularly when his steadfast friend Lord Yarborough, then the Hon. Mr. Pelham, sent his annual present of venison; and it is most surprising to consider how many persons of good sense and high talent visited Mrs. Nollekens, though it probably was principally owing to the good character her father and

[1] When she went to Oxford-market to beat the rounds, in order to discover the cheapest chops, she would walk round several times to give her dog Cerberus an opportunity of picking up scraps. However, of this mode of manœuvring she was at last ashamed, by the rude remarks of the vulgar butchers, who had been complained of to her Nolly, for having frequently cried out, 'Here comes Mrs. Nollekens and her bull-bitch!'

sister held in society. Dr. Johnson and Miss Williams were often there, and they generally arrived in a hackney-coach, on account of Miss Williams's blindness. When the Doctor sat to Mr. Nollekens for his bust, he was very much displeased at the manner in which the head had been loaded with hair, which the Sculptor insisted upon, as it made him look more like an ancient poet. The sittings were not very favourable, which rather vexed the artist, who, upon opening the street-door, a vulgarity he was addicted to, peevishly whined—'Now, Doctor, you *did* say you would give my busto half an hour before dinner, and the dinner has been waiting this long time.' To which the Doctor's reply was, 'Bow-wow-wow!'

The bust is a wonderfully fine one and very like, but certainly the sort of hair *is* objectionable; having been modelled from the flowing locks of a sturdy Irish beggar, originally a street pavior, who, after he had sat an hour, refused to take a shilling, stating that he could have made more by begging!

Doctor Johnson also considered this bust like him, but, whilst he acknowledged the Sculptor's ability in his art, he could not avoid observing to his friend Boswell, when they were looking at it in Nollekens's studio, 'It is amazing what ignorance of certain points one sometimes finds in men of eminence:'[1] though, from want of knowing the Sculptor, a visitor, when viewing his studio, was heard to say, 'What a mind the man must have from whom all these emanated!' Banks, in his tale of 'Every Man in his Way', commences with,

> One art, Philosophers maintain,
> Is full sufficient for one brain;
> And He who made us men, design'd
> For such a science such a mind.

---

[1] Dr. Johnson, upon hearing the name of an eminent Sculptor mentioned, observed, 'Well, Sir, I think my friend Joe Nollekens can chop out a head with any of them'.

Defective as he was in many particulars, Nollekens's fame for bust-making will never be diminished; and I would have this truth 'written as with a sunbeam'. Possessed of such distinguished talent, he now became extremely popular, though he never sought employment; and perhaps no man had less intrigue,

> As spiders never seek the fly,
> But leave him of himself, t' apply.

Most of his sitters were exceedingly amused with the oddity of his manner, particularly fine women, who were often gratified by being considered handsome by the Sculptor, though his admiration was expressed in the plainest language. I remember his once requesting a lady who squinted dreadfully, to 'look a little the other way, for then,' said he, 'I shall get rid of the shyness in the cast of your eye:' and to another lady of the highest rank, who had forgotten her position, and was looking down upon him, he cried, 'Don't look so *scorny*; you'll spoil my busto; and you're a very fine woman; I think it will be one of my best bustos.' I heard him ask the daughter of Lord Yarborough, in the presence of her husband, to prove to her that he had not forgotten all his Italian, if she did not recollect his dancing her upon his knee when she was a *Bambina*. He was very fond of speaking Italian, though I have been told it was exceedingly bad; and he would often attempt it even in the presence of the Royal Family, who good-temperedly smiled at his whimsicalities. Even the gravest of men, the Lord Chancellor Bathurst, when sitting to him for his bust for the Chancery Court, in his large wig, condescendingly endured the following collection of nonsense, in which at last his Lordship was obliged to join. *Nollekens*.—'Ah! there goes the bell tolling; no,—it's only my clock on the stairs: when I was a boy, you would have liked to have seen me toll the bell; it's no very easy thing, I can tell you;—look a little that way,—you must toll, that is to say, I did, one hour for a man, three times three; and three times two for a woman:—now, your Lordship must mind, there's a Moving-bell and a Passing-bell; these the Romans always attended to.' 'You mean the Roman Catholics, Mr. Nollekens,' observed his Lordship. 'Yes, my Lord, they call that the Moving-bell, which goes when they move a body out of one parish to the next, or so on. The Passing-bell, is when you are dying and going from this world to another place.' 'Ay, Mr. Nollekens,' observed his Lordship, 'there is a curious little book, published in 1671, I think by Richard Duckworth, upon the art of Ringing, entitled "Tintannologia".'

But simple and half-witted as this artist certainly was, yet he always knew how to take care of what is called the main chance, as will be proved by the following anecdote.

A lady in weeds for her dear husband, drooping low like the willow, visited the Sculptor, and assured him that she did not care what money was expended on a monument to the memory of her beloved; 'Do what you please, but do it directly,' were her orders. Industry was a principle riveted in Nollekens's constitution; he rose with the lark, and in a short time finished the model, strongly suspecting she might, like some others he had been employed by, change her mind. The lady, in about three months, made her second appearance, in which more courage is generally assumed, and was accosted by him, before she alighted, with 'Poor soul! I thought you'd come'; but her tripping down with a 'light fantastic toe', and the snorting of her horses, which had been hard-driven, evinced a total change in her inclination, and he was now saluted with, 'How do you do, Nollekens: well, you have not commenced the model?'—'Yes, but I have though,' was the reply. *The Lady*, 'Have you, indeed? These, my good friend, I own,' throwing herself into a chair, 'are early days; but since I saw you, an old Roman acquaintance of your's has made me an offer, and I don't know how he would like to see in our church a monument of such expense to my late husband; indeed, perhaps, after all, upon second thoughts, it would be considered quite enough if I got our mason to put up a mural inscription, and that, you know, he can cut very neatly.'—'My charge,' interrupted the artist, 'for my model will be one hundred guineas'; which she declared to be 'enormous'. However, she would pay it and 'have done with him'.

His singular and parsimonious habits were most observable in his domestic life. Coals were articles of great consideration with Mr. Nollekens, and these he so rigidly economized, that they were always sent early, before his men came to work, in order that he might have leisure time for counting the sacks, and disposing of the large coals in what was originally designed by the builder of his house for a wine-cellar, so that he might lock them up for parlour use. Candles were never lighted at the commencement of the evening, and whenever they heard a knock at the door, they would wait until they heard a second rap, lest the first should have been a runaway, and their candle wasted. Mr. and Mrs. Nollekens used a flat candlestick when there was any thing to be done; and I have been assured that a pair of moulds, by being well nursed, and put out when company went away, once lasted them a whole year! It happened one morning, that poor old Daphne, the large yard-dog, a constant market companion of Mrs. Nollekens, barked incessantly, until Mr. Nollekens, who was then taking in the milk, which was his constant practice, could go to the gate; where he was addressed by a raw-boned man full six feet in height, who said he was a cutter of funeral inscriptions come from the city of Norwich, and would be glad of a job. At this time the Literary Club, founded by Sir Joshua Reynolds, which met at the St. Luke's Head in Gerrard-street, had signed a Round-Robin, addressed to Dr. Johnson, requesting him to alter into English the inscription for Dr. Goldsmith's monument, at that time executing by Mr. Nollekens, who promised the man at the gate the cutting of it, as soon as it was sent back; and this I saw him execute under a shed in the yard near the dog, who constantly eyed his movements. Trifling as the incident may at first appear, this person became a valuable assistant to his new master, under whom he made what is called a very pretty fortune. His name was William Arminger, and he carved many of Mr. Nollekens's best busts; but farther particulars of him will be given in a future page.

The monument to Dr. Goldsmith was put up in Poet's Corner, Westminster Abbey, over the entrance to the Chapel of St. Blaize, which has long been used as a vestry to the edifice.

CHAPTER III

Friends of Mrs. Nollekens.—G. M. Moser, and his daughter Mary.—Her letters, and one from Fuseli in reply.—Angelica Kauffmann, and her marriage.—Mrs. Carter.—Old houses on Hampstead-heath.—G. Steevens and his portraits.—Nollekens's bust of George III.—Parsimonious management of Nollekens when a bachelor.—Personal appearance of him and his wife.—Economy of Mrs. Nollekens.—The Sculptor's figure and dress.—White's Coffee-house, and the Gamesters' Address to the King.

MRS. NOLLEKENS was honoured with the friendship of three highly celebrated ladies, Miss Moser, R.A. the famous Painter of flowers, afterwards Mrs. Lloyd; Mrs. Angelica Kauffmann, R.A., whose works are too well known to need any encomiums from me, both of whom were chosen Members of the Royal Academy upon its establishment; and Mrs. Elizabeth Carter, the well-known translator of Epictetus. Of the two former characters I shall now give a few anecdotes, which, from their being uncommon, at this distance of time may prove rather interesting.

Miss Mary Moser was the daughter of George Michael Moser, a truly worthy and clever man. He was originally a chaser, but when that mode of adorning plate, cane-heads, and watch-cases, became unfashionable, he, by the advice of his friend, Mr. Thomas Grignon, the celebrated watchmaker, applied himself to enamelling watch-trinkets, necklaces, bracelets, &c. from which occupation he became an excellent enameller of larger and more eminent works. He drew remarkably well, and was successively at the head of several drawing schools, until at last he was elected Keeper of the Royal Academy on its foundation; which situation he filled some considerable time with honour to himself and his brother Academicians.

Moser died at his apartments in Somerset House, on Friday, January 24th, 1783, aged seventy-eight, and was buried in the churchyard of St. Paul, Covent Garden.

Mr. Moser originally lived in Craven-buildings, Drury-lane; a street at the south end of the lane, which was built upon part of the premises of Craven House, in the year 1723, as appears by an inscribed stone let into the north-west corner house of the street, at the bottom of which, against the wall, was a large equestrian portrait of William Lord Craven, painted by Paul Van Somer the younger, for there were two painters of that name. This picture, which is now destroyed, I have engraven in my 'Antiquities of London'.

Miss Moser, though somewhat of a precise woman, was at times a most cheerful companion. My father knew her well, and was often delighted by hearing her relate the passing events of the day: specimens of which I now present to the reader, in two letters addressed to her friend Mrs. Lloyd, the wife of the gentleman whom she afterwards married; with the loan of which entertaining epistles I was favoured by Mrs. Nichols, who was for many years the faithful companion of the writer.

May 8th.

MY DEAR FRIEND,

Come to London and admire our plumes; we sweep the sky! a Duchess wears six feathers, a lady four, and every milk-maid one at each corner of her cap! Your mamma desired me to inquire the name of something she had seen in the windows in Tavistock-street: it seems *she* was afraid to ask; but *I* took courage, and they told me they were rattle-snake tippets; however, notwithstanding their frightful name, they are not very much unlike a beaufong, only the quills are made stiff, and springy in the starching. Fashion is grown a monster! pray tell your operator, that your hair must measure just three-quarters of a yard from the extremity of one wing to the other. I should not have said so much about fashions, but I suppose it makes part of the conversation of country ladies; I hope my advice will not be stale; French trimming is quite the bon-ton.

N.B. The Queen and her ladies never wear feathers: they say here, that the minority ladies are distinguished from the courtiers by their plumes. Mrs. Sheriff brought a terrible story of a trance, which I suppose your mamma has told you already; but I have since inquired into the merits of the case, and have been assured by some of the lady's relations, who are likewise cousins of mine by marriage, that the story is fabulous, and they fancy it was fabricated to amuse a good old aunt, who delights in the marvellous. Is there no ghostly story propagated at Carnarvon that would petrify one's friends? For Heaven's sake invent me some! let them be very wonderful indeed, that I may make a figure among the old ladies. I have found very good effects from telling a terrific story, when I have held a doubtful, low hand; pray keep this secret. I do not know one gossiping anecdote, or it should be at your service. My father and mother join in compliments to you and Capt. Lloyd, and

I remain, to all perpetuity,
Your sincere friend and humble servant,
MARY MOSER.

Somerset House, Jan. 9.

MY DEAR FRIEND,

YOUR 'Palace of Silence' has engrossed all my thoughts for these last six weeks; I dream of it, and cry 'Silence' in my sleep. If your printer should not have mercy on me, and bring it out shortly, I shall certainly die with impatience.

'The renewal of the year gives me an opportunity of wishing you in words, what I always wish you in thought —many, many, happy years. 'May you live as long as you deserve to live,' says Lord Chesterfield to his son. Give me leave to conclude my wish in the same manner; because, if my wish succeed, you will live for ever. Pray, if you have read Lord Chesterfield's letters, give me your opinion of them, and what you think of his Lordship: for my part, I admire wit and adore good manners, but at the same time, I should detest Lord Chesterfield, were he alive, young, and handsome, and my lover, if I supposed, as I do now, his wit was the result of thought, and that he had been practising the graces in the looking-glass. I cannot help smiling at the fine compliments he desires his son to make to the Duke of Newcastle, and the delicate turn of his epistle to Voltaire: witty sayings made yesterday, and compliments manufactured at leisure, I hate; so I will not allow my Lord Chesterfield to have been a wit, unless you speak in his defence, which I think you will not do, because he has said the best of us are little better than things in leading-strings and forehead cloths: however, as I have heard that it is generous to acknowledge the merit of those we do not love, I will declare, if all the good things in Lord Chesterfield's work were compiled in one volume, independent of his adoration of the Graces, it would be a most excellent little book.

I shall have the pleasure of seeing your mamma this afternoon at Mrs. Toussaint's; so adieu, my dear friend, and believe me,

Sincerely, with all love,
Your humble humble servant,
MARY MOSER.

To Mrs. Lloyd.

Mrs. Nichols has also indulged me with the loan of two other letters, one of which is warmly addressed by Miss Moser to Fuseli, when at Rome;[1] the other is Fuseli's answer, and is certainly coldly written. However, with these epistles the reader will be highly pleased, as they contain some truly interesting particulars respecting the Arts. I should have premised that Miss Moser was glancing at Fuseli, but his heart, unfortunately, had already been deeply pierced by Angelica Kauffmann.

If you have not forgotten at Rome those friends whom you remembered at Florence, write to me from that nursery

[1] Fuseli left England in December 1769, and arrived at Rome in January 1770; in September 1778, he left Rome for Switzerland, where he continued till the middle of 1779, when he returned to England.

of arts and raree-show of the world, which flourishes in ruins: tell me of pictures, palaces, people, lakes, woods, and rivers; say if Old Tiber droops with age, or whether his waters flow as clear, his rushes grow as green, and his swans look as white, as those of Father Thames; or write me your own thoughts and reflections, which will be more acceptable than any description of any thing Greece and Rome have done these two thousand years.

I suppose there has been a million of letters sent to Italy with an account of our Exhibition, so it will be only telling you what you know already, to say that Reynolds was like himself in pictures which you have seen; Gainsborough beyond himself in a portrait of a gentleman in a Vandyke habit; and Zoffany superior to every body, in a portrait of Garrick in the character of Abel Drugger, with two other figures, Subtle and Face. Sir Joshua agreed to give an hundred guineas for the picture; Lord Carlisle half an hour after offered Reynolds twenty to part with it, which the Knight generously refused, resigned his intended purchase to the Lord, and the emolument to his brother artist. (He is a gentleman!) Angelica made a very great addition to the show, and Mr. Hamilton's picture of Brisëis parting from Achilles, was very much admired; the Brisëis in taste, *à la antique*, elegant and simple. Coates, Dance, Wilson, &c. as usual. Mr. West had no large picture finished. You will doubtless imagine, that I derived my epistolary genius from my nurse; but when you are tired of my gossiping, you may burn the letter, so I shall go on. Some of the literati of the Royal Academy were very much disappointed as they could not obtain diplomas, but the Secretary, who is above trifles, has since made a very flattering compliment to the Academy in the Preface to the Travels: the Professor of History is comforted by the success of his 'Deserted Village', which is a very pretty poem, and has lately put himself under the conduct of Mrs. Hornick and her fair daughters, and is gone to France; and Dr. Johnson sips his tea, and cares not for the vanity of the world. Sir Joshua, a few days ago, entertained the Council and Visitors with callipash and callipee, except poor Coates, who last week fell a sacrifice to the corroding power of soap-lees, which he hoped would have cured him of the stone: many a tear will drop on his grave, as he is not more lamented as an artist than a friend to the distressed. (*Ma poca polvere sono che nulla sente!*) My mamma declares that you are an insufferable creature, and that she speaks as good English as your mother did High-German. Mr. Meyer laughed aloud at your letter, and desired to be remembered. My father and his daughter long to know the progress you will make, particularly

MARY MOSER,

Who remains sincerely your friend, and believes you will exclaim or mutter to yourself, '*Why did she send this d—d nonsense to me?*'

Rome, April 27, 1771.

MADAM,

I AM inexcusable. I know your letter by heart, and have never answered it; but I am often so very unhappy within, that I hold it matter of remorse to distress such a friend as Miss Moser with my own whimsical miseries;—they may be fancied evils, but to him who has fancy, real evils are unnecessary, though I have them too. All I can say is, that I am approaching the period which commonly decides a man's life with regard to fame or infamy; if I am distracted by the thought, those who have passed the Rubicon will excuse me, and you are amongst the number.

Mr. Runciman, who does me the favour to carry these lines, my friend, and in my opinion the best *Painter* of *us* in Rome, has desired me to introduce him to your family; but he wants no other introduction than his merit. I beg my warmest compliments to papa and mamma, and am unaltered,

Madam,
Your most obliged servant and friend,
FUSELI.

To Miss Moser,
Craven Buildings,
Drury Lane.

The late Queen Charlotte, whose real worth, as to private benevolence, was not known until after her death, took particular notice of Miss Moser, and for a considerable time employed her at Frogmore, for the decoration of one chamber, which her Majesty commanded to be called Miss Moser's Room, and for which the Queen paid upwards of 900*l*.

It having been asserted that Angelica Kauffmann studied from an exposed male living model, which Mr. Nollekens said he believed,—I was determined to gain the best information on the subject, by going to Mr. Charles Cranmer, one of the original models of the Royal Academy, now living, in his eighty-second year, at No. 13, in Regent-street, Vauxhall-bridge; and he assured me, that he did frequently sit before Angelica Kauffmann at her house on the south side of Golden-square, but that he only exposed his arms, shoulders, and legs, and that her father, who was also an artist and likewise an exhibitor at the Royal Academy, was always present. I have under my care, as Keeper of the Prints and Drawings in the British Museum, a most spirited study of her's, dated 1771, of a male academy model, recumbent and half draped; it is in black and white chalk, upon brown paper, and is in the splendid collection left to the Museum by the late Richard Payne Knight, Esq., a Trustee of that magnificent establishment, which will in a few years be the admiration of our own country and the envy of all the world.

Angelica, before she married Mr. Zucchi, the artist, was most artfully deceived by a discarded servant of Count Horn, who had imposed himself upon her smiles with the title of his late master; and, being a very fine handsome fellow, she was determined to show her friends, with whom she had flirted, that she had at last made a good hit, and therefore, without the least hesitation, immediately gave her hand to the impostor. The next time Angelica attended at Buckingham-house upon the Queen, who was pleased by seeing her paint, she communicated her marriage to her Majesty, upon which she received the most condescending congratulations, with an invitation to her husband to come to Court; who, however, was cunningly determined to keep himself within the house, from the sight of every one, until his baggage had arrived, which he expected every day. At last Count Horn himself came to England, and when at the levee, was much surprised by being complimented upon his marriage. Angelica, who soon received the mortifying information from the Queen, was for a time inconsolable; but at last, her friends prevailed upon the fortune-hunter to leave England upon a pension, and Angelica, who resumed the name of Kauffmann, which she retained till her death, was fortunately never troubled with him afterwards.

Mrs. Carter, of whom Mrs. Nollekens was in possession of a portrait, most exquisitely engraven by Hayward, from a picture by Lawrence, would often complain of her 'indefatigable head-ache'. She was a truly sincere woman, and will be introduced in a future page.

Mr. and Mrs. Nollekens took me one Sunday morning with them in a glass-coach, to pass a day with their friend Mrs. Haycock, a very aged lady, who resided near Hampstead-heath. She was quite of the old school in her dress, and so indeed was every thing in and about her house. Her evergreens were cut into the shapes of various birds, and Cheere's leaden painted figures of a shepherd and shepherdess were objects of as much admiration with her neighbours, as they were with my Lord Ogleby, who thus accosts his friend in the second scene of the 'Clandestine Marriage'.

> 'Great improvements, indeed, Mr. Stirling! wonderful improvements! the four Seasons in lead, the flying Mercury, and the basin with Neptune in the middle, are in the very extreme of fine taste. You have as many rich figures as the man at Hyde-Park-corner.'

The fine row of elms, which is now open upon the left hand of the green opposite to a garden wall, was, at the time we made the visit, within Mrs. Haycock's grounds; which were surrounded by a primly cut holly-hedge. After we had dined with this lady, who had lived several years beyond eighty, at which period she had received the small-pox, Mrs. Nollekens expressed a wish to view the grounds of her opposite neighbour, George Steevens, Esq. better known under the appellation of 'Shakspeare Steevens'; and she was more particularly anxious to see this spot, as she had often heard her father speak of its notoriety. It having been, too, a fashionable place of resort for the Londoners, when it was the Upper Flask Tavern; and Richardson having noticed it as the place where his Clarissa had fled to from Lovelace, the public at that time was generally talking of it.

Mr. Steevens ordered his gardener to show the grounds, which were beautiful beyond description.[1]

Steevens early in life was rather conceited of his person, and had a miniature of himself beautifully painted by the celebrated Meyer, the Enameller and Royal Academician. He also stood, being fond of private theatricals, in which he often took a part, for a whole-length portrait in oil, in the character of *Barbarossa*. Zoffany likewise painted a picture of him in oil, with a favourite little dog, which has been engraven for Boydell, for his edition of Shakspeare.[2]

[1] I received no small pleasure last summer, when—— Shepherd, Esq. the present possessor, politely gave me permission to revisit them, to find this highly enviable spot nearly in the same state in which it was in my youthful days.

[2] Fond as he was of having his portrait taken in early life, in his latter days he not only refused to sit, but actually took the greatest pains to destroy every resemblance of his features; and never suffered himself to remain in the company of an artist for any length of time, lest he should steal his likeness. Notwithstanding these precautions, however, he was seriously annoyed by receiving an impression of an etching of his face, though not a very good likeness, taken by stealth by Sayer, the caricaturist, at which liberty

I once heard Mr. Nollekens relate an anecdote in the presence of Mr. Richard Dalton, then Librarian to King George III, which will show how well his Majesty must have been acquainted with even the religious persuasions, as well as the faces and family connexions of his subjects.

'When I was modelling the King's busto,' observed Mr. Nollekens, 'I was commanded to go to receive the King at Buckingham House, at seven o'clock in the morning, for that was the time his Majesty shaved. After he had shaved himself, and before he had put on his stock, I modelled my busto. I *sot* him down, to be even with myself, and the King seeing me go about him and about him, said to me, "What do you want?"—I said, "I want to measure your nose. The Queen tells me I have made my nose too broad." "Measure it then," said the King.' 'Ay, my good friend,' observed Dalton, who had been intimate with

Steevens was so highly exasperated that he threatened 'to cane the fellow'; a mode of chastisement, which, with a raised arm and a clenched fist, he often declared he would inflict upon most of those persons who offended him. Steevens, who certainly had remarkably handsome legs, which he generally covered with white cotton stockings, would frequently pique himself upon having walked from his house at Hampstead, half over London, and back, without receiving a speck of dirt upon them.

Mrs. Swan, an aged woman, who lets ready-furnished lodgings in Hampstead, and who married Steevens's gardener, assured me that no creature on earth could be more afraid of death than Steevens; that on the day of his decease, he came into the kitchen where she and her husband were sitting at dinner, snatched at their pudding, which he ate most voraciously, at the same time defying the grinning monster in the most terrific language. However, he died, and Flaxman has placed his effigy on his monument in white marble, placidly seated contemplating a bust of Shakspeare, which is erected in the north chancel of the East India Company's Chapel in Poplar.

Nollekens during their stay at Rome, 'I have heard it often mentioned in the library; and it has also been affirmed that you pricked the King's nose with your said callipers. I will tell you what the King said of you when you did not attend according to command, one morning, "Nollekens is not come; I forgot, it is a Saint's day, and he is a Catholic."'[1]

The following anecdote is current, but on what authority it rests, I know not: allowing the story to be true, it could come only from an attendant on the King—certainly not from his Majesty, nor from Nollekens; however, I could name half-a-dozen persons who continue to relate it.

The story runs thus:—When Mr. Nollekens attended the King the following day, to receive his Majesty's commands as to the time for the next sitting, as he approached the royal presence, instead of making an apology on the Saint's account, he merely wished to know when he might be allowed to go on with his busto? The King, however, with his usual indulgence to persons as ignorant as Nollekens was of

[1] Although it is true that Nollekens followed the old family persuasion of his father, and possibly he might at that time, as it was just after his arrival from Rome, have paid more attention to Saints' days, yet I am quite certain that during his latter years he cared very little for the Catholic religion, nor indeed for any other. As for Mrs. Nollekens, though she pretended to be a staunch friend to the National Protestant Church, yet she never contributed much to its support; for she certainly never was known to indulge in the expense of a pew, or even a single seat. She generally contrived, by standing near the pew of some one of her tenants, to catch an eye of observation, when she was sure of being accommodated with a seat, not only in the church, but very often in a carriage home; and this latter attention often afforded her an opportunity of accepting an invitation to a card-party, or a seat in a box at the Opera, of which entertainment she always declared herself to be excessively fond.

the common marks of respect, observed, 'So, Nollekens, where were you yesterday?'

Nollekens.—'Why, as it was a Saint's day, I thought you would not have me; so I went to see the beasts fed in the Tower.'

The King.—'Why did you not go to Duke-street?'

Nollekens.—'Well, I went to the Tower; and do you know, they have got two such lions there! and the biggest did roar so; my heart! how he did roar!' And then he mimicked the roaring of the lion, so *loud* and so close to the King's ear, that his Majesty moved to a considerable distance to escape the imitation, without saying, like Bottom in the Comedy,

Let him roar again, let him roar again.

A modeller keeps his clay moist by spirting water over it; and this he does by standing at a little distance with his mouth filled with water, which he spirts upon it, so that the water is sent into all the recesses of his model before he covers it up: this, it is said, Nollekens did in the King's presence, without declaring what he was about to do. However, it was not the case with Mr. Bacon, the Sculptor, who had provided a long silver syringe for that purpose, before he attended the King, with which he could easily throw the water into the recesses of the model, without making so disagreeable a noise in his Majesty's presence. With the drapery of this bust of the King, Nollekens had more anxiety and trouble than with any of his other productions; he assured Mr. Joseph, the Associate of the Royal Academy, that after throwing the cloth once or twice every day for nearly a fortnight, it came excellently well, by mere chance, from the following circumstance. Just as he was about to make another trial with his drapery, his servant came to him for money, for butter; he threw the cloth carelessly over the shoulders of his lay-man, in order to give her the money, when he was forcibly struck with the beautiful manner in which the folds had fallen; and he hastily exclaimed, pushing her away. 'Go, go, get the butter.' And he has frequently been heard to say, that that drapery was by far the best he ever cast for a busto.

The reader is to be informed, that when Mr. Nollekens was engaged upon this bust of our late gracious King, Miss Mary Welch was not in possession of the power of managing his domestic concerns. He was then a single man, and his servant, for at that time he kept but one, always applied to him for money to purchase every description of article *fresh*, as it was wanted for the approaching meal; and by that mode of living, he concluded, as he kept his servant upon board-wages, he was not so much exposed to her pilfering inclinations, particularly as she was entrusted with no more money than would enable her to purchase just enough for his own eating. He generally contrived to get through the small quantity he allowed himself, never thinking of keeping any portion of a roll, or a pat of butter, for any one who might pop in at his breakfasting hour, or as a reserve for a friend as a bever before dinner.

I have frequently heard Miss Moser assure my father, that whenever she carried him a pot of jelly, or a quince marmalade, she always, upon opening his closet, found the last presented pot entirely emptied; so fond was he of any thing given to him, particularly when he had a sore throat, of which he frequently complained to those who made black-currant jelly.

Before the commencement of some other anecdotes, which may amuse the reader, I must indulge in a comparison betwixt the general appearance of Mr. and Mrs. Nollekens, certainly not cheek-by-jowl, but by the simile of placing a pair of compasses and a short pair of callipers, side by side; the first opened at ten degrees, or perhaps not quite so much, the latter at full fifteen; and then, I think, Mrs. Nollekens will stand pardoned for continuing to call her husband 'Little Nolly': which name, by-the-by, he originally received from her early admirer and sincere friend, Dr. Johnson, who never failed to visit her for the last three years of his life, at least three times a month, so that I had frequent opportunities of peeping at him. In the way in which the compasses and callipers will appear, when opened at the above degrees, so Mr. and Mrs. Nollekens's figures may be conceived:—the lady with *legs tall*, *thin*, and *straight*, the gentleman with *limbs short* and *bowed:* thus *proportioned*, they would slowly move, on a Sunday morning, till they arrived at a certain corner in Mortimer-street, where they then parted; the one turning to the right, the other to the left; he to the Roman Catholic chapel, and she to the Protestant church.

Sometimes in the evening, when they had no engagements, to take a little fresh air, and to avoid interlopers, they would, after putting a little tea and sugar, a French-roll, or a couple of rusks into their pockets, stray to Madam Caria's, a Frenchwoman, who lived near the end of Marylebone-lane, in what were at that time called the French Gardens, principally tenanted by the citizens, where persons were accommodated with tea equipage and hot-water at a penny a-head. Mrs. Nollekens made it a rule to allow one servant,—as they kept two,—to go out on the alternate Sunday; for it was Mr. Nollekens's opinion, that if they were never permitted to visit the Jew's Harp, Queen's Head and Artichoke, or Chalk Farm, they never would wash '*theirselves*'.

Had the facetious Samuel Foote witnessed the following scene, it is probable he would have given it a more humorous commemoration; but I shall endeavour to narrate it in the manner Mrs. Bland, who kept a Turner's shop, used to tell it to her customers. Mrs. Nollekens, upon opening Mrs. Bland's door, declared she had not seen her for some time, though they lived in the same street, and were close neighbours, only seven doors apart.—*Mrs. Bland.* 'No, Madam, I have not sold you a broom for these five years!' —*Mrs. Nollekens.* 'Five years! my dear Mrs. Bland, how time passes! though you don't look the worse for wear, my good friend.'—*Mrs. Bland.* 'I thank you, Ma'am, I have had my share of troubles, with my poor dear husband and my two boys.'—*Mrs. Nollekens.* 'Ah! so we all have. My house opposite has been to let a good while now, ever since the General left it: is it not a pity so good a house should remain empty? indeed, it must be a great loss to *you*, Mrs. Bland, for I understand they had all their turnery of you.'—*Mrs. Bland.* 'Yes; and what is more, they always gave me my price, and paid punctually!'—*Mrs. Nollekens.* 'I will now put it in your power to gain a customer; here is a bill, which I got *Little Smith*' (myself) 'to write in a large hand; allow it to occupy a pane of your shop-window, and as there is more sun upon this side of the street, the white paper will sooner catch the eye.'—*Mrs. Bland.* 'I have no objection.'—'Well, then,' rejoined the lady, 'do desire your girl to clean the glass, and then put it up while I stay. Bless me! I totally forgot to bring wafers; can you oblige me with one?' —*Mrs. Bland.* 'I will see; we have used them so little here since my poor dear husband died.'—*Mrs. Nollekens.* 'Pray don't mention the loss of him now; we should never repine. Bless me! what a miserable stock: stay, we will not mind the colours, we shall manage it.' The bill being stuck up, Mrs. Nollekens asked her neighbour what was the price of a good mop: Mrs. Bland, after taking one down, and striking it on the floor to make it appear bushy, and holding it as a buffetier would his halbert, replied, 'There, Ma'am, there's a mop! half-a-crown.'—*Mrs. Nollekens.* 'What! half-a-crown! my good woman, why, I only gave two shillings and three-pence for the last.'

'Yes, Ma'am,' observed the shopkeeper, 'but that was ten years ago.'—*Mrs. Nollekens.* 'Come, come, Mrs. Bland, don't be rude; *I* know pretty well when it was: but what will you allow me, now, for an old stick?'—'Three halfpence, Ma'am.'—'No, Mrs. —— what's your name; allow me three-pence, and I will give you two shillings, and you may send in your mop.' As Mrs. Bland would not agree to this, Mrs. Nollekens shut the door without wishing her a good morning; at the same time muttering loud enough to be heard, that she would go to the man round the corner, who had just opened a Turner's shop.

Perhaps it now may be better, by way of variety, to give a few of Mr. Nollekens's recollections; but before they are related, a description of his person may not be considered as out of place.

His figure was short, his head big, and it appeared much increased by a large-crowned hat, of which kind he was very fond; but his dress-hat, which he always sported when he went to Court, or to the Academy dinners, was nearly flat, and he brought it from Rome. His neck was short, his shoulders narrow, his body too large, particularly in the front lower part, which resembled that of Tenducci, and many other falsetto-singers; he was bow-legged and hook-nosed, —indeed, his leg was somewhat like his nose, which resembled the rudder of an Antwerp packet-boat—his hips were rather thin, but between his brows there was great evidence of study. He was very fond of his ruffles, and continued to wear them long after they had become unfashionable; indeed, until they were worn out. A drab was his favourite colour, and his suit was generally made from the same piece; though now and then he would treat himself with a striped Manchester waistcoat, of one of which he was so fond, that he sat to Abbot for his portrait in it; an engraving from which may be seen in Messrs. Cadell's Collection of interesting Contemporary Portraits, where he is represented leaning on his bust of Fox, which brought him into more notice than any other of his productions. His dress-stockings were also rather remarkable, being ornamented with blue and white stripes; similar to those constantly and so lately worn by Sir Thomas Stepney, an old member of White's in St. James's-street; of which house of notoriety the annexed anecdote, extracted from the Rev. W. Cole's MSS. in the British Museum, shall conclude this chapter, and may probably be found entertaining to the reader.

'The following humorous address was supposed to have been written by Colonel Lyttelton, brother to Sir George Lyttelton, in 1752, on his Majesty's return from Hanover, when numberless addresses were presented. White's Chocolate House, near St. James's Palace, was the famous gaming-house, where most of the nobility had meetings and a society. It was given to me December 8th, 1752.

The Gamesters' Address to the King.

MOST RIGHTEOUS SOVEREIGN,

MAY it please your Majesty, we, the Lords, Knights, &c. of the Society of White's, beg leave to throw ourselves at your Majesty's feet, (our honours and consciences lying under the *table*, and our fortunes being ever at stake,) and congratulate your Majesty's happy return to these kingdoms, which assembles us together, to the great advantage of some, the ruin of others, and the unspeakable satisfaction of all, both us, our wives, and children. We beg leave to acknowledge your Majesty's great goodness and lenity, in allowing us to break those laws, which we ourselves have made, and you have sanctified and confirmed; while your Majesty alone religiously observes and regards them. And we beg leave to assure your Majesty of our most unfeigned loyalty and attachment to your sacred person; and that next to the Kings of Diamonds, Clubs, Spades, and Hearts, we love, honour, and adore you.

To which his Majesty was pleased to return this most gracious answer.

MY LORDS AND GENTLEMEN,

I RETURN you my thanks for your loyal address; but whilst I have such rivals in your affection, as you tell me of, I can neither think it worth preserving or regarding. I look upon you yourselves as a *pack* of *cards*, and shall *deal* with you accordingly.

See Cole's MSS. vol. XXXI, p. 171, in the British Museum.

CHAPTER IV

Nollekens's dinner-parties and visitors.—Mr. Taylor.—Economical eccentricities of Mrs. Nollekens.—Dr. Johnson.—The Sculptor and the Snow model in Oxford-market.—Mr. White of Fleet-street.—Mrs. Nollekens and the Modeller in butter.—Salubrious air of Hampstead, and Artists residing there.—Manœuvres of Mrs. Nollekens in dress, &c.

One day, when some friends were expected to dine with Mrs. Nollekens, poor Bronze, labouring under a severe sore-throat, stretching her flannelled neck up to her mistress, hoarsely announced '*all the Hawkinses*' to be in the dining-parlour! Mrs. Nollekens, in a half-stifled whisper, cried, 'Nolly! it is truly vexatious that we are always served so when we dress a joint: you won't be so silly as to ask them to dinner?'—*Nollekens.* 'I ask them! let 'em get their meals at home; I'll not encourage the sort of thing; or, if they please, they can go to Mathias's, they'll find the cold leg of lamb we left yesterday.'—*Mrs. Nollekens.* 'No wonder, I am sure, they are considered so disagreeable by Captain Grose, Hampstead Steevens, Murphy, Nichols, and Boswell.'

At this moment who should come in but Mr. John Taylor, who will be often mentioned in this work; he looked around and wondered what all the fuss could be about.—'Why don't you go to your dinner, my good friend?' said he; 'I am sure it must be ready, for I smell the gravy.' Nollekens, to whom he had spoken, desired him to keep his nonsense to himself. *Taylor.* 'Well, well, well, I own, I ought to have nothing to do with family affairs. I see your dog Daphne has the mange! you should put some brimstone in his water; it is a very fine purifier of the blood; indeed I take it myself now and then; and I recollect my old friend Jonathan Tyers never suffered any of his dogs to be without it. Heighday!' looking behind the screen; 'why, here's a boy naked!—What! Tom, is it you?' —'Yes, Sir,' replied I.—*Taylor*. 'Why, what are you sitting for now? you were a Cupid the other day. Oh! a Mercury, I see; a pretty compliment, faith! Well, you must mind what you're about. However, Nollekens has made a god of you, you'll remember that. I say, who's coming here to dinner, do you know? he has never asked me to dine with him as yet; I don't know what he *may* do; nor did he ever send me a slice of the Yarborough venison: well, perhaps I am as well without it, though I must own I like venison: Quin was fond of it too. He and my master, Frank Hayman, knew the taste of it full well; and I recollect when Lord Sandwich gave a dinner to Lady Vane in Vauxhall Gardens, the haunches were fifty shillings apiece.'

This dispute had lasted so long, that perhaps the *Hawkinses* overheard it, for they had silently let themselves out without even ringing the bell. Shortly after, the *invited* party arrived, and I, who had been 'a very good lad', was allowed to remain in the studio to finish my drawing for admission into the Royal Academy. Now, as this room was next to the dining-parlour, I could not help hearing part of the conversation, for, as there was not much to eat, there were many talkers; but before the company sat down, they were requested to walk up stairs for a moment, to see Angelica Kauffmann's portrait of Mrs. Nollekens, who was painted in the character of Innocence, with a dove, of a three-quarter size, for which she had just received 15*l*. 15*s*. In the mean time, Bronze, who had been assisting the cook to put on the dishes, called to me through the key-hole, 'Bless you! Master Smith, come and see our set-out!' and as the scanty display for so many persons astonished me, I shall endeavour to describe the '*spread*',[1] as it is called at Cambridge.

[1] In English, 'A few things, sufficient to keep body and soul together.'

Two tables were joined; but as the legs of one were considerably shorter than those of the other, four blocks of wood had been prepared to receive them. The damask tablecloth was of a coffee-colour, similar to that formerly preferred by washers of Court-ruffles. I recollect that the knives and forks matched pretty well; but the plates of Queen's ware had not only been ill-used by being put upon the hob, by which they had lost some of their gadrooned-edges, but were of an unequal size, and the dishes were flat and therefore held little gravy. The dinner consisted of a roasted leg of pork, the joint scented by their friend Taylor; a salad with four heads of celery standing pyramidically; mashed turnips neatly spooned over a large flat plate to the height of a quarter of an inch; and, lastly,

——Lo! a lobster introduced in state,
Whose ample body stretches o'er the plate.

The side-dishes were a chicken and a rein-deer's tongue, with parsley and butter, but the boat was without a ladle, and the plate hardly large enough for it to stand in. Close to Mrs. Nollekens's left elbow, stood a dumb-waiter with cheese, a slice of butter, a few water-cresses, and a change of plates, knives, and forks.

The dinner being announced, there was a great rustling of silks for preference of places, and I concluded, by the party drawing their chairs close, they were ready to begin; but Bronze used to say, 'No one could eat till he was red in the face at master's table.' The set at the table consisted of Nollekens, his wife, and five on a side. No challenges at dinner that I heard of, nor do I think wine was even mentioned until the servants were ordered to '*take off*'. Much about this time there was a great bustle, in which I distinctly heard Mrs. Nollekens's voice vociferate, 'I will have it found!' At last Bronze entered, to whom she had given peremptory commands to fetch it. *Mr. Nollekens.* 'And, *arter* all, pray where did you find it?'—*Bronze.* 'Why, Sir, under the pillow of your bed.'—'There, Mr. N., I knew you had used it last night.' Nollekens ordered Bronze out of the room, saying 'he never liked that woman—her mouth looked so much like the rump of a chicken.' This nameless article was then caught first by one elderly maiden, and then by another; and as for Miss Welch, she declared a '*back-scratch*' to be the most agreeable thing imaginable, and she was glad it was found, as it had been her mother's; adding that Cowper was perfectly correct in his assertion upon things mislaid—

For 'tis a truth well known to most,
That whatsoever thing is lost,
We seek it, ere it come to light,
In every cranny,—but the right.

Mrs. Nollekens. 'My dear Nolly, you had no occasion to have wasted the writing-paper for the claret; for as it is the only bottle with a tall neck, we should have known it. My dear Mrs. Paradice, you may safely take a glass of it; for it is the last of twelve which Mr. Caleb Whitefoord sent us as a present; and every body who talks about wine, should know his house has ever been famous for claret.'—*Mr. Nollekens.* 'Don't crack the nuts with your teeth, Miss Moser; you'll spoil them.'—'Ay, and what would Mr. Fuseli say to that?' asked Mr. Saunders Welch, who now spake for the first time. The ladies at last retired, and Bronze soon declared tea to be ready; upon which the gentlemen went to the drawing-room, though without Mr. Nollekens, who remained to give orders for the salad to be put up again for the next day.

On the following morning, Mr. Taylor popped in as usual, and wished to know 'in the name of Fortune!' who had dined there yesterday; and being told of a few of the persons, one of whom had just lost his wife, his memory served him again as to his old master Hayman. 'Ay,' said he, 'my master, Frank Hayman, was a droll dog. I recollect when he buried his wife, a friend asked him why he expended so much money on her funeral?—"Ah, Sir!" replied he, "she would have done as much, or more, for me with pleasure."'

Mrs. Nollekens was a collector of prints, by receiving presents from those Engravers who were candidates for the Associates' chairs in the Royal Academy. She had several engravings after Claude, with whom she always expressed herself delighted; and whenever she had occasion to show them, would invariably make the following observation: 'It is very remarkable that Claude, Salvator Rosa, and Nicholas Poussin, lived close beside each other on the Trinità del Monte'.

Mrs. Nollekens, well knowing her dear father to be fond of a glass of Yorkshire ale, endeavoured economically to procure a little, though her attempts were unsuccessful; and indeed she was frequently heard to declare herself by no means obliged to her neighbour, Mr. Sparrow, for so often declining to allow her something for the odd bottles she had in her cellar. It was true that they were mostly of different shapes and sizes, but that she could not help, as they were all presents. 'However,' added she, 'as that is the case, they would better suit all sorts of purposes; he might have taken them, particularly as I have frequently told him Mr. Nollekens did not punish him for having his bills stuck against our yard-gates, when he advertised for his son:' a fine youth, who was afterwards discovered to have been drowned when bathing in Marylebone Basin.

Mr. and Mrs. Nollekens, who made a point of never visiting people at their country lodgings, where there was often too great a make-shift, had no objection to obey the truly kind commands of Sir Joshua Reynolds,

Sir William Chambers, or Mr. Wilton, at their delightful villas, where every thing was perfection itself; but they were more particularly pleased, when Sir Joshua accommodated Dr. Johnson and themselves with seats in his carriage.

By such an indulgence, they not only avoided the fare to Richmond, but by keeping the carriage some time at the door, to the great annoyance of the Doctor, who once roared out, 'Come, Nolly! Nolly!'—proved to the Rev. Mr. Martin,[1] and other neighbours in Mortimer-street, who were sure at that moment to be applied to for her lost cat, how much they were respected by the President of the Royal Academy and the renowned Doctor Johnson: the latter being at that time so popular, that gentlemen continued to pass and repass, purposely to feed their sight upon so excellent and learned a character.

During a severe frost, after a heavy fall of snow, an Oxford-market butcher meeting Nollekens at the barber's, requested him to visit a snow-house, which he and several other lads of the steel had erected, in which he said twelve pretty corpulent people could comfortably dine. Our Sculptor being always fond of sights, went with him; when a few greasy brothers of the knife surrounded him within, and swore they would not let him out unless he paid his footing. The R.A., however, gave them only sixpence, insisting that it was quite enough for a model in snow; which so exasperated the brutal architects, that the wickedest son of Palladio thawed with a warm, smoky poker, the name of Nollekens upon the outside of the hut,

[1] Of this most respectable clergyman, who for many years was Mr. Nollekens's next-door neighbour, there are two most admirable likenesses, both painted and engraved by Linnell. Mr. Martin, whose literary works are well known, for many years had a Chapel in Grafton-street, Soho, from whence he went to an entirely new one in Keppel-street, Russell-square.

which induced the observers to believe and report that he had made it. This most scandalous insinuation annoyed Mrs. Nollekens exceedingly, and the butchers insisted upon her giving them five shillings to take it out, which demand she paid, and afterwards went by the appellation of their Frosty Friend. Indeed, for a long time, Nollekens was bantered by Barry, the Painter,—who, though he could not bear a joke, knew pretty well where to pass one, and was perfectly master of wit enough to render it a nuisance to those at whose door he thought proper to throw it,—gave Nollekens the nick-name of a 'Frozen-hearted architect', who could 'so coolly, in such an inclement season, deliberately erect a mansion, with neither a door, a window, nor a fire-place. And how, in the name of Fortune, he could think of gaining a tenant to reimburse himself for two weeks together, was to his friends quite enigmatical. However, there was one thing which even his enemies could not charge him with, a fault too common among many modern builders,—he had not laid a rotten foundation.'

No friend could perplex Mrs. Nollekens more, than by presenting her with a turkey, when she was without a cook to draw the sinews of the legs; as every poulterer in the neighbourhood had repeatedly refused her custom, in consequence of her tiresome mode of offering them less than the market-price for their chickens, and always leaving their shops without once making a single purchase, so that her only means of procuring poultry was of the higglers: their fowls, she found out, were either so ill fed, or of such an enormous age, that there was no gravy to follow the knife; a sure proof, she observed, that they could neither be the genuine Dorking, nor the true 'barn-door birds'. There was one man, however, a cheesemonger, then living at the corner of Wells-street, who always got the whip-hand of her in an exchange for butter, whenever she had more game in the house than would well keep for use; for as to giving any away, that was an act she could not honestly record in her diary, whilst she could get Mr. Mason's butter in return; cheese being never allowed, nor seen in her house, but at set dinners; when, as there was a partition in the old family tray, she generally sported samples of two sorts, taking particular care that they should not be too heavy for Bronze to put on over the head of her master.

When straw-hats had become unfashionable, Mrs. Nollekens hinted to old White, the hatter of Fleet-street, who frequently came to show Nollekens one of his Roman medals, or a lamp, that possibly he could accommodate her with a Leghorn hat at a moderate rate. White, who was a cunning old fox, and well knew how to plough with another man's heifer, seldom visited Mr. Nollekens's studio, by way of getting the loan of a model, or a squeeze of something old or singularly curious, without first looking into the parlour to see how his dear friend Welch's daughter was; at the same time taking care to present her with an old-fashioned hat, well knowing that she cut them into more modern shapes, and covered them either with velvet from an old tippet, or a silk hatband. Nollekens, finding his wife always benefited by these visits, never refused White a squeeze of a patera, or any thing that would answer his purpose; and at the same time, when he was gone, he readily joined in the laugh against old Gerrard, and the other fools who had been for years duped by old White, who had turned his wine-cellars into manufactories for the produce of cast coins, and modern squeezes from Roman lamps. These imitations White put into auctions and venders' shops for sale, and they were actually bought with avidity by the profound judges and collectors of such trash; who would, when the secret was discovered, rather than acknowledge their own want of judgment in such matters, boldly insist upon their originality, and call the man who declared himself as their fabricator 'an impudent impostor'. White has not been the only one whose performances have deceived unwary collectors; and even the learned have sometimes been pleased to impose copies upon themselves, to the no little injury of the man of real taste and talent, who produced some of their boasted treasures from the rough material. There can be little doubt as to the possibility of deceiving collectors in almost every pursuit; and I should expect, that if the imitations of Greek and Roman art could declare themselves, many a curious tale could be told by some of those now hoarded up in cabinets, for which pretty heavy sums have been given by their happy possessors.

I must own Mrs. Nollekens had one quality which dignifies a superior woman—she seldom interfered in her husband's profession and concerns with the world; and during the whole of my observations upon that lady's deportment, I witnessed only two liberties, if, indeed, they may be called so, that she took with her Nolly's professional career: and one was when that great article of consumption, butter, was concerned. One morning, a very handsome woman, who lodged in the first-floor of No. 5, Oxford-market, modestly rapped at the door. Mr. Nollekens, who was giving me instructions to knead the clay for a bust of Mr. Mathias, according to his usual custom, answered the knock, and when he saw the beautiful creature, whom I had seen over the window-blinds, he said, 'Come in, my dear; who sent you to me?'—'No one, Sir; my friends tell me I have a peculiar talent for modelling in butter, and I have brought a few pigs and sheep in this butter-boat to show you.'—'Walk in, walk in, this is only my pupil, and he won't say a word about it.' —'I beg your pardon, Sir, for the intrusion; perhaps I ought to have informed you that I am a housekeeper in want of a situation, and finding that the knowledge of modelling animals in butter would greatly add to my recommendation, I have taken the liberty of submitting the little things I have done to your inspection.'

At this moment the studio-door was opened, and Mrs. Nollekens, with her usual precision of words, stepped up to her husband, and, putting her finger upon his sleeve, said, 'Surely, Mr. Nollekens will not suffer himself to be looked upon in the light of a pastry-cook! what have you, my dear Sir, to do with modelling in butter? the world will say that you have taught Mrs.—what is your name, my good woman?' —'Wilmot.'—'Mrs. Wilmot to model in butter! Pray, are you married, Mrs. Wilmot?'—'No, I can't say I am married, Ma'am.'—'Mr. Nollekens, I wish to speak with you in the next room.'—What was said there, I know not, but Mrs. Wilmot observed to me, 'She is jealous—so far my good looks are against me.'

In what way Mr. Nollekens was prevailed upon I cannot tell, but true it is, he did not return into the room, though his wife entered, who delivered the following address to the handsome housekeeper:—'Mr. Nollekens is extremely sorry to say, that his professional engagements, at this season of the year, will not permit him to attend to your wishes; but that, if you will leave your address with me, he will consider himself your debtor.' Mrs. Wilmot gave the address as before mentioned, and then, after replacing her lambs, sheep, and pigs in the butter-boat, retired gracefully; at least, in my opinion; though, at that time, I must own, my ideas of grace were not very extensive. It was curious to remark, that for some time after the visit from the beautiful butter-modeller of Oxford-market, Mrs. Nollekens made her husband pass the lady's door, in order to discover how far he had an inclination to improve her acquaintance.

After this rencontre, Mrs. Nollekens ventured occasionally to give an opinion as to the propriety of professional applications to Mr. Nollekens; for I recollect another intrusion upon him of a similar kind, by a person who cut out castles, rocks, and mountains upon the backs of shells, and all with a common pen-knife. Here, for the love of the true character of Nolly's professional life, she again interfered, observing to him, that he ought not to attend to such visitors. 'You might just as well,' continued she, 'praise the carvings upon a Wycherley comb, so carefully preserved by the collectors of old china and such gimcracks. Why, bless my heart! soon, Sir, you will have the man who dresses Doctor Lettsom's glass wig, to know how he ought to replace a deficient curl, or how much of its possessor's face it should cover, so that his forehead might be seen to the best advantage.'

Mrs. Nollekens, from her mother's experience, insisted that it was by far the cheapest and least troublesome plan for a single person, whose health required fresh air, and was unattended by a servant, to lodge at a regular boarding-house; as the lower class of people, in general, who let lodgings, were much addicted to pilfer from every article of consumption.

Towards the latter part of her life, she expressed a wish to go once more to Hampstead, a spot considered by most physicians and landscape-painters as the most salubrious and beautiful of all the Montpeliers of England; but she could neither make up her mind as to the enormous expense of its accommodations, nor as to the peculiar fragrance of its seven sorts of air, which of them she ought then to prefer. The latter perplexity afforded her at times much conversation; and when she was requested to name the seven airs, she, in an elevated voice, stated them thus. 'My dear Sir, there are the four sides of the hill, each receiving freely the air from the four quarters. There is the hill itself, very clear, but certainly often bleak. Then there is the "Vale of Health", as it is called, in a stagnate bottom; a pit in the heath, where, if a bit of paper is whirling in the air, it can never rise above the high ground about it. And is there not also the mild air of the centre of the town, where the situation, though high, is entirely sheltered by surrounding buildings?'

Wilson, Gainsborough, Loutherbourg, and Kirk, for several years had lodgings at Hampstead; and made that spot the seat of their morning and evening study: and Collins and Linnell, now inhabitants, are constantly seen culling its beauties. It is also, occasionally, the residence of Beechey, Phillips, and Westall; and I have seen Callcott, Arnald, the Reinagles, Burnet, and Martin, enjoying its luxuriant windings. Old Oram, the Landscape-painter, and member of the Board of Works, who was a man of some genius, inhabited the house south of Jack Straw's Castle. And it was to Hampstead that Hayley's friend, Romney, the Painter, retired in the decline of his life, when he built a dining-room close to his kitchen, with a buttery-hatch opening into it, so that he and his friends might enjoy beef-steaks, hot and hot, upon the same plan as the members of the Beef-steak Club are supplied at their room in the Lyceum.

No persons could more cordially hate each other than Romney and Nollekens; Mr. Greville, Hayley, and Flaxman, were staunch friends of the former, who, from some pique, objected to the latter modelling from any of his portraits. Flaxman, on the contrary, was so great a favourite with Romney, that, in his letters to Hayley, he absolutely idolizes him; and in one, written at the time he was hourly expected in London from Rome, he exultingly exclaims, 'Huzza! Flaxman's arrived!'

To return; Hampstead has been for years resorted to by Barret, Fielding, Glover, Hills, Hunt, Prout, Pyne, Robson, the Varleys, and all the other celebrated water-colour draughtsmen, whose productions have so astonishingly surpassed those of their predecessors, both in this and in every other country.

My old school-fellow, Smith, the Grocer, of Margaret-street, has been frequently heard to declare, that whenever Mrs. Nollekens purchased tea and sugar at his father's shop, she always requested, just as at the moment she was quitting the counter, to have either a clove or a bit of cinnamon to take some unpleasant taste out of her mouth; but she never was seen to apply it to the part so affected: so that, with Nollekens's nutmegs, which he pocketed from the table at the Academy dinners, they contrived to accumulate a little stock of spices, without any expense whatever.

Mrs. Nollekens's friends, after frequently wondering to see her in shoes so varied in their embroidery, and being well aware that she would never think of indulging in such expensive articles in a *spick-and-span* new state, all agreed that she certainly must have purchased them second-hand; and by their maids, who were encouraged to *pump* Bronze, were satisfied that it was really the fact; and were also informed that her muffs and parasols were obtained in the same way. Mrs. Nollekens would often plume herself with borrowed feathers; a shawl or a muff of a friend she never refused when returning home, observing, that she was quite sure they would keep her warm; never caring how they suffered from the rain, so that her neighbours saw her apparelled in what they had never before seen her wear.

CHAPTER V

Mr. Nollekens's fancies and his wife's jealousy.—Anecdote of the Sculptor, Dr. Johnson, and Mrs. Thrale.—Lord Besborough.—Charles Bannister.—The Sculptor's assistants and pupils.—Dr. Johnson's encouragement of the Author.—Instances of benevolence and eccentricity in Mr. Nollekens.—Notices of his relations.—Saunders Welch, his father-in-law.—Anecdote of Wilkes.—Henry Fielding, and his character from life.—Dr. Johnson's intimacy with the Welch family.—Death, epitaph, and will, of Mr. Welch.—Recollections of him by Mrs. Nollekens.—His prudence and resolution as a Magistrate.—Silver tea-pot, and other reliques of Dr. Johnson.—Mr. Welch's humanity.—Anecdotes of Wilson.

Of all the varieties of itinerant amusements before Mr. Punch came into vogue, none seemed to give Nollekens more pleasure than the Milk-maids' dance on May-day; of which he was so avowed an admirer, that Mrs. Crosdale, my old school-mistress and his opposite neighbour, assured me that she one May-day witnessed no less than five garlands, and their lasses, who had danced at his parlour window, to each of whom he had given half-a-crown.

This indulgence of his was considered by Mrs. Nollekens as a great piece of extravagance, until she discovered from Bronze that it was the custom of most of the abandoned women who sat to him for his Venuses, to hire themselves as dancers upon those occasions; and as he constantly promised to give each of them something when they came, he always made a point of staying at home to see them display their agility. Sometimes Mrs. Nollekens, whose exquisite feelings induced her to stand at a distance to watch their lascivious movements, would rate him for descending to such low pleasures. 'A man like you,' she would say, 'who could obtain orders at any time for the Opera House, where you could see Vestris, and who is visited by the Noveres; how you can agitate your feet as you do, at such strumming, is to me perfectly astonishing! See! look over the way at the first-floor window of the Sun and Horse-shoe, the landlord and his wife are laughing at you: and I declare, there is Finney, your brute of a mason, yes, and his son Kit, ay, and old John Panzetta, the polisher, looking over their shoulders. How can you so expose yourself, Mr. Nollekens? I wish, from my heart, Doctor Burney would come in just now! and I am quite sure that Miss Hawkins, poor as her ear is for music, whose playing, as the Doctor says, distracts one to hear,—even she, I say, could never be pleased with such trash as you are now listening to.' But he was deaf to all her remonstrances, and continued to move his head to the movement of the feet of the girls, with as much gratification as the man of real taste and feeling expresses at this day, when he is riveted to the magic sweetness of Samuel Wesley's voluntaries.

Bronze, my informant, also stated, that as soon as Nolly had left the room to get his half-crown, Mrs. Nollekens, after slowly and silently creeping to his abdicated place at the window, made the spot just in time to catch a hussey's wanton and decoying leer, intended for her husband, at the very tantalizing moment that the blind disciple of Geminiani was striking up Arnold's rondo of 'Come, thou rosy dimpled boy!' Upon his re-entering the room, her face being reddened and her anger raised, she recommenced her lecture with redoubled vociferation till the dance was over; after which, finding her jobations of no avail, and having paced the carpet pretty often, and as often convinced herself that her gloves fitted closely to her fingers, she, bursting with passion, vowed to tell her sister. 'So do,' returned Nolly; 'and then she'll tell you what a great fool you *was* for having me, as she always does.'—'You filthy thing!' rejoined Mrs. Nollekens, 'your grovelling birth protects you from my chastisement.'—'Come, I like that vastly,' rejoined her husband: 'true it is, your father possessed a *plum;* but then it was only a grocer's one. Why, I had five times the money he died worth when I made you my wife; and you know what you whispered to me in bed about your mother. Come, let us have no more of your impertinence; I won't stand it,—now, once for all, I tell you that.' Just as Mrs. Nollekens opened the door, she exclaimed, 'What, you're here, Mr. Eavesdropper! and pray, Mr. Christopher, what do you want?'—'Why, Ma'am, there's the woman that Mr. Cosway recommended at the yard-gate, dancing to Jack-in-the-Green, and wants to see master.'—'Indeed! There, Sir! there is another of your women! What! and you will go to her too! It's very well, Sir! mighty well, Sir! Oh fie! fie! The first year of our marriage, you told me you should dispense with such people; but you are like all the rest of your sex, always seeking for new beauties.'

Just as Nollekens had closed his leathern bag, and was about to leave Jack's lady, a high personage, who came to sit for her busto, was announced; and then the lecture rested till the nocturnal curtains were drawn, when Bronze heard the culprit mumble for some time, as is usual in such cases, before the curtains of his eyes were suffered to drop for the enjoyment of balmy and refreshing sleep.

Mrs. Thrale one morning entered Nollekens's studio, accompanied by Doctor Johnson, to see the bust of Lord Mansfield, when the Sculptor vociferated, 'I like your picture by Sir Joshua very much. He tells me it's for Thrale, a brewer, over the water: his wife's a sharp woman, one of the blue-stocking people.'—'Nolly, Nolly,' observed the Doctor, 'I wish your maid would stop your foolish mouth with a blue-bag.' At which Mrs. Thrale smiled, and whispered to the

Doctor, 'My dear Sir, you'll get nothing by blunting your arrows upon a block.'

The late Earl of Besborough was so well known to Nollekens's dog, that whenever the animal saw his Lordship's leg within the gate, he ceased barking, and immediately welcomed the visitor; who always brought a French-roll in his blue great-coat-pocket purposely for him, with which his Lordship took great pleasure in feeding him. But whenever he had been thus fed, Nollekens would say, when cutting his meat, 'There, that's enough for you, you have had a roll to-day; the other half will do for to-morrow.'

Whilst I am speaking of this truly benevolent nobleman, I will take the opportunity of observing, that I have heard my father relate the following anecdotes of him:—

His Lordship was once standing to see the workmen pull down the wooden railing and brick-work which surrounded the centre of Cavendish-square, when a sailor walked up to him and asked him for a quid of tobacco: his Lordship answered, 'My friend, I don't take tobacco.'—'Don't you?' rejoined the sailor; 'I wish you did, Master, for I have not had a bit to-day.' As he was turning away, his Lordship called to him and said, 'Here, my friend, here is something that will enable you to buy tobacco,' and gave him half-a-crown.

At another time, a poor woman, with two children, who appeared much distressed, but was remarkably clean, curtseyed to his Lordship as he was passing; he drew out his purse, but in attempting to give her two shillings, they dropped, and rolled into the kennel, upon which, his Lordship, after picking them up, wiped them with his pocket-handkerchief before he gave them to the distressed widow.

Mr. Nollekens, who was honoured with frequent visits from his Lordship, once asked his assistants in the studio, if they had noticed his diamond buckles;

adding, that as they had belonged to his wife, he had worn them in common ever since her Ladyship's death.

I was one time assisting Mr. Nollekens in the parlour, in piling up clay for a bust of General Paoli, when his attention was called away by Mrs. Nollekens, who cried out, 'Nolly! Nolly! come here; there's old Bannister over the way, who used to mimic the cats in the gutter at Marylebone Gardens, when my father's friend, Tommy Lowe, was Manager!'—*Nollekens*. 'He's a good-looking John Bull; his son was a student in our Royal Academy, he studied under Loutherbourg (called Leatherbag in the play): I remember he used to frighten our old John devilishly with his tragedy tricks.' Miss Moser and Mrs. Carter being present at these remarks, 'My father,' observed the former, 'was glad when he left the Academy, though he liked him so well, that he took a whole box at his first appearance; and he was nobly received, I assure you.' *Mrs. Nollekens*. 'He is a most excellent actor.' 'Ay,' observed the celebrated Mrs. Carter, as she was returning to the fire-side, 'and what is still more, he bears the *best of characters* off the stage, for he is known under the friendly appellation of Honest Jack.' It is related of Charles Bannister, that when returning to town from Epsom, in a gig, accompanied by a friend, they found themselves pennyless when they arrived at Kensington-gate, where the man would not let them pass without paying the toll. Bannister, however, offered to sing him a song, and immediately struck up the 'Tempest of War'; his voice was heard afar, and 'Bannister! Bannister!' was the cry. The gate was soon thronged, and he was loudly encored by the voters returning from Brentford; this he complied with, and the turnpike-man declared him to be 'a noble fellow', and that he would pay fifty tolls for him at any gate.

By this time, William Arminger, the young man

whom Nollekens had employed in cutting Dr. Goldsmith's epitaph, had become extremely useful to him, for he had, by slow degrees, improved himself in the art of cutting marble as a sculptor. My father was then Nollekens's principal assistant; and Delvaux, a nephew of the Sculptor of that name, Plara, the elder Gahagan, and Green,[1] were among his best workmen.

It is not because it has been stated that Mr. Nollekens was little more than one remove from an idiot, that I should omit mentioning an act of charity bestowed by him on a fellow-creature.

The first act of his relaxation from meanness which I witnessed, was the following. An artist, named George Richardson, who published several useful works, particularly upon architectural decorations, was an old man at the period I speak of, and lived at No. 105, Titchfield-street, for many years, during which time he occasionally walked around the studio. One day, he was asked by Mr. Nollekens, what made him look so dull: 'I am low-spirited,' he replied. 'Then go to the pump and take a drink of water,' was the advice in return. The poor old man, after remaining a few minutes looking vacantly about him, went

[1] The son of the celebrated actress, the daughter of Hippesley, and pupil of Kitty Clive. At this time Mr. Charles Townley was a constant visitor to the studio, and I remember him as being the first patron who ever gave me money as an encouragement to proceed in my studies; for upon his noticing a drawing which I was then making, he took out his purse and presented me with half a guinea to buy chalks and paper: but what is more singular in my humble history is, that Dr. Samuel Johnson came up to me the same day, and feeling for my head, put his hand upon it, and said, 'Very well, Aratus!' that being the bust I was copying. I can perfectly remember the figure of that awkward and mighty man, whose benevolence, loyalty, and strict religious principles will ever stand high examples to mankind; notwithstanding the numerous attacks which have frequently been made upon his reputation.

away in tears. Mr. Nollekens, who had just before been summoned to dinner, upon his return, observed to my Father, that Richardson 'looked glumpish'. 'Ah! Sir,' rejoined my Father, 'he is distressed, poor fellow! and you have hurt his feelings by desiring him to go to the pump for relief; he was in tears when he left us.'—'Bless me! I hurt him!' cried Nollekens, and hastily walked out with his head foremost, putting both hands into his pockets. The next morning Mr. Richardson was waiting at the studio for my Father, to whom he gratefully expressed himself for what he had said to Mr. Nollekens, who had been with him the preceding evening, and after asking if he were offended with him for recommending the pump, stated, that when he was low-spirited the pump always brought him to. Mr. Richardson, upon disclosing his circumstances, expressed a wish to leave the world in the same room in which his wife died: 'Well,' observed Nollekens, 'and why should you not die there? it's only a garret; let the rest of the house, man, you'll live rent free; one room will do for you; sell your furniture. Here, I have brought you twenty guineas, and I'll allow you the same sum every year as long as you live.'—Indeed my opinion of Mr. Nollekens is, that had he been led into good actions, he would have performed more; and it is only to be lamented, that some kind-hearted individual had not endeavoured to make him understand, in the latter part of his long life, when he had heaped up such immense sums, that he should have recollected his poor cousins at Antwerp, if they *were* his cousins. At all events, he should not have forgotten the near relations of his wife at Aylesbury; then, and now, declining in the deepest sorrow and aged infirmity, either within the walls or the precincts of the workhouse. It is, however, unaccountable, that, at the very time when he was so very humane to poor Richardson, he absolutely suffered his own uncle and aunt to sell their beds to support them in water-gruel; and it was not until the kind interference of Mr. Saunders Welch, who had, with his daughter Anne, seen them in Paris, that he allowed them thirty pounds a year. Their melancholy situation has been proved by several letters addressed to Mr. Nollekens, and lately produced before the Master in Chancery by Mr. Nelson Beechey, with a sight of which I have been favoured by John Stone, Esq. of Southampton-street, Bloomsbury, Solicitor to Mr. Jasper Peck, one of Nollekens's first cousins, to whom he had left some very trifling remembrances, considering his near relationship to his own mother. To the Rev. Mr. Kenrick Peck, another of his first cousins, nothing was left; and that gentleman has several children dependent on him for support.

In speaking of these relations, it seems proper that I should now lay before my readers some little account of Saunders Welch, Esq. the father of Mrs. Nollekens. He was born at Aylesbury, was educated in the workhouse of that town, and was apprenticed to one of the most popular men of his day, Mr. Clements, the celebrated Trunk-maker, at the corner of St. Paul's Church-yard, in London. But I must pass him on to manhood, for the want of intermediate information, with which his relative, Mr. Woodcock, is not able to furnish me,—and fix him in trade, for he was many years a grocer, occupying the shop, No. 1, at the south-west corner of Museum-street, late Queen-street. My worthy friend, William Packer, Esq. of Great Baddow in Essex, and many other venerable persons, recollect seeing him as High-Constable of Westminster, dressed in black, with a large, nine-story George the Second's wig, highly-powdered, with long flowing curls over his shoulders, a high three-cornered hat, and his black bâton tipped with silver at either end, riding on a white horse to Tyburn with the malefactors. Mr. Welch was a member of the Beef-steak Club, when founded by Mr. Rich and George Lambert, the Scene-painter, with whom he was intimate; and I have often heard Mrs. Nollekens say, it was her business to dress up for him a round hat with ribbons, similar to those worn by the Yeomen of his Majesty's Guard, which the gentlemen of that club then wore: she added too, that her father was so loyal a man, that when Wilkes was admitted a member, he withdrew himself.

My friend the late Mr. Thomas Grignon, of Russell-street, Covent-garden, informed me, that as Mr. Wilkes was passing the house in which he then lived, in a hackney-chair, his father tapped at the window to him, which notice Mr. Wilkes returned by kissing his hand; but he had not gone three yards, before he ordered one of the chairmen to go to the gentleman who had tapped at the window, and inform him that he wished to speak with him. Mr. Grignon immediately went to him, and was addressed in nearly the following manner. 'Grignon, you are intimate with Sir John Fielding. I am going to him upon a very singular business, will you accompany me?'—'Certainly,' he replied; 'let me fetch my hat.' They went, and Mr. Wilkes, to the great astonishment of his friend, addressed the sitting-magistrate, Mr. Spinnage, Sir John Fielding being absent, to this effect. 'Sir, *I demand a warrant* to arrest the persons of the Secretaries of State, by whose order my bureau, desk, and escritoire, have been broken open, and all my papers seized!'—'God bless me!' said Mr. Grignon; 'friend Wilkes, you are another John.'—'Whom do you mean? John Hampden?'—'No; John Lilburn,' he rejoined. —'*Well it's all one*,' observed Wilkes. Mr. Spinnage, however, refused to grant the warrant; and Mr. Wilkes, after persisting in his right, and threatening the Magistrate, went to Justice Welch, who smiled at his threats, and refused his request. It must be here observed, that Mr. Grignon was not aware of Mr. Wilkes's business or intention, when he first accompanied him; but, as he was a most liberal man, he would not desert him in a moment of difficulty. My friend Grignon assured me, that his father's inadvertence deprived him of many of his best customers; though he added, that his father had no other acquaintance with Mr. Wilkes, than that of frequently meeting him at the Beef-steak Club.

Mr. Henry Fielding, in his 'Journal of a Voyage to Lisbon', in 1754, published in 1755, when stating his great difficulty of moving himself, being dreadfully afflicted with the dropsy, says, 'By the assistance of my friend Mr. Welch, whom I never think or speak of but with love and esteem, I conquered this difficulty.' This was when he was getting into the vessel at Rotherhithe. When they were at Gravesend, Monday, July 1st, he says, 'This day Mr. Welch took his leave of me, after dinner.'[1]

[1] Henry Fielding was fond of colouring his pictures of life with the glowing and variegated tints of Nature, by conversing with persons of every situation and calling, as I have frequently been informed by one of my great-aunts, the late Mrs. Hussey, who knew him intimately. I have heard her say that Mr. Fielding never suffered his talent for sprightly conversation to mildew for a moment; and that his manners were so gentlemanly, that even with the lower classes, with which he frequently condescended particularly to chat, such as Sir Roger De Coverley's old friends, the Vauxhall watermen, they seldom outstepped the limits of propriety. My aunt, who lived to the age of 105, had been blessed with four husbands, and her name had twice been changed to that of Hussey: she was of a most delightful disposition, of a retentive memory, highly entertaining, and liberally communicative; and to her, I have frequently been obliged for an interesting anecdote. She was, after the death of her second husband, Mr. Hussey, a fashionable sacque and mantua-maker, and lived in the Strand, a few doors west of the residence of the celebrated Le Beck, a famous cook, who had a large portrait of himself for the sign of his house, at the north-west corner of Half-moon-street, since called Little Bedford-street. One day, Mr. Fielding observed to

Mr. Boswell states, that Dr. Johnson maintained a long and intimate friendship with Mr. Welch, who succeeded Fielding as one of his Majesty's Justices of the Peace for Westminster, and kept a regular Office for the Police of that district. The Doctor begins a letter addressed to Saunders Welch, Esq. at the English Coffee-house, Rome, dated February 3d, 1778:—'Dear Sir,—To have suffered one of my best and dearest friends to pass almost two years in foreign countries without a letter, has a very shameful appearance of inattention. But the truth is, that there was no particular time in which I had any thing particular to say; and general expressions of good-will, I hope, our long friendship is grown too solid to want.' The Doctor, speaking of Miss Welch in another part of the same letter, notices that lady thus: 'Miss Nancy has doubtless kept a constant and copious journal.' It was not, however, towards Miss Welch that the Doctor had serious thoughts, but of her sister Mary; and I have heard Mr. Nollekens say, that the Doctor, when joked about her, observed, 'Yes, I think Mary would

Mrs. Hussey, that he was then engaged in writing a novel, which he thought would be his best production; and that he intended to introduce in it the characters of all his friends. Mrs. Hussey, with a smile, ventured to remark, that he must have many niches, and that surely they must already be filled. 'I assure you, my dear Madam,' replied he, 'there shall be a bracket for a bust of you.' Sometime after this, he informed Mrs. Hussey, that the work was in the press; but, immediately recollecting that he had forgotten his promise to her, went to the printer, and was time enough to insert, in vol. III, p. 17, where he speaks of the shape of Sophia Western—

'Such charms are there in affability, and so sure is it to attract the praises of all kinds of people.

'It may, indeed, be compared to the celebrated Mrs. Hussey.' To which observation he has given the following note: 'A celebrated mantua-maker in the Strand, famous for setting off the shapes of women.'

have been mine, if little Joe had not stepped in.'—I must now, in order of time, state, that death spread his mantle over the family; and that every one grieved for the loss of Mr. Welch, who died at Taunton Dean, in the county of Somerset. Upon a mural monument, erected within the porch over the centre entrance of the Parish Church of St. George, Bloomsbury, is engraven the following inscription, written by Sir John Hawkins, Knt.[1]

'In the cemetery belonging to this Church lie the remains of Saunders Welch, Esq. late of this Parish, one of his Majesty's Justices of the Peace for the Counties of Middlesex, Surrey, and Buckingham, and for the City and Liberties of Westminster. He was born and educated at Aylesbury, in the County of Buckingham; and married Mary, the daughter of Will. Brotherton, Gent. by whom he had issue two surviving daughters, Maria and Ann. He departed this life 31st day of October, 1784, in the 74th year of his age.

As long as Themis with impartial hand
His blessings shall disperse throughout this land;
Or lenient statutes, or vindictive law,
Protect the good, or hold the bad in awe;
Or Mercy, blending Grace with Justice, shed
Her milder beams on the delinquent head;
While Probity and Truth shall be rever'd
And legal power as much belov'd as fear'd,
So long shall fame to each succeeding day
Thy virtues witness and thy worth display.'

Mr. Welch, in his will, dated December 10th, 1775, left his daughters Mary and Anne, equal proportions of his leasehold estates; but nearly all his moveables he bequeathed to Anne, for her tenderness towards him in his decline of life. Tillotson's Sermons, &c. fell to the lot of Mary. To Sir John Hawkins he left five guineas; to his son-in-law Nollekens he left fifteen

[1] Father of John Sidney Hawkins, Esq. one of the Editors of 'Ignoramus', Henry Hawkins, Esq., and Matilda Letitia Hawkins, with whose writings the public is well acquainted.

guineas, to be laid out in a set of silver castors; and to his steadfast friend Samuel Johnson, LL.D. whose memory must ever be revered, he left five guineas, which, says the entertaining Boswell, the Doctor 'received with tenderness as a kind memorial'. Mr. Welch's will has all the appearance of being genuine, and the greatest mass of the testator's property very properly devolved to his daughters. Indeed Mr. Welch was of such sound sense, that no one dared to direct his conduct, or even to delude him by flattery or presents.

Whenever Mrs. Nollekens related any anecdote of her father, she always elevated her person by standing upon her toes, at the conclusion of every extraordinary mark of his benevolence, courage, or sensible magisterial decision.

Mrs. Nollekens often spake of his going, in 1766, into Cranbourne-alley unattended, to quell the daily meeting of the journeymen-shoemakers, who had struck for an increase of wages. Immediately her father made his appearance he was recognized, and his name shouted up and down the Alley,—not with fear, but with a degree of exultation. 'Well,' said the ringleader, 'let us get him a beer-barrel and mount him;' and when he was up, they one and all gave him three cheers, and cried, '*Welch! Welch, for ever!*' In the mildest manner possible, Mr. Welch assured them that he was glad to find they had conducted themselves quietly; and at the same time, in the most forcible terms, persuaded them to disperse, as their meetings were illegal. He also observed to the master-shoemakers, who were listening to him from the first-floor windows, that as they had raised the prices of shoes on account of the increased value of provisions, they should consider that the families of their workmen had proportionate wants. The result was, that the spokesmen of their trade were called into the shops, and an additional allowance was agreed upon. The men then alternately carried Mr. Welch on their shoulders to his office in Litchfield-street, gave him three cheers more, and set him down. Welch was a tall man, and when in the prime of life, robust and powerful. But though his benevolence was unbounded in cases of distress, yet whenever necessity urged him to firmness, he was bold and resolute, as may be seen by the following anecdote.

When the streets were entirely paved with pebble-stones up to the houses, hackneymen could drive their coaches close to the very doors. It happened that Mr. Welch had good information, that a most notorious offender, who had for some time annoyed the Londoners in their walks through the green lanes to Mary-le-bone, and who had eluded the chase of several of his men, was in a first-floor of a house in Rose-street, Long-Acre. After hiring the tallest hackney-coach he could select, he mounted the box with the coachman, and when he was close against the house, he ascended the roof of the coach, threw up the sash of a first-floor window, entered the room, and actually dragged the fellow from his bed out at the window by his hair, naked as he was, upon the roof of the coach; and in that way carried the terror of the green lanes down New-street, and up St. Martin's-lane, amidst the huzzas of an immense throng which followed him to Litchfield-street.

Sir John Fielding took cognizance of those offenders who were nearest Bow-street, such, for instance, as the inhabitants of Lewkner's-lane, Vinegar-yard, and Short's-gardens; but more particularly that most popular of all gardens, I mean that which is within and in the middle of St. Paul's Parish; which garden became infamous, when its splendid inhabitants exchanged their residences for the newly-built mansions in Hanover, Grosvenor, and Cavendish-squares, and Holles, and the other streets adjacent. It was at that period, that Mother Needham, Mother Douglass;

(alias, according to Foote's 'Minor', Mother Cole,) and Moll King, the tavern-keepers, and the gamblers, took possession of the abdicated premises; so that Sir John Fielding was in the hot-bed of the three principal of all the vices.

Saunders Welch's attention was for the most part confined to the abandoned women and pickpockets who frequented Hedge-lane, the Hay-Market, Cranbourne-alley, and Leicester-fields; the last of which, from the rough and broken state of its ground, and the shadow of a lofty row of elms, which then stood in the road in front of most of the houses on the eastern side, was rendered a very dangerous part to pass, particularly before the streets were paved and publicly lighted.

In addition to these, Mr. Welch had visitors among the frequenters of Mary-le-bone gardens; the highwaymen who committed nightly depredations in the adjacent lanes; the pick-pockets who attended Whitfield's Meeting-house in Long Acre; and the thousands of his Sunday friends who congregated in Mary-le-bone-fields, before the New-road was made from Paddington to Islington; when the public newspapers announced an inhabitant of the city to have arrived safely at his house in Mary-le-bone! It was the practice of Mr. Whitfield, before his Chapel in Tottenham-court-road was finished in 1759, to preach of a Sunday evening in these fields; and I have been credibly informed by William Packer, Esq. a gentleman now living in his ninetieth year, that he was there when it was supposed 50,000 persons were present; so much were the Mary-le-bone fields frequented by the Londoners on a fine summer evening, and so great was the popularity of the preacher. Mr. Welch also derived no small share of business, from the depredators who attended the executions at Tyburn. His office on those mornings, as well as Fielding's, was thronged by gentlemen who had lost their watches and pocketbooks, or ladies who had been robbed of their velvet cardinals or purses.

Doctor Johnson soon followed his friend Welch to the grave, as he died on Monday the 13th of December, 1784, in the back room of the first-floor of his house in Bolt-court, Fleet-street; of which room I made a drawing, just before Mr. Bensley, the Printer, pulled that part of the house down to make way for a staircase.[1]

As few persons are aware of the following anecdote, I am sure that the curious reader will pardon my inserting it. Whilst I was assisting Mrs. Maria Cosway with my advice as to disposing of the collection of her late husband, and thus putting some thousands of pounds in her purse, I was one morning agreeably surprised by a letter which she put into my hand, written by W. Hoper, Esq. giving me permission to make a drawing of Dr. Johnson's silver tea-pot in his possession; an article which had been described to me by W. V. Hellyer, Esq. of the Middle-Temple, through whose kindness the owner had sent it to his friend Mrs. Cosway, first for me to have tea from, and then to draw it, both of which I did with no little delight. Upon the side of this tea-pot the following inscription is engraven: 'We are told by Lucian, that the earthen lamp, which had administered to the lucubrations of Epictetus, was at his death purchased for the enormous sum of three thousand drachmas: Why, then, may not imagination equally amplify the value of this unadorned vessel, long employed for the infusion of that favourite herb, whose enlivening virtues are said to have so often protracted the elegant and edifying lucubrations of Samuel Johnson; the zealous advocate of that innocent beverage, against its declared enemy, Jonas Hanway. It was weighed out for sale under the inspection of Sir John Hawkins, at the very

[1] There is not a vestige of the original house now remaining.

minute when they were in the next room closing the incision through which Mr. Cruickshank had explored the ruinated machinery of its dead master's thorax,—so Bray the Silversmith, conveyed there in Sir John's carriage, thus hastily to buy the plate, informed its present possessor, Henry Constantine Nowell; by whom it was, for its celebrated services, on the 1st of November, 1788, rescued from the undiscriminating obliterations of the furnace.'

The ensuing is an answer to one of my interrogatory epistles, affording me another opportunity of recording the fate of two other articles which had been the property of the late Dr. Johnson; and as it was received from my friend the Rev. Hugh Bailye, Canon of Lichfield, I shall print it with a double gratification.

Lichfield, May 1st, 1821.

DEAR SIR,

I CERTAINLY am in possession of the late Dr. Johnson's watch, which I purchased from his black servant, Francis Barber, (*vide* 'Boswell's Life', for an account of this watch.) Dr. Johnson's punch-bowl is likewise in my possession; and was purchased by the Rev. Thomas Harwood, the Historian of Lichfield; it was bought at Mr. Harwood's sale by John Barker Scott, Esq. banker, who afterwards presented it to me.

I am, dear Sir,
Your's faithfully,
HUGH BAILYE.

To John Thomas Smith, Keeper of the Prints in the British Museum.

In vol. xxiv, page 72, of Cole's MSS. in the British Museum, the reader will find a copy of a letter addressed to Mr. Cole by George Steevens, dated May 14th, 1782; and as it will afford the collector of the various portraits of Dr. Johnson, a notice of one little known, I have here inserted it.

'As some return for the portrait of Mr. Gray, and the specimen of his hand-writing, I present you with the original sketch Dr. Johnson made for his life of Pope. Be not angry when you find that the same parcel includes his "Deformities", a Scottish pamphlet, written by a club of Caledonian wits. Every bookseller of credit in London has refused to sell it. The Doctor (who, by-the-by, is very ill, and I have many fears about him) laughs at such ribaldry, and offered, by way of Frontispiece to it, a very ugly head of himself, which was meant to have been prefixed to his "Beauties", but was cancelled at my desire.'

Mr. Welch, who was never happier than when he was rendering assistance to those among his numerous friends who stood in need of it, once kindly blamed Wilson, the Landscape-painter, when he found him in a dejected state. 'You never come to dine with me now,' said he, 'though you used to partake of my round of beef, and I am sure we have had many pleasant hours together.' Poor Wilson, who had existed for some time without selling a picture, regretted that Mr. Welch was not a collector of paintings. 'I certainly do not understand them, my good fellow,' said he; 'however, if you will dine with me next Monday week, I will then bespeak a fifteen-guinea picture of you.' Wilson pronounced him to be a noble creature, and taking him by the hand, added, 'Heaven knows where I may be by that time.' Mr. Welch then asked him, 'Are you engaged to-morrow?'—'No,' replied he. 'Well, then,' returned his friend, 'if you will send a picture to my house, and join me at dinner, I will pay you the money.' What person possessing the feelings of an English artist, can hear the name of Wilson mentioned, without secretly exulting that he was a native of our envied Island? and those who have perused the works of Dr. Wolcot, must have been pleased at the homage which even that sarcastic genius paid to 'Red-nosed Dick'. With my humble share of knowledge in Painting, I must, without fear of depriving either Turner, Callcott, or Arnald of one jot of their high celebrity, affirm that Wilson was a

Leviathan in his profession; and this also was the opinion of a skilful practitioner, and one of the first judges of art—I allude to the late ever-to-be-lamented Sir George Beaumont, Bart.; who is deservedly entitled to the wreath of everlasting honour for presenting so choice a collection of pictures to our glorious National Gallery. Mr. Welch, in the course of a few months, repeated to Wilson the proposition of sporting a round of beef and of making another fifteen-guinea purchase; and in this manner he became possessed of the two beautiful pictures which descended to Mr. Nollekens, of which some farther particulars will be found in another part of this work. As to the picture of Dover Castle, which Mr. Nollekens also possessed, Mr. Welch purchased it at a furniture sale, by Wilson's recommendation, assuring him that it was the best picture he had ever painted. The town-residence of that excellent connoisseur, Richard Ford, Esq. boasts a most splendid collection of Wilson's pictures in every variety of his manner. This incomparable assemblage, which consists of nearly fifty specimens, had been the property of Lady Ford, his mother, who, upon his marriage, most liberally presented them to him; her Ladyship became possessed of them at the death of her father. The same gentleman has also many of Wilson's finest drawings from nature, which he principally made when studying at Rome; one of which is particularly interesting, since it contains Wilson's own figure, seated on the ground in his bag-wig, making a drawing of Raffaelle's villa. The late Paul Sandby, Esq. once showed me a fine collection of Wilson's drawings, to which he attached the following anecdote. Wilson, well knowing the frequent intercourse Mr. Sandby had with some of the highest persons in the country, solicited him to show a portfolio of his drawings to his pupils. Paul Sandby, with his usual liberality, did so, and spake highly in their favour; but found that the amateurs, or gentlemen-draughtsmen, preferred highly-finished drawings to mere sketches; and finding his repeated attempts to serve his old friend Wilson fruitless, was induced to make the purchase himself, without allowing him to know that he had been unsuccessful in his applications.

CHAPTER VI

Interview between Mr. Nollekens and Nathaniel Hone.—Hone's satirical picture on Sir Joshua Reynolds and Angelica Kauffmann.—Account of Hone's Exhibition of it, with extracts from his Statement.—Other Notices of Hone and his pictures.—Short stature of Garrick and Nollekens.—Anecdote by Mrs. Garrick of Dance's picture of her husband as Richard III.—Mrs. Nollekens's dog.—Sagacity of that of Mrs. Garrick.—Norman the Dog-doctor.—Mrs. Radcliffe's dogs.

ONE day, Daphne, the dog, announced the approach of a stranger in the yard, and a tall, upright, large man, with a broad-brimmed hat, and a lapelled coat buttoned up to his stock, with measured and stately steps entered the studio, walked up to Mr. Nollekens, who was then modelling a bust of Sir Charles Eyre Coote, and, full of self-importance, saluted him with 'Joseph Nollekens, Esquire, R.A., how do you do?' Nollekens, who never liked him, answered, 'Well, now, I suppose, you're come to get me to join you in the Academy to-night, against Sir Joshua, but you're very much mistaken; and I can tell you more, I never will join you in any thing you propose: you're always running your rigs against Sir Joshua; and you may say what you please, but I have never had any opinion of you ever since you painted that picture of the Conjuror, as you called it. I don't wonder they turned it out of the Academy. And pray what business had you to bring Angelica into it? You know it was your intention to ridicule her, whatever you or your printed paper and your affidavits may say; however, you may depend upon it *she* won't forget it, if Sir Joshua does.'

The visitor, who proved to be no other than Nathaniel Hone, the Enamel-painter, replied, 'Why now, how can you be so ill-tempered this morning? I have brought you two prints which I bought in a lot at old Gerard's.'—*Nollekens.* 'Well, I don't care; you don't bribe me in that way; I know what you are going to do to-night, and I'll vote against you, so you may take your prints back again.'

Hone. 'Why, one of them is by Captain Baillie, one of the Commissioners of the Stamp-Office.'

Nollekens. 'Ay, he's another swaggering fellow too: he was praising the print you have engraved in mezzotinto, of Grose and Forrest, from another picture that did you no good. It proves you to be a man of no religion, or you would not sport with the Roman Catholics in that way.' Here the dialogue ended, by Hone's wishing Joseph Nollekens, Esquire, R.A., a good morning.

As few people now living are aware of the particulars of Hone's attack upon Sir Joshua Reynolds, I shall here insert some extracts from a paper which had been industriously distributed by Hone, among those persons who he thought were most likely to take part with him in the abuse of the honourable President; but before I introduce them, the reader should be apprised of the following particulars. Mr. Hone, who had been a fashionable Miniature-painter in enamel, commenced oil-painting upon a large scale; but in that branch of the art he was not so successful as in the former. Indeed he found Reynolds carry away the principal patronage, which rendered him so jealous, that he took every opportunity of endeavouring to defame him; and well knowing that Sir Joshua had borrowed the attitudes of some of his portraits from those of Vandyke, &c., he painted a picture of an old man in a gown, holding a wand in his hand, in the act of commanding the very engravings which he affirmed Sir Joshua had used, to rise out of the flames, which picture Hone called the Conjuror. There was at first some indelicacy, which he had introduced in the centre of the picture, but which he afterwards painted out, respecting a slanderous report which had been whispered as to Sir Joshua and Angelica Kauffmann.

This picture of the Conjuror being considered by the members of the Royal Academy as a most malicious satire upon their President, they very honourably agreed in Council, that it should not be exhibited by them: upon which decision, Mr. Hone, as the picture had been the subject of much conversation, determined upon having an exhibition of his own works, consisting of sixty-six in number,[1] in which the re-

[1] '1. A frame containing fifteen enamelled pictures, portraits. 2. A frame containing eleven pictures in enamel, portraits. 3. A frame containing thirteen portraits in enamel, copied from various painters: not one of the foregoing enamels have been painted within these fifteen years, as Mr. Hone gave up his leisure-hours from that time to painting in oil. 4. An Old Man, in crayons, painted twenty-seven years ago. 5. A Girl Drawing, painted above twenty years ago; this picture is a proof how little the colours have changed. 6. A Brickdust-man, the work of a day, in the first exhibition-room belonging to the Society of Arts, &c. 1760. 7. A Chinese Man, the work of an hour, as may be seen by the touch. 8. A Boy Deliberating on his Drawing, in the exhibition at Spring-gardens, 1766. 9. A Girl with a Rabbit, 1767, at Spring-gardens. 10. Diogenes Looking for an Honest Man, in the exhibition at Spring-gardens, 1768. 11. Signora Zamperini, in the character of Cecchini, at Spring-gardens, 1768. 12. A small whole-length of a Gentleman, at the Royal Academy, Pall-mall, 1769. 13. A Candlelight, "as if she'd say, ''Tis time to bed, love, let's away,'" at the Royal Academy, 1769. 14. A Piping Boy, at the Royal Academy, 1769. 15. A Young Gentleman, at the Royal Academy, 1769. 16. The Tripoline Ambassador, 1770, at the Royal Academy. 17. Two Gentlemen in masquerade, at the Royal Academy, 1770; the cross is here restored as at first intended, instead of a punch-ladle, which was painted by order of the Council of the Academy for its admittance. 18. A mezzotinto print of the same, by Mr. Hone. 19. A Boy with a Garland, at the Royal Academy, 1771. 20. A Girl with a Dog, at the

jected one of the Conjuror held the most conspicuous place. The room in which they were exhibited, is

Royal Academy, 1771; in the collection of Richard Knight, Esq. 21. A Boy with a Portfolio, at the Royal Academy, 1771. 22. A Student with a plaster of Paris head in his hand, Royal Academy, 1771. 23. A Portrait of Mr. Hone's mother, in the eightieth year of her age; that of his father, in the back-ground, he copied from a picture of his own painting, when he was quite unacquainted with the Art, but was a strong likeness; at the Royal Academy, 1771. 24. David, when a shepherd, after he had freed his lamb from the lion, at the Royal Academy, 1771. 25. A Girl with a Cat, at the Royal Academy, 1772. 26. A Portrait of a Gentleman, at the Royal Academy, 1773. 27. A Fisherman, at the Royal Academy, 1773. 28. A Young Lady, in a round frame, 1773. 29. A Lady at Church, at the Royal Academy, 1774. 30. A Lady with a Nosegay, at the Royal Academy, 1774. 31. Portrait of an Officer, at the Royal Academy, 1774. 32. Portrait of a Sheep bleating within the rails, at the Royal Academy, 1774. 33. Portrait of a General Officer, at one sitting, unfinished. 34. Two Spaniels, belonging to John Bailey, Esq. of Ramridge. 35. A Lady, in profile, at one sitting. 36. A Profile of a Right Hon. Lady, copied from an enamelled miniature of Mr. Hone's painting several years ago. 37. A Portrait of a Gentleman. 38. Copied from a Landscape of Claude Lorraine, several years since, the original is in the collection of Lord Scarsdale, at Kedleston. 39. Copied from a Landscape of Salvator Rosa, in the collection of John Barnard, Esq. done at one painting, as it is supposed the original was. 40. A Winter Evening's Amusement, a drawing in bister several years since. 41. A ditto. 42. A ditto. 43. A ditto, in black chalk. 44. A View from one of the Huts on Sydenham Common, some years ago. 45. A Girl with a Shell, this is the original; the copy, at the Royal Academy, is done by a young gentleman who has not been seven months with Mr. Hone. 46. Mr. Hone's protrait, about five years ago, painted to imitate the old dress of Henry the Eighth's time, the dress unfinished. 47. A Hare. 48. A Pheasant, unfinished. 49. A Lady, with her Daughter.—These six following were intended to have been exhibited in the Royal Academy this year, and were actually hung now a workshop behind the house of Messrs. Mouchett and Wild, No. 70, St. Martin's-lane, opposite to Old Slaughter's Coffee-house. Upon my questioning the late Associate, Mr. Horace Hone, upon this transaction of his father, he favoured me with a sight of the original Catalogue; and as it is now considered the greatest rarity in the Academic annals, I insert the following extracts from it.

'The EXHIBITION of PICTURES, by Nathaniel Hone, R.A., mostly the Works of his Leisure, and many of them in his own possession. "Nisi utile est quod facimus, frustra est gloria." '—PHÆDRUS. MDCCLXXV.

Many false reports having been spread relating to a picture called the 'Conjuror', painted by Mr. Hone, and offered to the Royal Academy Exhibition this season, he is advised by some very respectable friends to give a short statement of facts to the public, which he hopes will clear his character from the malicious aspersions attempted to

---

up there. 50. The Daughter of a Peer, whole-length. 51. A Lady with a lyre. "Audire, et videor pios errare per lucos, amœnæ quos et aquæ subeunt, et auræ. Hor. Carmen ad Calliopen." 52. A Lady in a turban, with a musical instrument. 53. A Judge. 54. St. Paviarius; the head finished at one painting, from the same man who sat for the Conjuror.—This poor but honest fellow, was formerly a pavior, for which reason he is named, as have heretofore been St. Veronica, St. Christopher, &c. from some particular action. 55. The Conjuror, refused by the Council of the Royal Academy, though Mr. Hone had agreed to make some alterations in the picture. 57. A Drawing of a Lady and Child. 58. A Drawing in bister, from Jacob Ruisdael.* 59. A Candlelight, in enamel. 60. A Locust, in the month of *August*, 1748, was taken up in a street in *London*, in enamel. 61. A Shell, in enamel. 62. A Candlelight, from G. Dow, in enamel. 63. A Chinese figure, in enamel. 64. A Moth and Butterfly, in enamel. 65. A Candlelight drawing. 66. St. Catherine, unfinished, in oil.'

---

* So written by the artist himself upon his etchings—Fuseli spells it Ruysdaal.

be fixed on him; as well as excuse him from the presumption of making an exhibition singly of his own works.

After the picture in question had remained several days, and was actually hung up in the Royal Academy Exhibition, Sir William Chambers, with another gentleman of the Council of the Academy, came to Mr. Hone at his house, and informed him that it had been rumoured that he had made an indecent figure or caricature of an eminent female artist; and that they should be sorry such an indelicacy should be offered to the public; or words to this purpose. Mr. Hone was greatly surprised at the accusation, and assured the gentlemen that he had always had the highest esteem for the lady alluded to, both on account of her reputation as an artist, as well as for her other accomplishments; and that, to remove the possibility of such a suspicion, he would alter any figure she or they chose, the very next day, or before the exhibition; and that he did not intend to represent any female figure in that picture, except the child leaning on the conjuror's knee, and hoped they would do him the justice to remove any prejudice the lady might have. The next morning, two more gentlemen of the Council (with that other gentleman who had been the night before with Sir William) called upon Mr. Hone, who were all of them so obliging to do him justice to say, they had carefully looked at the figures, and would clear him of the supposition of there being any woman figure—that they were well assured they were intended to mean the contrary sex. Mr. Hone assured them, as before, of his respect for the lady; nor did he trust to this alone, but went himself twice that day to wait on the fair artist to convince her of the error, but was refused admittance. He thereupon sent a letter by his son, who delivered it into her own hands, and whereof the following is an exact copy.

'MADAM,

'THE evening before last, I was not a little surprised at a deputation (as I take it) from the Council of our Academy, acquainting me, that you was most prodigiously displeased at my making a naked Academy figure in my picture of the Conjuror, now at the Royal Academy, representing your person. I immediately perceived that some busy meddler, to say no worse a name, had imposed this extravagant lie, (of whose making God knows!) upon your understanding.

To convince you, madam, that your figure in that composition was the farthest from my thoughts, I now declare, I never at any time saw your works, but with the greatest pleasure, and that respect due to a lady whom I esteem as the first of her sex in painting, and amongst the loveliest of women in person. Envy and detraction must have worked strangely; for yesterday morning some more gentlemen from the Academy assured me, that your uneasiness was very great: I assured them, I would so far alter the figure, that it would be impossible to suppose it to be a woman, though they cleared me of such a supposition themselves, as they understood it to be but a male figure; and that I would put a beard to it, or even dress it to satisfy you and them. I did myself the honour of calling at your house twice yesterday, (when I had the misfortune not to meet you at home,) purposely to convince you, how much you have been imposed upon, as you will perceive when you see the picture yourself, and likewise to convince you with how much respect,

'I am, Madam,
Your most obedient,
and most humble servant,
'NATHANIEL HONE.'

'Pall Mall, 19th April, 1775.
To Mrs. Angelica Kauffmann.'

To which the day following this answer was returned.

'SIR,

'I SHOULD have answered yours immediately, but I was engaged in business. I cannot conceive why several gentlemen, who never before deceived me, should conspire to do it at this time; and if they themselves were deceived, you cannot wonder that others should be deceived also, and take for satire that which you say was not intended. I was actuated, not only by my particular feelings, but a respect for the arts and artists, and persuade myself you cannot think it a great sacrifice to remove a picture, that had even raised suspicion of disrespect to any person who never wished to offend you.

'I am, Sir,
Your humble servant,
'ANGELICA KAUFFMANN.'

'To Nathaniel Hone, Esq.
Pall Mall.'

Mr. Hone was exceedingly hurt to find the lady's prejudices were so strong, that she was averse to being convinced, and would not trust her own senses to be undeceived. So forcibly had malice and detraction wrought the mischief, that a whole city was to laugh at the imposition, whilst a party concerned was resolved to remain obstinate in error, and oppose the most condescending offer that could be thought of to break the spell that Mr. Hone's enemies ensnared her in. However, other motives worked the concluding part, though this was to be the ostensible reason for the extraordinary conduct of rejecting the works of an Academician, honoured by his Majesty's sign-manual, and whose character had been hitherto unimpeached by the breath of slander, during a residence in this capital of upwards of thirty years.

He was still in hopes that all ill-grounded prejudices would be dispersed; but how was he disappointed in his prospects, when to his astonishment he received the following letter from the Secretary of the Academy!

'Sir,

'I am directed to acquaint you, that a ballot having been taken by the Council, whether your picture called the Conjuror should be admitted in the Exhibition, it was determined in the negative.

'You are therefore desired to send for the picture as soon as it may be convenient.

'I am, Sir,
Your most obedient,
and most humble servant,
'F. M. Newton, R. A. Secretary.'

'Exhibition Room, Pall Mall.
Tuesday evening, 9 o'clock.
Nathaniel Hone, Esq.'

He was now reduced to a dilemma,—to acquiesce supinely under the heavy reproach of having offered a picture unfit for the public eye, and suffer the affront of his labours being rejected, and his character traduced. What in such a case could he do? but by appealing to the public, to whose candour and judgment he submits himself and his art, being sure that at that tribunal the mist will be dispelled, truth will be prevalent, and that his labours, which have for many years given satisfaction and pleasure to his employers, will not now be disapproved of on a more general inspection by the indulgent public.

He trusts, that this explanation, with the following affidavit, will prove, first, that the accusation was frivolous and nugatory, and that he is not in the least guilty of having given any real cause of offence to Mrs. Angelica Kauffmann; and secondly, that it will excuse the presumption of offering to the public an exhibition singly of his own labours.

'MIDDLESEX TO WIT. I, Nathaniel Hone, of the Royal Academy, do make oath, that in the picture of a Conjuror, offered for exhibition to the said Academy for the present season, I never introduced, or intended to introduce, any figure reflecting on Mrs. Angelica Kauffmann, or any other lady whatever; and I gave the most explicit declaration of this to Sir William Chambers, and three other gentlemen of the Academy, who called at my house for the purpose of examining into that circumstance; and I at the same time told them the figure they pitched upon as giving offence should be taken out.

'NATH. HONE.'

'Sworn before me this 2d day of May, 1775,

'W. ADDINGTON.'

N. B. The figure said to have been intended for Mrs. A. K. is not only taken out, but all the other naked figures, lest they should be said to be likenesses of any particular gentlemen or ladies, which Mr. Hone never meant, as the merit of the picture does not depend upon a few smoked Academy figures, or even those well-dressed gentlemen who supply the place of those figures which were said to be so indecent; though Mr. Hone had shown the picture to ladies of the most refined taste and sentiment at his own house.

The following is a copy of Mr. Hone's Advertisement which appeared in several of the public papers.

EXHIBITION, ST. MARTIN'S-LANE.

Mr. Hone's Exhibition of the Conjuror, and one hundred other pictures and designs, all by his own hands, may be seen every day, (Sunday excepted,) opposite Old Slaughter's Coffee-house, the upper end of St. Martin's-lane, from ten in the morning till seven in the evening. Admittance one shilling. Catalogues, with Mr. Hone's Apology to the public, gratis.

May 9th, 1775.

Hone's picture of a Brick-dust man, which was exhibited at Spring-gardens, first raised his name as a painter. In 1769, he was elected a Royal Academician, but in consequence of some pique against Sir Joshua Reynolds, he became a turbulent member. He died at his house, now No. 44, in Rathbone-place, in his sixty-seventh year, and was buried August 20th, 1784, at Hendon. Mr. Hone etched a portrait of the Rev. Mr. Greenaway, and engraved his own likeness in mezzotinto, as well as a large plate of Two Gentlemen in masquerade (Captain Grose and Theos. Forrest) number seventeen in the catalogue of his works, which the reader will find upon a subsequent page. This picture is now in the possession of Mrs. Graham, and hangs over the sideboard of her dining-room at her house on Clapham Common.

In the sale of his effects in Rathbone-place, was a plaster mask of King Charles the Second, taken from his face when dead. When his pictures were offered for sale at Mr. Hutchins's, in King-street, Covent Garden, in March 1785, I saw Sir Joshua Reynolds most attentively view the picture of the Conjuror for full ten minutes.

Whenever Garrick's name was mentioned, it was generally accompanied with the appellation of *little;* but I have often heard my father observe, that he never knew any one who spake of *little* Hogarth, though he was half a head shorter. Perhaps this appellation might have arisen from Garrick's appearing on the stage with tall men, such as Quin, Barry, Woodward, Reddish, John Palmer, William Smith, Charles Bannister, Brereton, Lewis, &c. Dodd was a little man, and he was often called 'Little Dodd'; and Quick is now often noticed, when walking in Islington

Fields, as 'Little Quick'. In like manner, Nollekens was called 'Little Nolly', by those who spake of him with freedom; and as 'Little Nollekens' by strangers, who knew nothing but his person; and yet he was the only one of that name in England, though there are several bearing it in Antwerp to this day, some of whom have boldly declared their relationship to him.[1] That great and good man, Flaxman, the 'Sculptor of Eternity', as Blake styled him, was often called 'Little Flaxman, the Sculptor', though there was no other Flaxman a Sculptor. Indeed, I was going to say, nor ever will be: and if I had, my opinion surely could not possibly be called in question in less than *five hundred years*. Hogarth has insisted upon it that Garrick, if seen alone, would have appeared as tall as Quin, on account of the former being a thin and neatly-made man, and the latter, though tall, an awkwardly large one. This assertion he has exemplified, as may be seen in an etching by F. Cook, from a sketch by himself,[2] entitled 'Fac-simile of the proportions of Garrick and Quin'. Hogarth's assertion, as to this point, is also most glaringly visible in J. Dixon's engraving of Garrick in the character of Abel Drugger, from a picture by Zoffany, in which there is nothing to enable the observer to draw a comparison, as Garrick is the only object in the print. Now, the impression made upon the spectator is quite the contrary, when he is viewing him in the company of Subtle and Face, where a chair is also introduced; which, without any other auxiliary, acts as a tolerably good scale for the height of figures. For a farther corroboration of this remark, the reader has only to look at the large print by J. Dixon, also after Zoffany's picture from the same play, in which Barton, Palmer, and Garrick,

[1] It has recently been proved that these pretended relatives are from a different stock and of another country.

[2] The original drawing was in the possession of the late J. P. Kemble, Esq.

form the composition, and in consequence of Palmer's height, Garrick appears *small*. Garrick might have appeared as a *large man*, if he had taken a hint from Zoffany, who has painted him in the 'Farmer's Return', where he is seated in his kitchen, relating the sights he had witnessed in London, and particularly the story of the Cock-lane ghost,—to his *little* wife and *short* children. In this beautiful picture, Garrick is represented as a man of good height, as may be seen in J. G. Haid's engraving from it, published by Boydell, March 1st, 1766.

But I must not forget Nollekens in these ramblings: he also appeared tall when warming his hands in the hall of the Royal Academy, surrounded by the young students, who were listening to his good-natured stories of what happened to him when at Rome.

As he was once enjoying himself in this manner, Mrs. Malum, the housekeeper, applied to him for the poker, adding, 'You always hide my poker; why, you need not care how many coals we burn:—you don't buy them here.'

So good-natured, indeed, was Mr. Nollekens during his conversations with the students, that his familiarity sometimes exposed him to the ridicule of those who knew not or forgot the respect which they ought to have entertained for him as an Academician. Once an impudent fellow brought an old brown worsted-stocking, similar to one worn by the R. A. when he had a sore throat; which, to the great amusement of a few of his fellow-students, he tied round his neck, and stood by the side of Mr. Nollekens, when he was Visitor in the Life-Academy. However, it should be observed, to the honour of the well-disposed part of the students, that the ignorant scoffer was sent to Coventry,—and for a twelvemonth three-fourths of them would not speak to him.

I must acknowledge that at the time Mr. Carlini was Keeper, the Royal Academy students took those liberties with their superiors, which would not be noticed now but by expulsion; and it must give every well-thinking parent pleasure to know that their moral conduct was strictly noticed by the late worthy Keeper, Henry Thomson, Esq. R. A., and that that gentleman's successor, William Hilton, Esq. R. A. will most assiduously promote the same rectitude of conduct.

Mrs. Garrick visited the Print-room of the British Museum on the 21st of August 1821, for the purpose of looking over the volume of Mr. Garrick's portraits, which had been collected by the late Dr. Burney. When she came to J. Dixon's print from Dance's picture of her husband in the character of Richard the Third, now in the front drawing-room of Sir Watkin Williams Wynne's house, she looked at me, and with a firm emphasis whispered, 'Ay, Sir, Mr. Dance used me scurvily as to this picture; it was to have been mine at one hundred guineas, and a place was cleared for it, when to my great astonishment, he informed Mr. Garrick at our dinner-table, where he had been always welcome, that he could sell it for fifty or a hundred guineas more to Sir Watkin Williams Wynne. "Well, Sir," observed Mr. Garrick, "and you mean to take it?"—"Yes," replied Mr. Dance, for he was not then Sir Nathaniel, "I think I shall."—"Think no more of the picture," whispered Mr. Garrick to me; "in a short time you shall see a better one there:" which was the case, though he meant the compliment to me; for the first morning after, he had a looking-glass to the value of one hundred and twenty-five guineas put up in the place which had been allotted for Dance's picture: he requested me to go in and look at it, when he with his usual playfulness peeped over my shoulder. Sir Watkin, who never knew a word of Dance's ingratitude to Mr. Garrick,—who had introduced him to all his friends,—purchased the picture, and bestowed a most splendid frame upon it, at an enormous expense.'

Mr. Dance, in this picture of Garrick, has been guilty of an egregious anachronism. He has actually given Richard the Third the star of the Order of the Garter, when he ought to have known that it was not introduced before the reign of King Charles the First.[1]

Mrs. Nollekens had a little dog, which her father brought as a present to her from France: it was considered a great beauty of its kind, being perfectly white, having a long curled woolly mane, and its body half shorn from its hinder parts; the extremities of its tail and legs were left tufted, like an heraldical lion, and the eyelids were rather of a red colour, as those of the French breed generally are. With this animal, I formed a particular acquaintance; and, as she was very good-tempered towards me, I used to lay out my

[1] See Ashmole's *History of the Order of the Garter*, Lond. 1672, folio, chap. 7 pages 215, 216. The origin of the Star, according to that authority, was a badge consisting of the cross of the Order, surrounded by the Garter, to be worn upon the left side of the ordinary cloaks, &c. of the Sovereign and Knights-Companions. This was added to the insignia by King Charles I. at a Chapter held April 27th, in the second year of his reign, 1626. 'And,' adds Ashmole, 'it seems it was not long after ere the glory, or star, as it is usually called, having certain beams of silver that spread in the form of a cross, was introduced and added thereunto,—in imitation, as it is thought, of the French, who, after that manner, wore the chief ensign of the Order of the Holy Ghost, being the resemblance of a dove, irradiated with such like beams.' The anachronism of introducing the Star of the Garter before it was invented, has, however, been committed by a much better antiquary than Dance; since it is introduced in the year 1578, in the Romance of *Kenilworth*, by the Author of *Waverley*. Edit. Edinburgh: 1821, vol. I, ch. 7 page 149. 'The embroidered strap, as thou callest it, around my knee,' says the Earl of Leicester, 'is the English Garter, an ornament which Kings are proud to wear. *See, here is the Star which belongs to it*, and here is the diamond George, the jewel of the Order.'

pocket-money in buying, alternately, a pink and a blue ribbon to make her a collar, with which Mrs. Nollekens was highly delighted. I recollect Mr. George Keate,—whose politeness always procured him the good opinion of the ladies,—making much of this animal; and telling it that he had written some lines upon Mrs. Garrick's little dog, not unlike her in feature, of which *Favorie*—for she sometimes went by that name—ought to be very proud, since they were considered extremely beautiful. At this, Mrs. Nollekens caught the bait, and in polite terms declared she would send for his Poems, concluding that the lines were to be found there. 'Yes, Madam,' said he, 'I have introduced them in the book, and I will send it, not only for your inspection, but acceptance.' 'You are extremely polite,' answered Mrs. Nollekens, 'I shall be most happy to possess what you have said of Mrs. Garrick's dog.'

Before I entirely leave this subject, to prove the wonderfully sagacious and retentive memory of Mrs. Garrick's little dog, Biddy, and how much she must have noticed her master when rehearsing his parts at home, I shall give the following most extraordinary anecdote, as nearly as I can, in the manner in which Mrs. Garrick related it to me a short time before her death. 'One evening, after Mr. Garrick and I were seated in our box at Drury-lane Theatre, he said, "Surely there is something wrong on the stage," and added, he would go and see what it was. Shortly after this, when the curtain was drawn up, I saw a person come forward to speak a new prologue, in the dress of a country bumpkin, whose features seemed new to me; and whilst I was wondering who it could possibly be, I felt my little dog's tail wag, for he was seated in my lap, his usual place at the Theatre, looking towards the stage. "Aha!" said I, "what, do you know him? is it your master? then you have seen him practise his part?" '

When I last had the gratification of conversing with the relator of this anecdote, she spake in the highest terms of his present Majesty George IV., and said, that the last time she had the honour of seeing him, when Prince of Wales, the kind and condescending manner in which his Royal Highness sat by her side at Hampton, and asked after her health, gave her heartfelt pleasure: 'and I am not a little proud,' added she, 'of the privilege of being allowed to drive through St. James's Park.'

Lieut.-Colonel Phillips, whose venerable age is not beyond his politeness, has also favoured me with the following anecdote of the late Queen Charlotte and Mrs. Garrick. By some mistake the Queen was announced to Mrs. Garrick, at her house at Hampton, without the usual notice previous to a royal visit. Mrs. Garrick was much confused at being caught in the act of peeling onions for pickling. The Queen, however, would not suffer her to stir; but commanded a knife to be brought, observing that she would peel an onion with her, and actually sat down, in the most condescending manner, and peeled onions. The Colonel, who often relates anecdotes of his youth and the distinguished characters whom he has known, never forgets to observe, when speaking of Queen Charlotte, 'Ay, very few persons knew the goodness of her Majesty's heart, and the great good she had done, until after her death.'

I shall now give a dialogue which was held, as nearly as I can recollect, between Mrs. Nollekens and Mrs. Norman, the wife of a celebrated Dog-doctor, who, at the time I was with Sherwin, lived in Fox-court, St. James's-street; into one of the houses of which court, Sherwin's premises extended, and were used by him and his pupils as engraving-rooms. The name of Norman was so extensively known, that I consider it hardly possible for many of my readers to be ignorant of his fame; indeed, so much was he in requisition, that persons residing out of town would frequently order the carriage for no other purpose than to consult Doctor Norman as to the state of Biddy's health, just as people of rank now consult Partington or Thompson as to the irregularities of their children's teeth. The room in which Sherwin's pupils were placed, was on the first-floor, looking immediately into the court, so that it was impossible for them to be unacquainted with the patient's complaints, which were made known in the court either to the Doctor or his wife, who always answered from an upper casement. *Bijou*, Mrs. Nollekens's favourite lap-dog, was put under the Doctor's regimen by Nollekens, who, it appeared, had left her early one morning, before we had taken possession of our room. One day, about noon, we heard a female, who had tapped at the Doctor's door with the stick of her parasol, inquire if Mr. Norman was at home. 'Who calls?' interrogated Mrs. Norman from within. 'Mr. Norman, I ask if he lives here?' Mrs. Norman, who had then put her head out at the window, answered, 'Yes, he does, good woman; what's your pleasure?' ' "Good woman, what's your pleasure!" is that the way to speak to a lady? know, then, my name is Nollekens.'—'Oh dear, I beg your pardon: you are the person who sent a little man here with a French dog the other day: how does she do?'—'Do! why don't you come down, Mrs. Norman?'—'I come down! what, and leave all my dogs! bless you, there'd be the devil to pay when Norman comes home! You don't know the *disponsibility* I am in: why, we have got Mrs. Robinson's mother Mrs. Derby's dog; and we have got the Duke of Dorset's French lady's dog, Fidelle, just come from Duke-street. Mrs. Musters, of Portland-place, has sent three dogs, and we have Monsieur Goubert's from South Molton-street.—What! but is your bitch ill again? I am sure we brought it about—it was fed upon nothing but bread and milk.'—'Bread and milk!'

exclaimed Mrs. Nollekens; 'why we give it some of the best bits of our yard-dog's paunches.'—'Bless you, good woman! then it will never be well: the Doctor can do nothing for it, that I can tell you.' By this time, a fellow silenced Mrs. Nollekens, by inquiring in a rough voice if Doctor *Normandy* was at home. 'No,' was the reply.—'Well, then, when he comes home, he must come to Lady Bunbury's; one of her dogs has had no rest for these three nights, and her life is despaired of.'

I do not wish to reflect upon Mrs. Nollekens, or the peculiar attachment of any other lady to the brute creation, as there are, I am certain, tens of thousands, who, though many of them pet their dogs, also find delight in walking miles to alleviate the wants of their fellow-creatures with the balmy hand of sincere benevolence. Mrs. Radcliffe, the justly-celebrated Authoress of 'The Romance of the Forest', 'The Mysteries of Udolpho', &c. was one of that description, and she had two pets. The name of one was Fan, that of the other Dash; both obtained board and lodging, not as presents from Lady Sarah Bunbury, or Mrs. Garrick, but taken up by her in the streets, when they were outcasts and unowned; when, as poor old Bronze would frequently say of her master's broken antiques, no one would think of offering a brass farthing for their services. Mrs. Radcliffe's attention was one day arrested by a boy who stood silently weeping under the gateway of the Little Stableyard, St. James's; he held a cord, to the end of which a most miserable spectacle of a dog was tied, shivering between him and the wall. She requested to know the cause of his grief, and the poor little fellow, after sobbing for some time, with a modest reluctance stammered, 'My mo-mo-mo-mother insists upon my hanging Fan; she won't keep her because her skin is bare. Don't touch her, Ma'am, she has got the mange.'—'Well, my little fellow, if you will walk back with me, I will not only give you half-a-crown, but will keep your dog, and you shall come and see it.' When the poor animal was safely lodged at No. 5, Stafford-row, Pimlico, her new mistress placed her under proper care; and when she was again coated, she became excessively admired for her great beauty, and, being under the tuition of so amiable a protectress, she so improved in manners as to be often noticed by the late Queen and the Princesses, when walking with her mistress in Windsor Park, at the time Mrs. Radcliffe had a small cottage in the town. My informant related the following proof of Fan's good-breeding and respect for a dog under superior protection.

One of the Princess's dogs, a spaniel exactly of Fanny's size, caught one end of a long bone, at the moment Fan had found it; who, instead of snarling as a dog generally does when an interloper attempts to carry off a prize, very good-temperedly complied with the playfulness of the Princess's dog by continuing to walk by her side, just like two horses in a curricle, each holding the extreme end of the bone, to the no small amusement of the royal equestrians, who frequently recognized and noticed Mrs. Radcliffe as the Authoress and Fanny's mistress.

The other dog was of a large size, and the latter part of his history is as follows. One day it happened, as Mr. and Mrs. Radcliffe were walking along the Strand, to visit the Exhibition of the Royal Academicians at Somerset-place, they saw a poor half-starved dog that had just been drawn upon the pavement, a coach-wheel having broken one of its legs. When they got up to the crowd, as there was no master near or willing to own it, each person was giving his opinion as to the most expeditious mode of putting the unfortunate animal out of his misery. Upon this Mrs. Radcliffe, with her accustomed humanity, requested her husband to procure a coach; and instead of proceeding to the Exhibition to feast upon the works of art, they preferred following the impulse of good-nature, by ordering the coachman to Stafford-row, where, by skilful attention, the once-wretched animal was not only in a short time restored to perfect health, but repaid his life-preserver with the most frolicksome agility, who ever after called him 'Dash'.

CHAPTER VII

Anecdotes of Seward and James Barry.—Conversations in Westminster Abbey, on waxen figures, fees, alterations, monuments, and the Gate-house.—Norfolk-House, the birth-place of George III.—Mr. Nollekens's restoration of the Townley Venus.—Colonel Hamilton.—Conversation between Mr. Nollekens and Panton Betew, on artists and the China manufactories at Bow and Chelsea.—Characteristic anecdotes of Betew.—Early engravings by Hogarth.

Mr. Seward, of anecdotic memory, who lodged at the Golden Ball, No. 5, Little Maddox-street, where the sign is still pendent, was perpetually complimenting those persons of eminence who appeared to him most likely to contribute to his budget. I recollect, when I was a student in the Royal Academy, seeing him one night make up to Barry, who was descending from the rostrum, and hearing him, after he had expressed his admiration of his lecture, solicit the pleasure of walking part of the way home with him. Mr. Nollekens and I overtook them at a baker's shop in Catherine-street, when Barry, who detested Seward for his avowed attachment to Fuseli, requested him to wait while he purchased a loaf, and when he came out, had the audacity to ask Seward to assist him in stuffing it into a ragged pocket of his long great-coat. When he had accomplished the task, Barry exclaimed, 'It's in: that's the way to be independent; I have no fixed baker, so where I like the appearance of the bread, I buy it.' Nollekens, who had stopped with me to notice them, observed, 'Ay, Tom, when they get themselves under the Piazza, Jem will lose him; I know his tricks well, when he dislikes a man. Why, do you know, that fellow Seward sadly wanted me the other day to give him my Michel Angelo model of Venus!'[1]

Mr. Nollekens having received an order for a monument, similar in size to one which his employer had pointed out, erected in Westminster Abbey, asked my father to accompany him thither, and they took me with them to assist in the measurement. I recollect the morning with pleasure: the sun enabled us to look into every corner of the Abbey; and I now wish I had then been older, to have benefited more by the interesting remarks by my parent and friend.

Mr. Nollekens, during the time his men were moulding parts of monuments in Westminster Abbey, had the following conversation with the late Mr. John Catling, the Verger, to the great amusement of my father, who was also present. *Mr. Nollekens.* 'Why, Mr. Catling, you seem to be as fond of the Abbey as I am of my models by Michel Angelo. My man, Finny, tells me you *was* born in it.'—*Catling.* 'No, not in the Abbey; I was born in the tower, on the right hand, just before you enter into the little cloisters.'—*Nollekens.* 'Oh! I know; there's some steps to go up, and a wooden rail to hold by. Now, I wonder you

[1] This beautiful little gem now sparkles over the chimney-piece of Sir Thomas Lawrence's front parlour, a room enviably rich in inestimable jewels. The cabinets are filled with the choicest drawings, by Michel Angelo, Raffaelle, Rubens, and Rembrandt, many of which were formerly dispersed through the portfolios of King Charles the First, Rubens, the Earl of Arundel, Sir Peter Lely, the two Richardsons, Hudson, Moser, Sir Joshua Reynolds, Barnard, Ralph Willett, Udney, Earl Spencer, West, and several grand collections abroad, from which they were selected, and brought into this country by Mr. Ottley and Mr. Samuel Woodburn; two most excellent judges of art, to whom England is much indebted for numerous works of the old and great masters, which might at this moment have been locked up in foreign cabinets, had it not been for their zeal and liberality.

don't lose that silver thing that you carry before the Dean, when you are going through the cloisters. Pray, why do you suffer the schoolboys to chalk the stones all over? I have been spelling pudding, grease, lard, butter, kitchen-stuff, and I don't know what all.' —*Catling*. 'Why, thereby hangs a tale: do you know that the Dean married a woman?'—*Nollekens*. 'Well, so he ought; the clergy are allowed to marry now-a-days; it is not as it was formerly: you know I have been at Rome, and know enough about their customs.' Here Mr. Catling gave Mr. Nollekens an admonitory pinch upon the elbow, for at that moment the Bishop was passing through Poet's Corner from the Deanery, on his way to the House of Lords. *Nollekens*. 'What does he carry that blue-bag with him for?'—*Catling*. 'It contains his papers upon the business of the day.'—*Nollekens*. 'Oh! now you talk of papers, Mrs. Nollekens bid me to ask you where Ashburnham House is, that held the Cotton paper, I think it was.'—*Catling*. 'Your good lady means the Cottonian Manuscripts, Sir; it is in Little Dean's-yard, on the north side; it has a stone entrance, designed by Inigo Jones, and is now inhabited by Doctor Bell, who was Chaplain to the Princess Amelia.'—*Nollekens*. 'Oh! I know, he was robbed by Sixteen-string Jack, in Gunnersbury-lane; thank ye. And she wants to know what you've done with the wooden figures, with wax masks, all in silk tatters, that the Westminster boys called the "Ragged Regiment": she says they *was* always carried before the corpse formerly.'—*Catling*. 'Why, we had them all out the other day, for John Carter and young Smith to draw from; they are put up in those very narrow closets, between our wax figures of Queen Elizabeth and Lord Chatham in his robes, in Bishop Islip's Chapel; where you have seen the stained-glass of a boy slipping down a tree, a slip of a tree, and the eye slipping out of its socket.'—*Nollekens*. 'What! where the Poll-Parrot is?

I wonder you keep such stuff: why, at Antwerp, where my father was born, they put such things in silks outside in the streets. I don't mind going to Mrs. Salmon's Wax-work, in Fleet-street, where Mother Shipton gives you a kick as you are going out. Oh, dear! you should not have such rubbish in the Abbey: and then for you to take money for this foolish thing, and that foolish thing, so that nobody can come in to see the fine works of art, without being bothered with Queen Catherine's bones, the Spanish Ambassador's coffin, the Lady who died by pricking her finger, and that nasty cap of General Monk's you beg of people to put money into, just like the money-box that I recollect they used to put down from the Gate-house. You had better tell Mr. Dean to see that the monuments don't want dusting, and to look after the Westminster boys, and not let them break the ornaments off to play at sconce with in the cloisters. Now, at Rome, and all other churches abroad, a man may go in and draw; but here he must write and wait, and be brought up like a criminal before the Dean. Why, do you know, I have been told that Stothard, one of our Academicians, had a great deal of trouble with the man; and then he talked about the proper fees! Bless my heart! it's very bad!'[1]—*Catling*. 'My good Sir, you are very severe with us this morning. Let me ask you what would become of the gentlemen of the choir, and myself, as well as the Dean, if we did not take money?'—

[1] When all the demands for viewing the various curiosities of Westminster Abbey are added together, the sum will amount to a *little more now* than it did one hundred and fifty-one years ago, as can be proved by a reference to Peachan's truly interesting tract, entitled, 'The Worth of a Penny', published in the year 1667, in which the author says:—

'For a penny, you may hear a most eloquent oration upon our English Kings and Queens, if, keeping your hands off, you will seriously listen to David Owen, who keeps the monuments in Westminster.'

Nollekens. 'What's become of that curious old picture that used to hang, when I was a boy, next to the pulpit?'—*Catling*. 'You mean the whole-length portrait of King Richard II. in his robes: that is now put up in the Jerusalem Chamber in the Deanery: I have a print of it by Carter.'—*Nollekens*. 'My mother had one by Vertue: she was acquainted with him, and at that time he lived in Brownlow-street, Drury-lane. Well, and what has become of Queen Catherine's bones?'—*Catling*. 'Oh, the remains of her bones have been gone long ago!'

They were now interrupted by old Gayfere, the Abbey-mason, who exclaimed, as he came toddling on, 'Ah, Mr. Nollekens, are you here?'—*Nollekens*. 'Here! yes; and why do you suffer that Queen Anne's altar to remain here, in a gothic building? send it back to Whitehall, where it came from. And why don't you keep a better look-out, and not suffer the fingers of figures and the noses of bustos to be knocked off by *them* Westminster boys?'—*Gayfere*. 'Why, what an ungrateful little man you are! don't it give you a job now and then? did not Mr. Dolben have a new nose put upon Camden's face the other day at his own expense? I believe I told you that I carried the rods when Fleetcraft measured the last work at the north tower when the Abbey was finished.'—*Nollekens*. 'There's the bell tolling; Oh, no, it's the quarters; I used to hear them when I was in the Abbey working with my master Scheemakers. There's a bird flying!'—*Gayfere*. 'A bird? ay, you may see a hundred birds; they come in at the broken panes of glass.'—*Nollekens*. 'Here comes Mr. Champneys. Well, you have been singing at St. Paul's, and now you are come to sing here: why don't you put a little more powder in your wig? why it's as brown as my maid Bronze's skin now is: that's what is called a Busby, an't it?'—*Champneys*. 'It is, Mr. Nollekens. Pray how is Mrs. Nollekens? I was once a beau of hers.'—*Nollekens*. 'Oh dear! I was looking at his monument, to see if it was the same wig, but he has a cap on.'—*Champneys*. 'That's a fine monument, Mr. Nollekens.'—*Nollekens*. 'Yes, a very good one; it was done by Bird. Mrs. Nollekens says he was fond of flogging the Westminster boys.'—*Champneys*. 'It is said so. Our friend Roberts, of the Exchequer, has Busby's house at Ealing, where Busby's Walk still remains, on which the Doctor used to exercise of a morning, to "wash his lungs", as he used to say.'—*Nollekens*. 'What have you done with the old gothic pulpit?'—*Catling*. 'It has been conveyed to our vestry, the Chapel of St. Blaize, south of Poet's Corner; a very curious part of the Abbey, not often shown—did you ever see it? it's very dark; there is an ancient picture, on the east wall, of a figure, which can be made out tolerably well, after the eye is accustomed to the dimness of the place. Did you ever notice the remaining colours of the curious little figure that was painted on the tomb of Chaucer?'—*Nollekens*. 'No, that's not at all in my way.'—'Pray, Mr. Nollekens,' asked Mr. Champneys, 'can you give me the name of the Sculptor who executed the basso-relievo of Townsend's monument? I have applied to several of my friends among the artists, but I have never been able to obtain it: in my opinion, the composition and style of carving are admirable; but I am sorry to find that some evil-minded person has stolen one of the heads.'—*Nollekens*. 'That's what I say. Dean Horsley should look after the monuments himself. Hang his wax-works! Yes, I can tell you who did it—Tom Carter had the job, and he employed another man of the name of Eckstein[1] to model the tablet. It's very clever. I don't know what else he has done besides; his brother kept a public-house, the sign of the Goat

[1] In 1762, the above artist, Mr. John Eckstein, received from the Society of Arts, for a basso-relievo in Portland-stone, the premium of 15*l*. 15*s*. and in 1764, for a basso-relievo in marble, the sum of 52*l*. 10*s*.!

and Star, at the corner of Tash-court, Tash-street, Gray's Inn-lane. Bartholomew Cheney modelled and carved the figures of Fame and Britannia for Captain Cornwall's monument; Sir Robert Taylor gave him four pounds fifteen shillings a week.'

One afternoon, whilst I was drawing in the cloisters of Westminster Abbey, Mr. Gayfere observed that he had met Flaxman. 'Yes,' answered I, 'he has just been so good as to point out to me those beautiful little figures that surround the tomb of Aymer de Valence, which he advises me to draw from.'—*Gayfere*. 'He is a very clever man, and bears a good character.'—I can safely venture to say, that had Mr. Gayfere been living now, he would have said he was a great man, and bore the best of characters.—*Gayfere*, 'Pray, did your Father ever see a print or a drawing of the Gate-house?'—'No, he never did; I have often questioned him about it. I remember it, Sir; it stood, as you well know, across the street, at the end of the houses opposite to the west entrance of the Abbey; one archway led into Tothill-street, and another, to the left, was opposite the entrance to Dean's Yard. I recollect walking under it with my grandmother, and seeing a tin box that was let down with a string for money out of one of the windows of the prison, and hearing a person in a hollow voice cry, "Pray remember the poor prisoners!" So I have at Old Newgate. That building stood across Newgate-street, near the south-east corner of St. Sepulchre's Church. Both these gates were not very unlike the old gate now remaining of St. John Clerkenwell, in St. John's-lane, where Mr. Cave, the predecessor of the house of Nichols, first printed the Gentleman's Magazine.'—*Gayfere*. 'Did you ever hear the echo on the centre of Westminster-bridge? If you go to one of the middle alcoves, and speak in a whisper, putting your mouth close to the wall, to a friend on the opposite side, after he has placed his ear close to the centre of the other alcove, he will hear every syllable you utter as distinctly as he would if you had both been in the gallery of St. Paul's.'

When going with Mr. Nollekens one Sunday morning to see Mr. Gainsborough's pictures, he stopped at the Duke of Norfolk's house in St. James's-square, and said, 'There! in that very house our King was born: my mother used to show it to me.' Recollecting this remark, I applied for confirmation of it to the Rev. James Dallaway,[1] who had been the late Duke of Norfolk's chaplain, and with his usual liberality, he immediately favoured me with the following very satisfactory information, which I now give in that gentleman's own words. 'Arundel House was taken down in 1678, and its site converted into Norfolk, Surrey, Arundel, and Howard-streets, including what had been called Arundel-rents. The present Norfolk House, in St. James's-square, was built from a design of R. Brettingham, in 1742, by Thomas Duke of Norfolk, and finished by his brother Edward in 176—.

'It had been previously the site of St. Albans House, built by Henry Jermyn, Earl of St. Albans, and was sold by Henry Duke of Portland for 10,000*l*. In 1738, only the buildings on the north side of the inner court were completed, which were lent to Frederick Prince of Wales, as a temporary residence till Leicester House was finished. On the 24th of May, 1738, the late King George was born, and, being very sickly, was baptized the same day. He was a seven-months' child. Prince Frederick presented the Duchess of Norfolk with miniatures in enamel of himself and the Princess, set in brilliants.'

[1] This gentleman has just completed a new edition of 'Walpole's Anecdotes of Painters', in which, I trust, there are not only many of Lord Orford's errors corrected, but new information given of English artists, of whom his Lordship appeared ignorant: there certainly is a more interesting account of Vandyke than any that has yet appeared.

As we were turning round to proceed to Pall Mall, Mr. Charles Townley accosted Mr. Nollekens, who immediately, in the open street, loudly commenced his observations in what he thought the Italian language; but as he was very noisy in his jargon, Mr. Townley requested him to confine himself to English, or the people in the street would notice them. Mr. Townley then desired him to send for his small Venus, in order to model a pair of arms to it. That gentleman also wished him to try them in various positions, such as holding a dove, the beak of which might touch her lips; entwining a wreath; or looking at the eye of a serpent.—*Nollekens*. 'Well, I'll send for it, then; shall you be at home when my man comes?'—*Mr. Townley*. 'Send to-morrow at ten o'clock, when I shall be at home.'—*Nollekens*. 'Which way now are you going?' —*Mr. Townley*. 'This way, Mr. Nollekens;—good-morning to you!' Nollekens called after him, 'Well, I'll send.' Strange to tell, I stood to Mr. Nollekens for all the various positions he could devise for the arms, and after six changes the present ones were carved;[1] the right one of which is too much like one of the arms of the Venus de' Medici, which are looked upon as the work of Baccio Bandinelli.

Upon our arrival at Mr. Gainsborough's, the third west division of Schomberg-house, Pall Mall, the artist was listening to a violin, and held up his finger to Mr. Nollekens as a request of silence. Colonel Hamilton was playing to him in so exquisite a style, that Gainsborough exclaimed, 'Now, my dear Colonel, if you will but go on, I will give you that picture of the boy at the stile, which you have so often wished to purchase of me.' Mr. Gainsborough, not knowing

[1] This statue is now in the British Museum, and measures three feet six inches and five-eighths, including the plinth. A modern editor has roundly asserted, that Gavin Hamilton directed Mr. Nollekens in his restoration of the arms of this statue. Gavin Hamilton was in Rome at the time.

how long Nollekens would hold his tongue, gave him a book of sketches to choose two from, which he had promised him. As Gainsborough's versatile fancy was at this period devoted to music, his attention was so riveted to the tones of the violin, that for nearly half an hour he was motionless; after which, the Colonel requested that a hackney-coach might be sent for, wherein he carried off the picture.[1] Mr. Gainsborough, after he had given Mr. Nollekens the two drawings he had selected, requested him to look at a model of an ass's head which he had just made.—*Nollekens.* 'You should model more with your thumbs; thumb it about, till you get it into shape.'—'What,' said Gainsborough, 'in this manner?' having taken up a bit of clay; and looking at a picture of Abel's Pomeranian Dog which hung over the chimney-piece —'this way?'—'Yes,' said Nollekens, 'you'll do a great deal more with your thumbs.'

Mr. Gainsborough, by whom I was standing, observed to me, 'You enjoyed the music, my little fellow, and I am sure you long for this model; there, I will give it to you;'—and I am delighted with it still. I have never had it baked, fearing it might fly in the kiln, as the artist had not kneaded the clay well before he commenced working it, and I conclude that the model must still contain a quantity of fixed air.

Colonel Hamilton above-mentioned, was not only looked upon as one of the first amateur violin-players, but also one of the first gentlemen pugilists. I was afterwards noticed by him in my art as an etcher of landscapes; and have frequently seen him spar with the famous Mendoza in his drawing-room, in Leicester-street, Leicester-square.

The following dialogue took place in Greenwood's auction-room, during the sale of Barnard's collection of drawings, between Mr. Nollekens and Panton Betew. Mr. Betew had been a silversmith of the old

[1] It has been engraven by Stow, a pupil of Woollett.

school, and also a dealer in pictures, drawings, and other works of art. I recollect him well in my boyish days, at his house in Old Compton-street, Soho, at which time he was generally accosted by his old friends under the free and easy appellation of Panny.—*Mr. Panton Betew*. 'Well, Mr. Nollekens, time has made little difference in your looks; you walk just in the same way with your cane and your ruffles, as you did twenty years ago, when I sold you Roubilliac's model, which he designed for General Wolfe's monument: Wilton was the successful candidate, he gained the order.'—*Nollekens*. 'I remember it very well; you would have the odd sixpence of me. Pray what became of that poor fellow, Chattelain, who used to work for Vivares? I once saw several of his drawings in your window.'—*Betew*. 'Yes, I bought many drawings of him, and there's a great deal of spirit in what he did. But he died at the White Bear in Piccadilly: the landlord came to me, knowing that I knew him, to ask me to attend his funeral. Poor fellow! the parish buried him in the Pest-fields, Carnaby-market: I went, Vivares went, and so did M'Ardell, and several others. I recollect well, he was a Roman Catholic, and all the common people who frequented the Romish Chapel in Warwick-street, followed; and the boys called it an Irish funeral, for there were very few of us in black coats.'—*Nollekens*. 'Poor fellow! I lost sight of him for some years, and could not tell what had become of him. I remember a tallow-chandler used to lend me some of his drawings to copy when I was quite a youngster.'—*Betew*. 'Ay, I had many drawings and pictures by young artists, very clever fellows; but they are nearly all gone now. There was Brooking, the Ship-painter; he died, poor fellow, just as he was getting into full song, as the saying is; and there was Tull, the Landscape-painter, he was a genius: he married the King's butcher's daughter, in St. James's-market, and became the schoolmaster at

Queen Elizabeth's School in Tooley-street, in the Borough. I have a few of his pictures by me now; his style was an imitation of Hobbima's. Vivares has engraved four of them, and very pretty they are. His colouring was rather black; but he was a self-taught artist, as people call those who don't regularly study under others, but pick up their information by degrees. Well, and then there was your great Mr. Gainsborough, I have had many and many a drawing of his in my shop-window before he went to Bath; ay, and he has often been glad to receive seven or eight shillings from me for what I have sold: Paul Sandby knows it well.'—*Nollekens*. 'What do you want for that model of a boy? I suppose you have got it still.'—*Betew*. 'Why now, why can't you say Fiamingo's boy? you know it to be one of his, and you also know that no man ever modelled boys better than he did:—it is said that he was employed to model children for Rubens to put into his pictures.'—*Nollekens*. 'Well, what must I give you for it?'—*Betew*. 'Fifteen shillings is the money I want for it.'—*Nollekens*. 'No; ten.'—*Betew*. 'Now, my old friend, how can you rate art in that manner? you would not model one for twenty times ten, and if you did, you could not think of comparing it with that;—why, you are obliged to give more at auctions when Lord Rockingham or Mr. Burke is standing by you. No, I will not 'bate a farthing.'—*Nollekens*. 'Well, I'll take it. Do you still buy broken silver? I have some odd sleeve-buttons, and Mrs. Nollekens wants to get rid of a chased watch-case, by old Moser, one that he made when he used to model for the Bow manufactory.'—*Betew*. 'Ay, I know there were many very clever things produced there: what very curious heads for canes they made at that manufactory! I think Crowther was the proprietor's name; he had a very beautiful daughter, who is married to Sir James Lake. Nat. Hone painted a portrait of her, in the character of Diana, and it was one of his best pictures. There were some clever men who modelled for the Bow concern, and they produced several spirited figures: Quin in Falstaff; Garrick in Richard; Frederick Duke of Cumberland, striding triumphantly over the Pretender, who is begging quarter of him; John Wilkes, and so forth.'—*Nollekens*. 'Mr. Moser, who was the Keeper of our Academy, modelled several things for them. He was a chaser originally.'—*Betew*. 'Bless you! I knew him well; my friend Grignon, the Watch-maker, in Russell-street, Covent-garden, advised him to learn to enamel trinkets for watches; and he succeeded so well, that the Queen patronized him, and he did several things for the King: it is said, his Majesty was so pleased with him, that he once ordered him a hatfull of money for some of his works.'—*Nollekens*. 'So I've heard.'—*Betew*. 'Chelsea was another place for China.'—*Nollekens*. 'Do you know where that factory stood?'—*Betew*. 'Why, it stood upon the site of Lord Dartery's house, just beyond the bridge.'—*Nollekens*. 'My father worked for them, at one time.'—*Betew*. 'Yes, and Sir James Thornhill designed for them: Mr. Walpole, at Strawberry-hill, has a dozen plates by Sir James, which he purchased at Mrs. Hogarth's sale in Leicester-square. Paul Ferg painted for them. Ay! that was a curious failure: the cunning rogues produced very white and delicate ware, but then they had their clay from China; which when the Chinese found out, they would not let the captains have any more clay for ballast, and the consequence was, that the whole concern failed.'

Many of my readers may recollect Fielding's description of the Man of the Hill, in his 'Tom Jones', and such another human form Nature displayed in Panton Betew: his dress differed from the general mode; he wore a loose dark-brown great-coat, with, generally, a red cloth waistcoat, black shalloon small-clothes, dark-grey worsted stockings, easy square-toed shoes, with small silver buckles, and a large slouched hat with a close round crown, without the least nap, being often brushed, for cleanliness-sake, with the shoe, shining, or table-brush. He was well-known to all the fish-vendors in Lombard-court, Seven-dials, as a purchaser of fish for two; which provender he was not ashamed to carry home in a dark snuff-coloured silk handkerchief, always taking care to hold it in his right-hand, that he might display a brilliant ring, which he said he wore in memory of his mother. The watchman shut and opened his shop. I remember his leaving old Compton-street for one of his mother's houses in Nassau-street, St. James's-market, and afterwards his living in a house in Chelsea, beyond what was formerly called the Five-Fields: upon which a new city of most magnificent mansions is now in a course of building, to the wonderful increase of the princely income of the Earl Grosvenor.

In his house at Chelsea, where Betew died, my father and I have often visited him. Independently of his knowledge of the origin of the artists of the last century, he was a well-informed person upon the general topics of conversation; and he has been heard to say, that he liked to converse with a man whom he could *swop* an idea with. He was intimate with Hogarth, and frequently purchased pieces of plate with armorial bearings engraved upon them by that artist, which he cleared out for the next possessor; but, unfortunately for the Stanleyean Collection, without rubbing off a single impression. This was not the case with Morison, a silversmith, who at that time lived in Cheapside; he took off twenty-five impressions of a large silver dish, engraved by Hogarth, which impressions he not only numbered as they were taken off, but attested each with his own signature. Should this page meet the eyes of any branches of the good old-fashioned families, which have carefully preserved the plate of Oliver their uncle, or Deborah their aunt,

I sincerely implore them, should the armorial bearings be the production of the early part of the last century, to cause a few impressions to be taken from them; for I am inclined to believe it very possible, that some curious specimens of Hogarth's dawning genius may yet in that way be rescued from future furnaces.

The following use was made of Hogarth's plates of the Idle and Industrious Apprentices, by the late John Adams, of Edmonton, Schoolmaster. The prints were framed and hung up in the school-room, and Adams, once a month, after reading a lecture upon their vicious and virtuous examples, rewarded those boys who had conducted themselves well, and caned those who had behaved ill.

CHAPTER VIII

Mr. Nollekens's opinion of Colossal Sculpture.—Restorations of the paintings at Whitehall.—Increase of the value of modern pictures.—Remarkable old houses and customs.—Mrs. Nollekens's visits.—Ireland's Vortigern.—London cries.—Sir Peter Lely's sale.—Nollekens at the Academy Club, and at Harrowgate.—His Venus model.—Meanness of Mrs. Nollekens.—Miss Hawkins and her Anecdotes.

NOLLEKENS at all times strongly reprobated colossal sculpture, more especially when commenced by the too-daring student in the art; and, indeed, whenever any one led to the subject, he would deliver his opinion, even to persons of the first fashion and rank, with as much freedom as if he were chiding his mason's boy, Kit Finny, for buying scanty paunches for his yard-dog, Cerberus. 'No, no, my Lord,' he would vociferate, with an increased nasal and monotonous tone of voice, 'a grand thing don't depend upon the size, I can assure you of that. A large model certainly produces a stare, and is often admired by ignorant people; but the excellence of a work of art has nothing to do with the size, that you may depend upon from me.' In this, he unquestionably was correct; as the graceful elegance of a Cellini cup, or a bell for the Pope's table, does not consist in immensity. I have a cast from an antique bronze figure only three inches in height, which, from its justness of proportion and dignity of attitude, strikes the beholder, when it is elevated only nine inches above his eye, with an idea of its being a figure full thirty feet in height.

I well recollect my play-fellow, John Deare, the Sculptor, powerfully maintaining that grandeur never depended upon magnitude. A preposterously large figure, like Gog or Magog in Guildhall, or the giant and giantess of Antwerp, would, without dignity and breadth of style and just proportion, exhibit nothing beyond a mass of overwhelming lumber. 'What!' he would exclaim, 'is not that beautiful gem of Hercules strangling the lion a work of grand art? and that figure is contained in less than the space of an inch.' This is also my own humble opinion; for I think that Simon's Dunbar medals, of which I have now some beautiful casts before me, are quite as grand as any of the finest busts by Nollekens.[1] That a figure should be of increased dimensions the higher it is placed above the eye of the spectator, is beyond a doubt; since, if it were only the size of life, it would dwindle into insignificance, particularly if placed on the top of the monument on Fish-street-hill; for that pillar being two hundred and two feet in height, it would require a statue of full fourteen feet. The figures of the Apostles sculptured by Bird on the top of St. Paul's, are more than twice the height of a man; but what appeared most astonishing to me when a boy, was the enormous magnitude of the figures surrounding the apotheosis of King James I., painted upon the ceiling of Whitehall by Rubens. My father being intimately acquainted with Cipriani, took me up to the scaffold when that artist was repairing the picture, and to our great astonishment they measured the enormous height of nine feet. This appears hardly credible, as they look no larger than life when viewed from the

[1] I am quite certain, that if a talented medallist were to execute a series of heads from the finest of Nollekens's busts of persons of the highest eminence, his labours would meet with great encouragement; but he must honestly copy and not attempt even the slightest alteration, for by such sophistications he would make a botched medal; for which he never should, if I had my wish, receive more than the weight of the metal. Many of Chantrey's finest busts have been in this manner most disgracefully misrepresented.

floor.[1] Cipriani excelled as a draughtsman; his style of colouring in oil-pictures was rather cold, and sometimes hard, particularly when compared with the luxuriantly sunny glow of Rubens's pictures. However, it was a very profitable employment for him, as it is said he had one thousand pounds for repairing it, and an enormous sum for re-touching it only. I verily believe he must have repainted it wholesale, or such an amount would never have been sanctioned by the officers in whom payment was invested. I am quite certain such a charge would be closely looked into at present.

It is a curious fact, that though this ceiling of Whitehall is so grand in its design, and is, indeed, I believe, the only work of such magnitude from the mind of Rubens in England,—few people, comparatively with the tens of thousands who pass the building daily, know any thing about it. However, I consider it but fair for the high reputation of Rubens as a colourist, to state, that this picture has been *restored*, *re-painted*, and *refreshed*, not fewer than three times. In the reign of King James II., 1687, Parrey Walton, a Painter of

[1] Upon an investigation, in consequence of a report that there was a very fine copy of this work of Rubens, as a fixture, in a house on the south side of Leicester-fields, I found that the curiously ornamented *papier-maché* parlour ceiling of No. 41, had been painted, though very indifferently, by some persons who had borrowed groups of figures from several of Rubens's designs, which they had unskilfully combined. This ceiling is divided into three compartments; in the centre one there is a figure, with a head resembling King Charles I.; and in that at the south end of the room is another of King James I., evidently painted from recollection, as it is so ill done, of that of the same sovereign at Whitehall. I consider this visit, however, as well bestowed, since it may possibly, in some measure, set at rest the assertion so roundly and fallaciously propagated, should the premises ever be destroyed, and the loss of the ceiling be deplored by those who had never seen it.

still life, and Keeper of the King's Pictures, was suffered to re-touch this grand work of art, which then had been painted only sixty years; as appears by the Privy Council book, in which Mr. Parrey Walton's demand of two hundred and twelve pounds for its complete restoration, was considered by Sir Christopher Wren 'as very modest and reasonable'. Mr. Cipriani, as above stated, repainted it a second time; and last of all, Rigaud was employed to refresh it.

There is a most excellent engraving of this ceiling, in three sheets, by Gribelin, the same artist who executed that pretty set of prints from the Cartoons, by Raffaelle, at Hampton-court. This *design* of Rubens, —for, as it has been so often cleaned and painted upon, there can be but little of his *colouring* visible at this moment,—would still afford employment to the living; at least to the novelist, who might, by stating all its multifarious vicissitudes under Folly's innovations, render it a subject for a work fully as entertaining, and equally lucrative as 'The History of a Guinea', 'A Shilling', or, 'A Gold-headed Cane'. For instance, let us suppose Rubens, shocked at the contaminated effect of his own canvas, petitioning his great and liberal patron, Charles I., to invoke St. Luke to leave his easel, and to order an investigation into the conduct of the Surveyors-general; commencing with Sir Christopher Wren, and proceeding with others of the craft, who have flourished from his time to the late reign; in order, if possible, to discover how they could ever have sanctioned so bare-faced a change. This inquiry should be wholly confined to the honour of Rubens' pencil, and in no degree whatsoever as to the orders given, for the barbarously smearing, or refreshing, as Rigaud termed it, of the lively portraiture of King James I.; a Monarch whom no one could possibly think of sending to Heaven for *his patronage of the Fine Arts;* nor would Saint Luke be willing to introduce him there, though that Saint, according to

Spence's anecdote, had some influence with Saint Peter, when Sir Godfrey Kneller was admitted. The umpires ought to consist of Sir Peter Paul's seven brother Knights of the pallet, who have practised from the Reign of the above Monarch to the present day; viz. Sir Anthony Vandyke, Sir Peter Lely, Sir Godfrey Kneller, Sir James Thornhill, Sir Joshua Reynolds, Sir William Beechey, and lastly, Sir Thomas Lawrence, who, like Rubens, was honoured with a gold chain from the hand of a King of England. By such chronological arrangement, and as the four first-named gentlemen must, beyond a reprieve, agree to the execution of the culprits, the latter three would not be under the necessity of signing for the rope for two of the Scrubbers and Smudgers. As several of those fraternities, which are now fitly nick-named '*Painters and Glaziers*', so impudently recommend old pictures that have been thus 'restored', 'repainted', and 'refreshed', as the *only things* worthy the attention of the man of fortune, I have great pleasure in recording the triumph lately obtained over them, in the sale of Lord De Tabley's pictures, by modern English artists; which actually produced twenty-five per cent. more than they cost his Lordship, though they were purchased of the artists at what they considered most liberal prices. On this occasion, the pretenders alluded to were severely exposed by Mr. Christie. Mr. Nollekens also died possessed of three pictures by an English artist, Richard Wilson, which cost his father-in-law, Mr. Welch, only about a tenth part of the sum the said Mr. Christie sold them for.

One spring morning, as I was passing through Covent-garden, I was accosted by Mrs. Elizabeth Carter, who had accompanied Mrs. Nollekens thither for the purpose of purchasing some roots of dandelion, an infusion of which had been strongly recommended to her husband by Dr. Jebb. Twigg, the Fruiterer, to whom Mr. Justice Welch, during his magistracy, had often been kind, was at all times gratefully attentive to Miss Welch and her sister, Mrs. Nollekens. He procured the roots she wanted from that class of people called 'Simplers', who sit in the centre of the garden. The fruiterer was a talkative man, and was called by some of his jocular friends the 'Twig of the Garden'; he had been cook at the Shakspeare Tavern, and knew all the wits and eccentric characters of his early days.

Mrs. Carter, though she was seldom fond of noticing strangers, fell by degrees into a conversation with Twigg, and asked him which house it was in Tavistock-row that Miss Wray, who was shot by the Rev. James Hackman, occupied before she resided with Lord Sandwich: to which he replied, 'It was that on the south-west corner of Tavistock-court, next to the one in which the famous William Vandevelde, the Marine-painter, died.' This corner house, No. 4, is now occupied by a tailor; and that in which Vandevelde lived, now No. 5, is inhabited by Irish Johnstone, as he is usually called, that once delightful singer and excellent actor of the characters of Irishmen. 'Pray,' continued the lady, 'which was Zincke's, the celebrated Enameller's?'—'Why, Ma'am,' said he, 'it is No. 13, that in which Mr. Nathaniel Dance, the Painter, afterwards lived. Meyer, another famous Miniature-painter, resided in it; and the garrets are now occupied by Peter Pindar.' (Doctor Wolcot.) 'I recollect, Ma'am,' continued the fruiterer, 'Old Joe, who was the first person who sold flowers in this Garden: his stand was at that corner within the enclosure, then called Primrose Hill,[1] opposite to Lowe's Hotel. Lowe had been a hair-dresser in Tavistock-street before he took that large house, which he established as a family hotel, the earliest of that description in London, where he distributed medals, which procured

[1] This spot was so named in consequence of its being the station of those persons who brought primroses to the Garden.

him many lodgers.' Mrs. Nollekens then requested to know which house it was in James-street, where her father's old friend, Mr. Charles Grignon, resided; the engraver so extensively, and for so many years, employed upon the designs of Gravelot, Hayman, and Wale. 'No. 27,' said Twigg; 'I recollect the old house when it was a shop inhabited by two old Frenchwomen, who came over here to chew paper for the *papier-maché* people.'—*Mrs. Nollekens.* 'Ridiculous! I think Mr. Nollekens once told me that the elder Wilton, Lady Chambers's grandfather, was the person who employed people from France to work in the *papier-maché* manufactory, which he established in Edward-street, Cavendish-square.'—*Twigg.* 'I can assure you, Ma'am, these women bought the paper-cuttings from the stationers and bookbinders, and produced it in that way, in order to keep it a secret, before they used our machine for mashing it.'—*Mrs. Carter.* 'I recollect, Sir, when Mr. Garrick acted, hackney-chairs were then so numerous, that they stood all round the Piazzas, down Southampton-street, and extended more than half-way along Maiden-lane, so much were they in requisition at that time.'—*Twigg.* 'Then, I suppose, Ma'am, you also recollect the shoe-blacks at every corner of the streets, whose cry was "Black your shoes, your Honour?" '—'Yes, Sir, perfectly well; and the clergyman of your parish walking about and visiting the fruit-shops in the garden in his canonicals; and I likewise remember a very portly woman sitting at her fruit-stall in a dress of lace, which it was said cost at least one hundred guineas, though a greater sum was often mentioned.'

Here this dialogue about old times ended, by the entrance of several other customers; upon which Mrs. Carter and Mrs. Nollekens left the shop to pay a morning visit to Mrs. Garrick, and I made my bow.

Mr. Nollekens's uncultivated manners were at times

so truly disagreeable to his sister-in-law, Miss Welch, —whose talents were highly appreciated by the literati of the day,—that whenever she received her friends at a card-party, he was seldom invited; but Mrs. Nollekens, whom her sister was very fond of showing off, always attended them. To please her economical husband, she would appear to acquiesce in his opinion, that her shape was better shown by a close simple dress; for, in doing this, she could save a shilling in coach-hire, by going early in a plain gown, time enough to dress at her sister's, where she had by slow degrees conveyed various articles of finery, until she had lodged a pretty good wardrobe in one of the spare upper closets. Upon entering the drawing-room close behind those who had last knocked, her name was announced, as if just arrived, and she has been seen to make as formal a curtsey to her sister as to the rest of the party. At these ceremonious card-parties, Mrs. Nollekens, who, the reader will recollect, played the strict Hoyle game, would remain till she found herself in possession of more than she sat down with, and then inquired if her servant were below. Poor Bronze then attended her to the upper chamber, where, after changing her dress, she remained in her camlet-cloak till the whole of the visitors were gone; and then the foot, which had been that evening graced with a silver-spangled slipper, was pressed into a wooden clog. Thus equipped, Mrs. Nollekens, on leaving the house, placed her delicately-formed arm upon that of her faithful servant; whose swarthy hue her mistress could scarcely by daylight bear to look upon, but upon these occasions she condescended to rest upon her with perfect confidence.

Nollekens was at times so ridiculously soft, that, in several instances, he approached what was formerly called the 'Colley-Molley' class of beings; men who were fond of lacing the stays, and carrying the fans or pattens of their spouses; whose character is so admirably pourtrayed by Foote in his Jerry Sneak. In the exercise of some of his accommodating attentions to the will of his fair partner, his good-natured weakness exposed him to the notice of a friend, who was induced to watch him one night, in Bloomsbury-square, dangling a lantern, in attendance upon his wife and her sister Miss Welch, on their economical pedestrian return home from a formal cribbage-party. Nollekens, anxious to get home to bed, was generally foremost, and often proceeded, though with a toddling gait, so much too fast for the clogged ladies behind him, that Mrs. Nollekens was often heard to cry, 'Stop, Sir, pray stop;' but Miss Welch, of late years, seldom spoke to him. He would then, with due obedience, slacken his pace into a dawdling creep, suffer them to pass, and lag so considerably behind, that he was now and then openly and roundly charged with indulging in a nap. Upon these occasions they thought it wisest to wait his coming up with the lantern, upon pretence of seeing that all the umbrellas were safe under his arm; but, in reality, for fear of a rude embrace from some boisterous perambulator of the streets, under the influence of Bacchus or Thrale's Entire; and whenever there was a wide puddle to cross, Mrs. Nollekens always made a point of seeing her husband safe over first, by insisting upon his maintaining a proper precedence on such occasions.

Samuel Ireland had entreated Mrs. Nollekens to persuade her husband to go to the representation of what he called Shakspeare's play of Vortigern; and when he informed her that my father and I were going, she acquiesced, fully relying upon our taking care of him. The crowds which had assembled at the doors of Drury-lane Theatre, long before the hours of admission, were immense, and the anxiety of Ireland for the success of the play was so great, that he caused a hand-bill to be printed and thrown crumpled up, by hundreds, among the people; and as that bill is now esteemed rather a rare theatrical relique, the reader is presented with a copy of one which fell to my lot.

'VORTIGERN.

'A malevolent and impotent attack on the Shakspeare MSS. having appeared on the eve of representation of the play of Vortigern, evidently intended to injure the interest of the proprietor of the MSS.; Mr. Ireland feels it impossible, within the short space of time that intervenes between the publishing and the representation, to produce an answer to the most illiberal and unfounded assertions in Mr. Malone's Inquiry. He is therefore induced to request, that the play of Vortigern may be heard with that candour that has ever distinguished a British audience.

'*** The play is now at the press, and will in a very few days be laid before the public.'

After great patience and much crowding, we moved in, and, when safely seated in the pit, congratulated ourselves upon the possession of our shoes; whilst Mr. Nollekens recognised Miles Petit Andrews, Flaxman, and several others whom he knew. The play went on pretty well until Kemble appeared, when the noise of disapprobation commenced, and, being considered by the audience as an atrocious fraud, it was at length completely condemned.

Frequently, when Mr. Nollekens has been modelling, he has imitated the cries of the itinerant venders as they were passing by. I recollect the cries of two men pleasing him so extravagantly, that he has continued to hum their notes for days together; even when he has been engaged with his sitters, measuring the stone in the yard for a bust or a figure, feeding the dog, putting up the bar of the gate, or improving the attitudes of his Venuses.

The late Dr. Kitchiner, whose musical powers were so very generally acknowledged, kindly condescended to note down the following music of these cries, from my recollection, whereby I am enabled to gratify the reader with the very sound itself.[1]

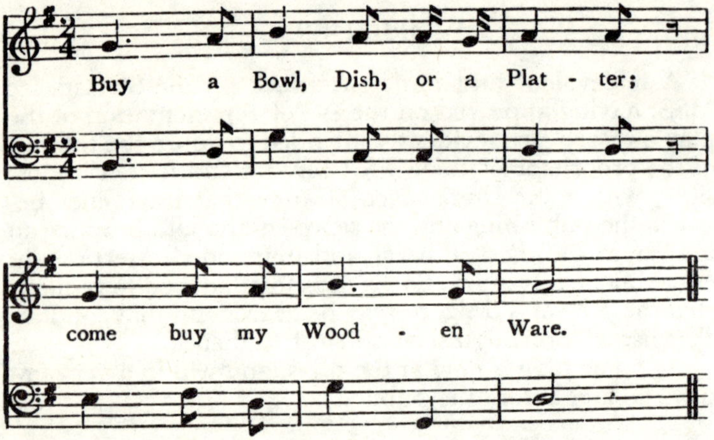

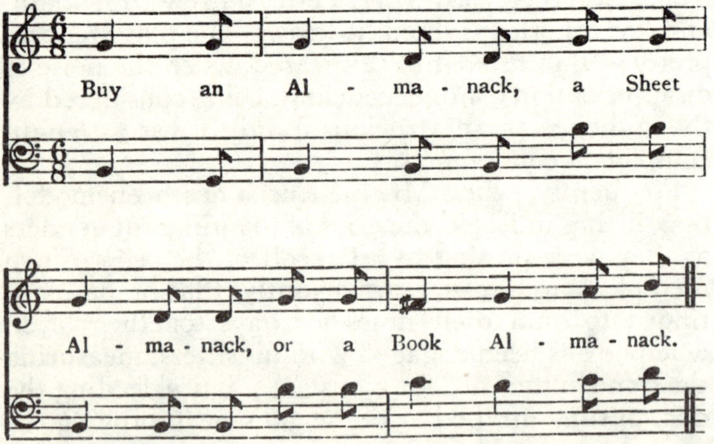

[1] During the last nine years, Dr. Kitchiner wrote the following works:—'Economy of the Eyes; Part I. Of Spectacles; Part II. Of Telescopes.' 'The Cook's Oracle.'

In a copy of Hawkins's 'History of Music', in the British Museum, in page 75, in the fifth volume, there is the following *manuscript* note respecting the famous Tom Britton, the musical small-coal man. 'The goodness of his ear directed him to the use of the most perfect of all musical intervals, the diapason or octave: his cry being, as some relate that remember it,'

The public have frequently been amused at the Theatres by actors who have mimicked the cries of London. I remember hearing Baddeley whine the cry of 'Periwinkles, a wine quart a penny, periwinkles. Come buy my shrimps, come buy my shrimps: a crab, will you buy a crab?' I have also heard that excellent comedian John Bannister cry,

Come, neighbours, see and buy; here's
Your long and strong scarlet ware;
Scarlet garters two-pence a pair,
Two-pence a pair! two-pence a pair!

Upon my mentioning this to Mr. Bannister, he did not immediately recollect it; though in a few moments he said, 'You are right, and it was at the Little Theatre in the Haymarket. Did you ever, my good fellow, hear of Ned Shuter's imitations of the London

'Art of Invigorating Life.' 'Observations on Singing.' 'National Songs of England.' 'Life, and Sea Songs of Dibdin.' 'Housekeeper's Ledger.' 'Century of Surgeons.' 'Traveller's Oracle.' The Doctor composed and selected the music of the Opera of 'Ivanhoe', for Covent-garden Theatre; composed the whole of the music for 'Love among the Roses', for the English Opera. 'Fifty English Ballads', 'An Universal Prayer', 'The Hymn of Faith', 'The English Grace', and 'The Lord's Prayer'. Number sold, 55,250 volumes.

cries? He was the most famous chap at that sort of thing; indeed, so fond of it, that he would frequently follow people for hours together to get their cries correctly. I recollect a story which he used to tell of his following a man who had a peculiar cry, up one street and down another, nearly a whole day, to get his cry, but the man never once cried; at last, being quite out of temper, he went up to the fellow, and said, "You don't cry; why the d——l don't you cry?" The man answered in a piteous tone "Cry! Lord bless your heart, Sir, I can't cry; my *vife* 's dead; she died this morning."'

Besides the musical cries mentioned above, about sixty years back, there were also two others yet more singular, which, however, were probably better known in the villages round London than in the metropolis itself. The first of these was used by an itinerant dealer in corks, sometimes called 'Old Corks', who rode upon an ass, and carried his wares in paniers on each side of him. He sat with much dignity, and wore upon his head a velvet cap; and his attractive cry, which was partly spoken and partly sung, but all in metre, was something like the following fragment:—

Spoken. Corks for sack
I have at my back;

Sung. All handy, all handy;
Some for wine and some for brandy.

Spoken. Corks for cholic-water,
Cut 'em a little shorter;
Corks for gin,
Very thin;
Corks for rum,
As big as my thumb;
Corks for ale,
Long and pale:

Sung. They're all handy, all handy,
Some for wine and some for brandy.

The other cry, which was much more musical, was that of two persons, father and son, who sold lines. The father, in a strong, clear tenor, would begin the strain in the major-key, and when he had finished, his son, who followed at a short distance behind him, in a shrill falsetto, would repeat it in the minor, and their call consisted of the following words:—

Buy a white-line,
Or, a jack-line,
Or, a clock-line,
Or, a hair-line,
  Or, a line for your clothes here.

In order to render this little work a book of reference to the London topographer as well as to the historian, I have occasionally given, and shall continue to give, the residences of persons of notoriety, as well as their places of birth, death, and burial; points which, I am sorry to say, are not always attended to by biographers.

The house in Great Queen-street, now divided into two, Nos. 55 and 56, was that in which Hudson lived; it was afterwards the last habitation of Worlidge, the Etcher, who died in it. Hoole, the Translator of Tasso, and the beloved friend of Dr. Johnson, next resided in it, and he was succeeded by Richard Brinsley Sheridan, who after Garrick's funeral, passed there the remainder of the day in silence with a few select friends. It was lately inhabited by Mr. Chippendale. This house is one of those built after a design of Inigo Jones, and still retains much of its original architecture. The street was named Queen-street in compliment to Henrietta-Maria. '*My* old friend,' Mr. Batridge, the barber, as Mr. Hone in his 'Every Day Book' has been pleased to call him, informed me that he very well recollected the gate-entrance into Great Queen-street from Drury-lane. It was under a house, and was so long and dark that it received the fearful appellation of 'Hell-gate'. Through this gate the

Dukes of Newcastle and Ancaster drove to their houses in Lincoln's Inn-fields, at that time the seat of fashion; which can readily be conceived, when the reader recollects that Grosvenor-square was building when Mr. Nollekens was a little boy.

Covent-garden was the first square inhabited by the great; for immediately upon the completion of the houses on the north and east sides of Covent-garden, which were all that were uniformly built after the design of Inigo Jones, they were *every one* of them inhabited by persons of the first title and rank, as appears by the parish-books of the rates at that time.

The chambers occupied by Richard Wilson were portions of the house successively inhabited by Sir Peter Lely, Sir Godfrey Kneller, and Sir James Thornhill; and, by way of rather a curious treat to the connoisseur, I shall insert the advertisement for the sale of Sir Peter Lely's collection of works of art, which I copied from 'The London Gazette', of February 16th, 1687.

'Upon Monday, in Easter-week, will be exposed by Public Auction, a most curious and valuable collection of Drawings and Prints, made with great expense and care, by Sir Peter Lely, Painter to his Majesty. The Drawings are all of the most eminent Masters of Italy, being originals and most curiously preserved. The Prints are all the works of Mark Antoine, after Raphael, and the other best Italian Masters, and of the best impressions and proof Prints in good condition and curiously preserved, some are double and treble.

The Sale will be at the house in Covent-garden, where Sir Peter Lely lived.'[1]

Covent-garden, even so late as Pope's time, retained its fashion, as may be seen by the following extract from 'The Morning Advertiser', for March 6th, 1730.

1 It was not the custom formerly to mention the name of the auctioneer in advertisements of sales.

'The Lady Wortley Montague, who has been greatly indisposed at her house in Covent-Garden for some time, is now perfectly recovered, and takes the benefit of the air in Hyde-Park every morning, by advice of her physicians.'

The tracing out and examining the peculiar manners and customs of the inhabitants and visitors of the parish of St. Paul, Covent-Garden, is a source of knowledge of considerable importance to every class of historian; both on account of the immense number of persons of the highest rank and title, as well as artists of the very first eminence, who at one time rendered it the most, and indeed the only fashionable part of the town; and also from the immense concourse of wits, literary characters, and other men of genius, who frequented the various and numerous coffee-houses, wine and cider-cellars, jelly-shops, &c. within its boundaries, the list of whom particularly includes the eminent names of Butler, Addison, Sir Richard Steele, Otway, Dryden, Pope, Warburton, Cibber, Fielding, Churchill, Bolingbroke, and Dr. Samuel Johnson; Rich, Woodward, Booth, Wilkes, Garrick, and Macklin; Kitty Clive, Peg Woffington, Mrs. Pritchard, the Duchess of Bolton, Lady Derby, Lady Thurlow, and the present Duchess of St. Alban's; Sir Peter Lely, Sir Godfrey Kneller, and Sir James Thornhill; Vandevelde, Zincke, Lambert, Hayman, Hogarth, Wilson, Dance, Meyer, &c. The diversified pleasure of procuring this information from numerous authentic sources, both written and related, together with several curious events which have fallen under my own observation, has occupied many years of my early life; and I now find myself in possession of a truly interesting mass of intelligence, sufficiently extensive for a publication of two volumes, containing some curious collections toward the history of that most frequented of parishes; which I hope, with the blessing of health and continuance of memory, (for the possession of which organ the friendly Doctor

Spurzheim has given me some credit,) to live to see published.

But at present I must not lose sight of Mr. Nollekens. He for many years made one at the table of what was at this time called the Royal Academy Club; and so strongly was he bent upon saving all he could privately conceal, that he did not mind paying two guineas a-year for his admission ticket, in order to indulge himself with a few nutmegs, which he contrived to pocket privately; for as red-wine negus was the principal beverage, nutmegs were used. Now it generally happened, if another bowl was wanted, that the nutmegs were missing. Nollekens, who had frequently been seen to pocket them, was one day requested by Rossi, the Sculptor, to see if they had not fallen under the table; upon which Nollekens actually went crawling beneath upon his hands and knees, pretending to look for them, though at that very time they were in his waistcoat pocket. He was so old a stager at this monopoly of nutmegs, that he would sometimes engage the maker of the negus in conversation, looking at him full in the face, whilst he slyly and unobserved, as he thought, conveyed away the spice: like the fellow who is stealing the bank note from the blind man in that admirable print of the Royal Cockpit, by Hogarth.

I believe it is generally considered, that those who are miserly in their own houses, almost to a state of starvation, when they visit their friends or dine in public, but particularly when they are travelling, and know that they will be called upon with a pretty long bill,—to lay in what they call a good stock of every thing, or of all the good things the landlord thinks proper to spread before them. This was certainly the case with Nollekens when he visited Harrowgate, in order to take the water for his diseased mouth. He informed his wife that he took three half-pints of water at a time, and as he knew the bills would be pretty large at the inn, he was determined to indulge in the good things of this world; so that one day he managed to get through 'a nice roast chicken, with two nice tarts and some nice jellies'. Another day he took nearly two pounds of venison, the fat of which was at least 'two inches thick'; at breakfast he always managed two muffins, and got through a plate of toast; and he took good care to put a French roll in his pocket, for fear he should find himself hungry when he was walking on the common by himself.

Our Sculptor would sometimes amuse himself on a summer's evening, by standing with his arms behind him at the yard-gate, which opened into Titchfield-street. During one of these indulgences, as a lady was passing most elegantly dressed, attended by a strapping footman in silver-laced livery, with a tall gilt-headed cane, she nodded to him, and smilingly asked him if he did not know her. On his reply that he did not recollect her, 'What! Sir,' exclaimed she, 'do you forget Miss Coleman, who brought a letter to you from Charles Townley, to show legs with your Venus? why I have been with you twenty times in that little room, to stand for your Venus!'—'Oh! *lauk-a-daisy*, so you have!' answered Nollekens: 'Why what a fine woman you're grown! Come, walk in, and I'll show you your figure; I have done it in marble.' After desiring the man to stop at the gate, she went in with him; and upon seeing Mrs. Nollekens at the parlour-window, who was pretending to talk to, and feed, her sister's bullfinch, but who had been informed by the vigilant and suspicious Bronze of what had been going on at the gate—she went up to her, and said, 'Madam, I have to thank—' Mrs. Nollekens then elevated herself on her toes, and with a lisping palpitation began to address the lady. 'Oh, dear,' observed Miss Coleman, 'and you don't know me:—you have given me many a basin of broth in the depth of winter, when I used to stand for Venus.' Mrs. Nollekens, not knowing what to think of Joseph, shook her head at him as she slammed the window, at the same time exclaiming, 'Oh! fie! Mr. Nollekens, fie! fie!'—Bronze assured me that when her master went into the front parlour he had a pretty warm reception. 'What!' said her mistress, 'to know such wretches after you have done with them in your studio!' The truth is, that Mrs. Nollekens certainly *did* contrive to get a little broth ready for the models, such as it was, and she likewise condescended to take it into the room herself; and this I am sorry to say, whatever her motives or other charitable intentions might have been, is the only thing I can relate of her that bears the semblance of kindness.

It is probable that Mrs. Nollekens never experienced that inexpressible delight which diffuses itself through the benevolent heart, when alleviating the wants of others; indeed, she would often remain at the window looking over the blind, and tantalizing the piteous supplicants who every moment expected relief from her hand; and she would indulge in this practice, that passers-by might suppose the inhabitants of the mansion to be charitably inclined. One winter morning, when the weather was so severe that the blackbirds fell from the branches, two miserable men, almost dying for want of nourishment, implored her charitable aid; but little did the unhappy mendicants suppose that the only heart which sympathised in their afflictions was that of Betty, in the kitchen, who silently crept up stairs and cheerfully gave them her mite. At this delicate rebuke, Mrs. Nollekens hastily opened the parlour-door, and vociferated, 'Betty! Betty! there is a bone below with little or no meat on it; give it the poor creatures!' upon which the one who had hitherto spoken, steadfastly looking in the face of his pale partner in distress, repeated, 'Bill, we are to have a bone with little or no meat on it.' When they were gone, the liberal-hearted Betty was seriously rated by her mistress, who was quite certain she would come to want. 'What good will your wages do you, child, if you give alms so often to such people? Doctor Johnson has done all our servants more injury by that constant practice of his, of giving charity, as it is called, than he is aware of—and I shall take an opportunity of telling him so when I next see him at Sir John Hawkins's; and I know Sir John and all his family will be on my side, for they are far from being extravagant people.'

My worthy friend, the late Dr. Hill, assured me that a gentleman of the faculty, who lectured upon medical electricity, and gave advice gratis to the poor twice a-week at his house in Bond-street, was visited by a woman dressed shabbily-genteel, who received the shock, until one of the patients informed the Doctor that she was no less a person than Mrs. Nollekens, the wife of the famous Sculptor. He was therefore determined to expose her the next day, by getting all the poor into the room before she was admitted; and what her *shock* was may easily be conceived, if we allow her to have possessed common feeling. When she was seated in the electrical chair, in the centre of the room, the Doctor stood before her, and making her a profound bow, addressed her as Mrs. Nollekens. 'I wonder, Madam,' said he, 'that a lady of your fortune, and the wife of a Royal Academician, could think of passing yourself off as a pauper; you, who ought to enable me to relieve these poor people: you are welcome, Madam, to the assistance which I have given you; but I hope and trust that you will now distribute the amount of my fees from persons in your station, to your distressed fellow-creatures around you in this room.' Mrs. Nollekens, after this electrifying shock, distributed the contents of her purse, which, unfortunately on this occasion, amounted only to a few shillings; though she left the room with a promise to send more. After this reproof, however, she was noticed to dress a little better, and to walk with her high-caned parasol as usual.

Mrs. Nollekens was not very fond of Miss Hawkins; she said that she was always giving her tongue liberties when speaking of Dr. Johnson, and, whenever Mr. Boswell's name was mentioned, she would throw herself into such a rage, because that gentleman had asserted, that Sir John Hawkins, her father, was the son of a carpenter. Poor Mrs. Nollekens! what would she have said, had she lived to have seen the three volumes of Anecdotes, in one of which Miss Hawkins says, 'Now, as to the carpenter's son, I am almost shocked at using lightly a term that exists in Holy Writ.' But, in my humble opinion, as she was not unconscious of overstepping sacred bounds, she ought to have been *quite shocked* for even glancing at Holy Writ upon such an occasion. There would have been an appearance of good sense in Miss Hawkins, had she adopted the ingenuous manner in which Mr. Gifford, in his account of himself, speaks of his own origin prefixed to his translation of Juvenal; since he there tells us, that he was apprenticed to a shoemaker. Again, too, she would also have done well, had she recollected that Doctor Hutton had been a common workman in a coal-mine in the north of England; and, indeed, there are innumerable instances of other great and good men who have arisen from the most humble callings to the pinnacle of fame and honour. That highly-respected character, the late Mr. Deputy Nichols, one of the Editors of the Gentleman's Magazine, informed me that Cave, the original Mr. Urban, often, when he made a visit, desired the servant to tell his master, that 'The Cobbler's son had called.' Samuel Richardson, the author of 'Clarissa', had no such feelings of false pride, since he scrupled not himself to say, 'My father's business was that of a Joiner.'

As Miss Hawkins did not think proper to exempt me from Mr. Sherwin's 'pupils in punch', and as I have no wish to leave the world and my family with the slander of drunkenness attached to my memory, when at no period of my life have I merited that stigma, I shall endeavour to show how little this lady, who is so fond of running a tilt at others, is to be believed in some of her assertions. At page 32, in the second volume of her Memoirs, she states, when speaking of Sherwin's eccentricities and follies, (and well knowing that I was his pupil at that time,) that 'He fired pistols out of his window half the night, and half drowned his pupils; for, sad to say, he had pupils in punch.' Miss Hawkins states on the same page, that 'Sherwin expired, forlorn and comfortless, in a poor apartment of a public-inn, in Oxford-street:' whereas the fact is, that Sherwin died in the house of the late Mr. Robert Wilkinson, the print-seller, in Cornhill, who kindly attended him, afforded him every comfort, and paid respect to his remains; his body having been conveyed to Hampstead, and buried in a respectable manner in the church-yard, near the north-east corner of the front entrance, in the very grave where his brother George had been interred. Miss Hawkins states that her mother's portrait was painted 'by Prince Hoare of Bath'; she should have said *William* Hoare, Esq. R. A., Prince Hoare's father. Miss Hawkins, who so often considers herself obliged to her brother for a *good* thing, allowed the following to be printed in page 218 of the first volume of her Memoirs.

(H. H. *loquitur.*)

Speaking of Doctor Johnson, H. H. says, 'Calling upon him shortly after the death of Lord Mansfield, and mentioning the event, he answered, "Ah, Sir, there was little learning and less virtue!"'

Now, unfortunately for Miss Hawkins and her brother H. H., this fabricated invective can never stand, for that highly respected and learned Judge, Lord Mansfield, died on Wednesday March 20th, 1794, ten years after the death of Dr. Johnson, with whom H. H. so roundly declares he conversed upon his Lordship's death. As Miss Hawkins states in a note at the foot of page 227 of the first volume of her Memoirs, that 'violation of truth cannot be treated too harshly', I trust that I shall stand pardoned for what I am doing: especially as in volume I. page 150, she says, 'Brought up, as my brothers and myself were, in strict regard to truth, and in abhorrence of all insincerity, even that of fashion.'

I think, in charity I ought to plead Miss Hawkins's chronological ignorance, or she never would have acknowledged that she applied to her brother, as she does in page 258 of volume I. of her Memoirs, for more of his anecdotes of Lord Mansfield and Dr. Johnson. In Dr. Birch's Life of Lord Bacon, it is said of a biographer, that 'he is fairly to record the faults as well as the good qualities, the failings as well as the perfections of the dead'; but here the assertion begins with the emphatic word *fairly*. All I have to add to these remarks is, that whether Miss Hawkins's grandfather, or her father, had been a carpenter or not,—since she has asserted her descent from Sir John Hawkins, who fought against the Spanish Armada, her time would have been innocently employed, if she had made out and favoured the public with her own pedigree, and proved that descent.

CHAPTER IX

Mr. Nollekens's favourite amusements.—Children's head-cloths and go-carts.—Bethlehem Hospital and Cibber's figures.—Anecdotes of Dr. Wolcot and Mr. Nollekens, Boswell, H. Tresham, R.A., and Fuseli.—Eccentricities of Lord Coleraine.—Mr. Nollekens and his barber.—Anecdotes of the Rev. John Wesley.—Mr. Nollekens's restoration of antiques at Rome.—Drawings at Rome by Mosman.—Tailors.—Family quarrels.—Mr. Nollekens's manœuvres for importing a picture.—Coarseness of his manners.—Mr. Charles Townley and the Abbé Devay.—Portrait, house, and antique marbles of Mr. Townley described.—The Royal Cockpit.—Immorality of Hogarth.

During my long intimacy with Mr. Nollekens, I never once heard him mention the name of the sweetest bard that ever sang, from whose luxuriant garden most artists have gathered their choicest flowers. To the beauties of the immortal Shakspeare he was absolutely insensible, nor did he ever visit the theatre when his plays were performed; though he was actively alive to a pantomime, and frequently spake of the capital and curious tricks in Harlequin Sorcerer. He also recollected with pleasure Mr. Rich's wonderful and singular power of scratching his ear with his foot like a dog; and the street-exhibition of Punch and his wife delighted him beyond expression.[1] In this

[1] He would probably have equally enjoyed the sight of the Traveller Twiss's large poodle dog walking in the open streets, with an immense pair of spectacles upon his nose, cut out in pasteboard, between his master and that admirable organist, Samuel Wesley, when they have been perambulating Camden Town in close conversation: and have beheld the scene with as much pleasure as those who witnessed the attentive gravity of the traveller's dog, with his long shaggy hair hanging over his head, and a sagacity of look as if he was to decide the not unfrequently knotty points upon which these celebrated originals frequently conversed during their pedestrian relaxations.

gratification, however, our Sculptor did not stand alone; for I have frequently seen, when I have stood in the crowd, wise men laugh at the mere squeaking of Punch, and have heard them speak of his cunning pranks with the highest ecstasy. Indeed, I once saw two brothers of the long robe involuntarily stop and heartily enjoy the dialogue of that merry little fellow with Jack Ketch, who was about to hang Punch for the murder of his wife and his innocent babe. These *Brothers-in-Law* discovered, however, before long, that they had not only lost their handkerchiefs when they had been elbowing the motley group for the best places, but that they had deprived a baker, to whom they had too closely attached themselves, of his *flowery* influence.

Nollekens, when noticing nursery-maids with little children, would always make most anxious inquiries as to the cutting of the child's teeth; and so addicted was he to accosting strangers in the streets, that I remember once his stopping to express his sense of the kindness of a mother who had made a pudding for her child's head, by saying. 'Ay, now, what's your name?' —'Rapworth, Sir.'—'Well, Mrs. Rapworth, you have done right; I wore a pudding when I was a little boy, and all my mother's children wore puddings.' This pudding consisted of a broad, black silk band, padded with wadding, which went round the middle of the head, joined to two pieces of ribband crossing on the top of the head and then tied under the chin; so that by this most excellent contrivance, children's heads were often preserved uninjured when they fell. As to the antiquity of this cap, which is now seldom seen, and I believe totally unknown in the nurseries of the great, I can safely observe that the child of the great Painter Sir Peter Paul Rubens wore one; as those mothers who are fond of showing their good sense by taking care of their children, may see in that truly beautiful mezzotinto engraving by M'Ardell, of Rubens, his wife and child, walking in a garden.[1]

By those readers who are fond of old household furniture, and also recollect the sensible uses of several articles of that denomination, many of which are now nearly thrown aside, the following notice of the go-cart may not be deemed irrelevant to the subject of this page. It was unquestionably one of the safest and most useful of all the comforts of the nursery and the infantile play-ground: and elderly persons will recollect that it was so constructed, that it safely enclosed and supported the child in an upright position, a little below its arms, which were allowed to be entirely free above it. As this machine moved upon castors, the child was enabled with ease to go forward, whilst, in consequence of its extending so widely at the feet, there was no danger whatever of its overturning; and I fully expect, as most things come round again in their use, that the affectionate and considerate mother will take this most valuable invention again into favour. The go-cart is supposed to be of considerable antiquity, since a figure of it appears upon a sarcophagus of a child, engraven in Montfaucon,[2] and it was also much used in Germany and Holland before it was known in England. In the British Museum, among the early German Masters of the fifteenth century, there is a rare folio sheet wood-cut, representing a man nearly bent double by age, with a long flowing beard, placed in a square go-cart, supported by six legs, tastefully and curiously carved with foliage. Upon a shelf at the top of the go-cart, which projects in front of him, is placed an hour-glass, surmounted by a human skull; but these he does not appear to notice,

[1] The painting from which this engraving was made, is now at Blenheim.

[2] Supplement au Livre L'Antiquité Expliquée, vol. V, Paris, 1724, fol. book V, ch. 1, sec. ii, pp. 105, 106, plates xlii, xliii.

as his eye is looking straight forward, and considerably above them. He is seemingly obeying the allurements of a boy who is riding on a stick, with a horse's head at the top. On one side, a little in advance of him, and immediately before him, is a grave, which, if we may judge by the spade which is left on the ground, has been recently dug purposely for his reception. Behind him is another child pushing on the go-cart, seemingly with little exertion; and, in the distance, there is a buck, which appears to be bounding back again, after he had accompanied this aged man to the brink of Eternity, into which the infant is so easily pushing him.[1] In Quarles' 'Emblems' there is also a go-cart introduced; and Rembrandt has etched one, where a nurse or mother is inviting the child who is in it to walk to her. This print is numbered 186, in Daulby's Catalogue of Rembrandt's Etchings, and is there called the Go-cart. When I was a boy, the go-cart was common in every toy-shop in London; but it was to be found in the greatest abundance in the once far-famed turners' shops in Spinning-wheel Alley, Moorfields: a narrow passage leading from those fields to the spot upon which the original Bethlehem Hospital stood in Bishopsgate-street, and upon which site numerous houses were erected, and formerly called Old Bethlehem. In 1825–26, however, both Spinning-wheel Alley and Old Bethlehem were considerably altered and widened, and subsequently named Liverpool-street.

Upon the establishment of the late Bethlehem Hospital, and indeed down to the time of King Charles II.,

[1] A design, almost similar, has been attributed to Michel Angelo, of which there are two different prints, one being without any engraver's name or year of publication though the other is dated 1538, and was published by Antonio Salamanca. Mr. Duppa, in his Life of Michel Angelo Buonarroti, London 1806, has given an outline copy of this subject.

the men and women were crowded together in one ward. I have seen, by favour of Dr. Haslam, several of the early manuscript account-books of this Hospital, in one of which there was the following entry:—'This day the neighbouring flax-dressers were called in, who gave the unruly patients a good dressing.' Whenever Nollekens heard the figures of Raving and Melancholy Madness mentioned, which were carved by Gabriel Cibber for the piers of the gates of Bethlehem Hospital, built in Moorfields, he never expressed himself pleased with them. This was not the case with Roubiliac, the Sculptor, who never left the city, when he went there to receive money, without going round, sometimes considerably out of his way, to admire them. It is said that Cibber carved these figures, which are now preserved in the hall of the new Hospital in St. George's fields, at once from the block, without any previous drawing or model whatever. An instance of similar talent for extemporary productions, I have heard mentioned by Mr. Joseph Cauldfield, a music-engraver, and a most excellent teacher of the piano-forte; who has declared, that the celebrated Charles Dibdin assured him, that he had frequently composed a song, with all its musical accompaniments, and played it in public on the evening of the same day entirely by memory, without the slightest written memoranda.

Those who recollect the figure of Dr. Wolcot in his robust upright state, and the diminutive appearance of Mr. Nollekens, can readily picture to themselves their extreme contrast, when the former accosted the latter one evening at his gate in Titchfield-street, nearly in the following manner. 'Why, Nollekens, you never speak to me now; pray what is the reason?'—*Nollekens*. 'Why, you have published such lies of the King, and had the impudence to send them to me; but Mrs. Nollekens burnt them, and I desire you'll send no more: the Royal family are very good to me, and are great friends to all the artists, and I don't like to hear any body say any thing against them.' Upon which the Doctor put his cane upon the Sculptor's shoulder, and exclaimed, 'Well said! little Nolly; I like the man who sticks to his friends; you shall make a bust of me for that.' 'I'll see you d—d first!' answered Nollekens, 'and I can tell you this besides, no man in the Royal Academy but Opie would have painted your picture; and you richly deserved the broken head you got from Gifford in Wright's shop: Mr. Cook, of Bedford-square, showed me his handkerchief dipped in your blood: and so now you know my mind. Come in, my Cerberus, come in.' His dog then followed him in, and he left the Doctor at the gate, which he barred up for the night.

Nollekens, who always expressed the highest pleasure when seeing French and Italian women dance, congratulated himself upon the burning down of the Opera-house in the Haymarket, by observing, 'Now the managers have hired the Pantheon in Oxford-street, I shall not have so far to go in the rain!' When he first was a frequenter of the Opera, which he never missed when '*bones*' of admission were sent to him, gentlemen were obliged to go in swords and bags in full-dress, which custom, however, was dropped, on the removal to the Pantheon; so that Nollekens was more at home, as he was now and then seen to take out a worsted stocking and tie it round his neck, whenever he had a sore throat, to which he was often subject. James Boswell, the faithful biographer of Dr. Johnson, meeting him in the pit of the Pantheon, loudly exclaimed, 'Why, Nollekens, how dirty you go now! I recollect when you were the gayest dressed of any in the house.' To whom Nollekens made, for once in his life, the retort-courteous of 'That's more than I could ever say of you.' Boswell certainly looked very badly when dressed; for, as he seldom washed himself, his clean ruffles served as a striking contrast to his dirty flesh.

Tresham, the Royal Academician, who had been employed to decorate the front of the stage at the Pantheon, filled the tympanum with a profusion of figures, displaying the Sciences, of which performance he was not a little proud. Having taken his seat in the front to see the effect of his pencil, on looking behind him, he found his nearest companion was Fuseli, to whom he addressed himself with, 'Well, Mr. Fuseli, how do you like my pedimental colouring?' to which he received no answer; but at last, after putting several other questions with as little success, he roused him by the interrogative of, 'How do you like the drawing of my figures?' To which Fuseli, who heard the bell ring, observed, 'The drawing bespeaks something clever; I mean the drawing of the curtain,' which the mechanists were just at that moment engaged in raising. Fuseli, however, soon alleviated the embarrassment of his brother R. A. by remarking, that the conceited scene-painter, Mr. Capon, to whom Sheridan had given the nick-name of 'Pompous Billy', had 'piled up his lump of rocks as regularly on the side-scenes, as a baker would his quartern-loaves upon the shelves behind his counter to cool.'

I believe every age produces at least one eccentric in every city, town, and village. Be this as it may, go where you will, you will find some half-witted fellow under the nick-name either of Dolly, Silly Billy, or Foolish Sam, who is generally the butt and sport of his neighbours, and from whom, simple as he may sometimes be, a sensible answer is expected to an unthinking question: like the common children, who will, to our annoyance, inquire of our neighbour's parrot what it is o'clock. In some such light, Nollekens was often held even by his brother artists; and I once heard Fuseli cry out, when on the opposite side of the street, 'Nollekens, Nollekens! why do you walk in the sun? If you have no love for your few brains, you should not melt your coat-buttons.'

The eccentric character is, however, sure to be found in London; where there are several curious varieties of this class of persons to be met with. In our walks, perchance, we may meet a man who always casts his eyes towards the ground, as if he were ashamed of looking any one in the face; and who pretends, when accosted, to be near-sighted, so that he does not know even the friend that had served him. Indeed, he draws his hat across his forehead to act as an eye-shade, so that his sallow visage cannot immediately be recognised, which makes him look as if he had done something wrong: whilst his coat is according to the true Addison-cut, with square pockets, large enough to carry the folio 'Ship of Fools'. Nollekens, though simple, was entirely free from any artful singularity of this kind, and he walked as if he meant to give every one he met the good-morrow; and if he had a fault in his latter perambulations, it was that of exposing himself to the cunningly-inclined.

No man was more gazed at than the late Lord Coleraine. That eccentric and remarkable character, who lived near the New Queen's Head and Artichoke, in Marylebone-fields, never met Nollekens without saluting him with, 'Well, Nolly, my old boy! how goes it? you never sent me the bust of the Prince:' to which Nollekens replied, 'You know you said you would call for it one of these days, and give me the money, and take it away in a hackney-coach.' I remember seeing his Lordship, after he had purchased a book, entitled 'The American Buccaneers', sit down close by the shop from which he had bought it, in the open street in St. Giles's, to read it. I also once heard Lord Coleraine, as I was passing the wall at the end of Portland-road, when an old apple-woman, with whom his Lordship held frequent conversations, was packing up her fruit, ask her the following question:—'What are you about, mother?'—'Why, my Lord, I am going home to my tea; if your Lordship wants any information, I shall come again presently.'—'Oh! don't baulk trade. Leave your things on the table as they are; I will mind shop till you come back;' so saying, he seated himself in the old woman's wooden chair, in which he had often sat before whilst chatting with her. Being determined to witness the result, after strolling about till the return of the old lady, I heard his Lordship declare the amount of his receipts by saying, 'Well, mother, I have taken three-pence half-penny for you: did your daughter Nancy drink tea with you?'

Mr. Nollekens, on entering his barber's-shop, was always glad to find another shavee under the suds, as it afforded him an opportunity of looking at his favourite paper the 'Daily Advertiser'. When his turn arrived, and he was seated for the operation, he placed one of Mrs. Nollekens's curling-papers, which he had untwisted for the purpose, upon his right shoulder, upon which the barber wiped his razor. Nollekens cried out, 'Shave close, Hancock, for I was obliged to come twice last week, you used so blunt a razor.'—'Lord! Sir,' answered the poor barber, 'you don't care how I wear my razors out by sharpening them.' Mr. Nollekens, who had been under his hand for upwards of twenty years, was so correct an observer of its application, that he generally pronounced at the last flourish, 'That will do;' and before the shaver could take off the cloth, he dexterously drew down the paper, folded it up, and carried it home in his hand, for the purpose of using it the next morning, when he washed himself.

The following is a verse of a *droll* song which Nollekens used to sing when I was a boy, and with which he was always highly delighted.

So a rat by degrees
Fed a kitten with cheese,
    Till kitten grew up to a cat;
When the cheese was all spent,
Nature follow'd its bent,
    And puss quickly ate up the rat.

He observed that his mother, who was fond of curious sights, once took him to see 'Adams's Rarities', at the sign of the Royal Swan, in Kingsland-road, where he saw a pillory for a rat.

Nollekens's manners and sentiments were such, if we may with the least degree of propriety be permitted to denominate his deportment *mannerly*, that though he would often hold long, and sometimes entertaining, conversations with the commonest people with the utmost good-nature, he would never suffer himself to be persuaded to model a bust of any of the sectarians in religion. The dignified clergy, and all persons holding high offices in the affairs of Government, were the characters he delighted to model. I recollect that several of the friends of John Wesley often applied to him for a portrait of their pastor; but he never would listen to their importunities, though they repeatedly declared to him that he was one of the worthiest members of any society existing. I have been assured that Wesley never wished to make money by preaching, unless it were to enable him to extend his acts of charity to the poor; in proof of which, I beg leave to repeat the following anecdote, nearly, I believe, as I heard it from his nephew, Mr. Samuel Wesley. An Order was made in the House of Lords, in May 1776, for the Commissioners of His Majesty's Excise to write circular letters to all persons who they had reason to suspect had plate, and also to those who had not regularly paid the duty on the same. In consequence of this Order, the Accountant-General for Household-Plate sent to the Rev. John Wesley a copy of it, and the following was the answer returned to him :—

SIR,

I HAVE two silver tea-spoons in London, and two at Bristol. This is all the plate which I have at present; and I shall not buy any more, while so many around me want bread. I am, Sir,

Your humble servant,

JOHN WESLEY.

When the death of Deare, the Sculptor, (of whom a memoir will be found in the second volume of this work)[1] was communicated to Nollekens, he observed, 'He's dead! is he? That palavering fellow, Fagan, promised me some of his drawings, but I never had any. I have got two of his four basso-relievos of the Seasons, and the two oval basso-relievos of Cupid and Psyche: they are very clever, I assure you; but he was a very upstart fellow, or he ought to have made money by sending over some antiques from Rome. I told him I'd sell 'em for him, and so might many of 'em; but the Sculptors now-a-days never care for bringing home any thing. They're all so stupid and conceited of their own abilities. Why, do you know, I got all the first, and the best of my money, by putting antiques together? Hamilton, and I, and Jenkins, generally used to go shares in what we bought; and as I had to match the pieces as well as I could, and clean 'em, I had the best part of the profits. Gavin Hamilton was a good fellow; but as for Jenkins, he followed the trade of supplying the foreign visitors with Intaglios and Cameos made by his own people, that he kept in a part of the ruins of the Coliseum, fitted up for 'em to work in slyly by themselves. I saw 'em at work though, and Jenkins gave a whole handful of 'em to me to say nothing about the matter to any body else but myself. Bless your heart! he sold 'em as fast as they made 'em. Jenkins had a great many pictures by many of the old Masters. Mosman, the German, made drawings of 'em in black chalk for Lord Exeter, who was his encourager for many years.'

The cause of Mosman being thus employed was related by his patron, the late Earl of Exeter, nearly to the following effect.—His Lordship, when at Rome, having entered a church, was surprised by seeing a common soldier making a most elaborate drawing from one of the altar-pieces. He complimented him upon his talent, and at the same time expressed his

[1] [Omitted in this edition.]

astonishment in seeing a man of his extraordinary powers in the dress of a common soldier. 'Sir,' said the draughtsman, 'you are welcome to look at my drawing; but you have no right to remind me of my condition.' Lord Exeter, whose dress did not upon every occasion bespeak his rank, assured him of his power to serve him if he stood in need of a friend; and when Mosman found by whom he had been questioned, he stated, in a few words, that for eighteen years he had been tormented by a vixen of a wife, till at last he left her in full possession of all his household property, pictures, drawings, &c. and enlisted into a foreign regiment as a common man; that his officer, who had heard his story, was very kind to him, and gave him leave to make the drawing he was then engaged upon. Lord Exeter purchased his discharge, and employed him to make drawings of various fine pictures, of which at that time there were no engravings. These drawings now fill four immensely large volumes, and were given by his Lordship to the British Museum; and at the commencement of the first of these splendid books is the following note:—

Mr. Nollekens, Statuary, in Mortimer-street, London, assured me that he was at Rome when the drawings in this book were made by one Mosman, a German,[1] who was recommended to Brownlow, Earl of Exeter; and he worked at them several years at five shillings a-day. Afterwards, Lord Exeter gave him half-a-guinea. Lord Exeter told Mr. Nollekens the book cost him 2000*l*. Mosman was a pupil of Mengs.

FRA^{s}. ANNESLEY.

---

[1] It appears on the manuscript title-page of the first volume of these drawings, that Joseph was considered as Mosman's christian name; but in numerous, and indeed all instances where the artist has written his own name upon the drawings, he signs Nicholas Mosman. The same title-page states, that he was a native of Rous, in Lorraine, and died the 14th of August 1787, aged fifty-eight years, two months, and eleven days.

One day, what some persons would call 'an old-fashioned boy' brought Mr. Nollekens home a pair of inexpressibles, that his master, a botching tailor, who worked in an opposite stall, had seated for him. Nollekens, after paying him the eighteen-pence, which was the sum agreed upon for the job, asked the boy how old he was; 'Sixteen,' answered he. 'Why, you're rather short of your age,' rejoined the Sculptor; upon which the boy put the same question to the master of the small-clothes, who having answered 'Near sixty;' 'Why, you're *very* short for *your* age, I am sure!' retorted the son of Accutus.—The great warrior, John Accutus, was originally a tailor. Those invaluable historians of everlasting reference, John Stow and John Speed, were also tailors; and I could introduce the names of many other worthy men now living of the highest talents, who have exchanged the needle, thimble, scissors, and shop-board, for poetry and painting.

I shall now give my reader a sketch of one of the family disputes in which Mr. and Mrs. Nollekens sometimes freely indulged.

One day Bronze heard a more violent disputation than usual between her master and mistress: 'What!' cried he, 'what! Madam, you're at your old tricks again? two-pence, indeed! I say I paid you the two-pence for the letter, and I'll take my 'davy of it!'—'Very well, Sir; very well: it's mighty well, perfectly correct, and perfectly just, *Mr. Positive*, I dare say,' retorted Mrs. Nollekens; 'you shall see, Sir, from this very moment I will never pay for a letter of your's again!' Then, after a pause, her bit of slate was thrown on the floor, and the lady in a whining tone, which convinced Bronze she was wound up to the highest pitch, cried with a half-stifled sob, 'You know—you know—you vile little thing! you paid me only two-shillings and seven-pence on last Thursday's account.'—'I tell you this, and now mind what I say,' replied Nollekens, 'that if it was so, it's your own fault; for I never will pay a farthing more when you have once smeared the slate: that I tell you.' A knock at the door induced Bronze to go in, and say, 'Hush! hush! there's a knock at the street-door.'—'I don't care,' exclaimed the Sculptor, 'she sha'n't collywabble me: go and see who it is.'—'Want any fish today?' asked an Irish fishwoman; 'it's Friday, bless ye!'—'I don't care for Friday.[1] I've had dinner enough, quite enough,' answered Nollekens, who walked out of the room with only one slipper on. 'Betty! Betty! shut the door, it is very odd that people will not take an answer,' rejoined Mrs. Nollekens.

At three o'clock, however, some chops were produced, and the half-sullen pair began both to be sorry for their *little heat;* but after the table-cloth was removed, upon Bronze going into the parlour with coals, she found them so perfectly reconciled, that her master was patting her mistress's cheek with the backs of his fingers, and they both appeared

> Still amorous, and fond, and billing,
> Like Philip and Mary on a shilling.

Or,

> Like dogs that snarl about a bone,
> And play together when they've none.

Nollekens, though his cunning was truly amusing, particularly whenever he could gain the whip-hand of his wife, yet at times, like Sir Giles Overreach, he overreached *himself;* and this he did most completely when he returned from Rome, as will appear from the fol-

[1] Whatever a man's religion may be, some praise is due to him for his attention to the tenets of that faith. I fear Nollekens was not entitled to much credit for observances to what *he* called *his Mother Church*, for I have often heard him declare, that the patronage of his friend Cardinal Albani, a great lover of sculpture, secured him from the observations of many persons, as to his neglect of religious duties.

lowing anecdote, which was communicated to me by one of his relations.

When he was preparing to leave Italy for England, he wished to bring, among a quantity of other things, a large picture, but after reflecting upon the immense duty that might be put upon it on account of its enormous size, he very ingeniously hit upon the *sensible* expedient of cutting it into several pieces; cunningly concluding that the inspector at the Custom-house would pass them over as useless mutilations. But lo! when these cuttings were inspected, the officer, in placing them together, detected his countryman's intended deception, and by making it known to the Commissioners, he was made to pay for every portion as a distinct picture!

What will not some men do when money is their object! The honest concerns of the world—nay, every respect for religion, are given up, when money, 'the infernal solicitor to evil', is their tempter.

Nollekens knew so little of what is generally denominated good-breeding, that when he had been at the country-house of any of his employers putting up a monument, his conversation has been often so unguarded and vulgar, as to occasion a table to be ordered for him in a room by himself, which deprived him of the agreeable society he might otherwise have been entitled to. I know this to have been the case when he was at the seat of a certain Nobleman; of which he complained to Mrs. Nollekens on his return to town. Mr. Charles Townley, however, did not follow this plan; for that gentleman, who had noticed Nollekens at Rome, kindly continued for years to entertain him at his house, No. 7, in Park-street, Westminster; and whenever any person spake of good eating, Mr. Nollekens always gave his friend Mr. Townley the highest credit for keeping a most excellent table. 'I am sure,' said he, 'to make a good dinner at his house on a Sunday; but there is a little man, a great deal less than myself, who dines there, of the name of Devay, a French Abbé, who beats me out and out: he is one of the greatest gormandizers I ever met with; though, to look at him, you would declare him to be in the most deplorable state of starvation.' The Abbé Devay was an excellent man; he conversed and wrote in many languages; and his reading and memory were so extensive and useful, that Mr. Townley, who referred to him in his literary concerns, always called him his 'walking library'. The high qualifications of the Abbé were also known and acknowledged by other men of learning; he was frequently present at the breakfast-table and *conversazioni* of Sir Joseph Banks, and instructed several persons of eminence in the classics.

The Sunday dinners of Mr. Townley, mentioned above, were principally for professors of the Arts; and Sir Joshua Reynolds and Zoffany generally enlivened the circle. The last-mentioned of these celebrated characters painted a picture called 'Mr. Townley's Gallery of statues'; it was a portrait of the Library, though not strictly correct as to its contents, since all the best of the marbles displayed in various parts of the house were brought into the painting by the artist, who made it up into a picturesque composition according to his own taste. The likeness of Mr. Townley is extremely good. He is seated, and looks like the dignified possessor of such treasures: at his feet, lies his favourite dog 'Kam', a native of Kamtschatka, whose mother was one of the dogs yoked to a sledge which drew Captain King in that island. Opposite to Mr. Townley is Monsieur D'Hancarville, seated at a table with a book open before him, behind whose chair stand two others of his friends, Thomas Astle, Esq. and the Hon. Charles Grevile, conversing.[1] This

[1] There is a large engraving of this picture, but unfortunately it is in an unfinished state. The painting itself has lately been sent to Townley Hall.

picture is of the same description, in point of subject and colouring, as the one painted by the same artist of the Florentine Gallery, for the late King George III. That excellent Monarch, having heard this collection of marbles much spoken of, so highly respected Mr. Townley, that his Majesty declared his intention of visiting him, though he never did. It happened, however, that when Mr. Townley petitioned the Board of Works to allow a tree in the Birdcage-walk, which darkened his house, to be cut down, the King, to whom this petition was submitted, at once most liberally gave permission; observing, that Mr. Townley should have every possible accommodation. It is very remarkable, that this gentleman was not only obliged by the King, but afterwards by an easterly wind, which, according to the proverb, seldom proves beneficial; for no sooner was the tree cut down, than a tremendous hurricane arose which tore up the one that had stood next to it, by which his rooms received an extensive and uninterrupted light from the north.

From what I have seen and heard described, in no instance can a private residence be found to equal that of the late Charles Townley, Esq. The possession of taste and an affluent fortune qualified and enabled that enlightened and elegant gentleman to indulge, in the course of his travels, in the purchase of those antiques which now grace the Townley Gallery of the British Museum, which will do eternal honour to his memory, as well as to the Government which so liberally purchased them. These treasures still keep their estimation with the public, notwithstanding the Elgin Marbles are now considered by the Professors, in every branch of the Polite Arts, to comprise the Artists' primer. I shall now endeavour to anticipate the wish of the reader, by giving a brief description of those rooms of Mr. Townley's house, in which that gentleman's liberality employed me when a boy, with many other students in the Royal Academy, to make drawings for his portfolios.

As the visitor entered the hall, his attention was arrested by an immense sarcophagus on his left-hand, measuring seven feet in length, opposite to which were two heads of lions, the size of life, one on either side of the chimney-piece. This hall was also adorned with bas-reliefs, sepulchral monuments, inscriptions, cinerary urns, &c. from the villas of Fonsega, Montalto, Pullucchi, Antoninus Pius, the Justiniani Palace, &c. The staircase was enriched with sepulchral urns and numerous Roman inscriptions, and a very curious and ancient chair of Pavonazzo marble. In the space over the dining-room door, was a bas-relief of a mystical marriage.[1] The parlour, or dressing-room, in Park-street, contained a rich display of votive altars, sepulchral urns, and inscriptions. Among the Marbles, was a most spirited statue of a Satyr, the thumb of whose right-hand is enclosed between his two fore-fingers; it is now numbered 24 in the Townley Gallery in the British Museum; and this small but excellent specimen of ancient art was presented to Mr. Townley by his friend Lord Cawdor.[2] The dining-parlour looking over St. James's-park was a room in which Mr. Townley has entertained personages of the highest rank in this kingdom, as well as visitors from all nations who were eminent for the brilliancy of their wit or their literary acquirements; and it contained

[1] When the Marbles were conveyed to the British Museum, this space was filled up with a cast of a boar, taken from the celebrated one at Florence.

[2] The ancient, rare, and truly interesting collection of Terracottas, brought from Rome by Nollekens, which has been already noticed in an early page of this volume, was let into the walls of this room. Of the female figures in these specimens, the tasteful Cipriani was so extremely fond, that he has been heard to declare to Mr. Townley, that they afforded him so much pleasure that he never knew when to leave them.

the greater part of his statues. Here stood those of Libera, Isis, Diana, the Discobolus, a drunken Faun, and an Adonis; but, above all, that most magnificent one of Venus, which measures six feet four inches in height. Mr. Nollekens informed me that, in the conveyance of this statue to England, the following singular stratagem to save the immense duty upon so large and so perfect a figure was resorted to. In consequence of it having been discovered that the figure had been carved from two blocks, and put together at the waist, at the commencement of the drapery, it was separated, and sent at different times; so that the duty upon each fragment amounted to a mere trifle. It is now numbered 14 in the Townley Gallery in the British Museum. Among the busts was that of Caracalla, and one of the most beautiful vases, perhaps, in the world: it is embellished with Bacchanalian figures, and was brought from the Villa of Antoninus, where other treasures of art have been discovered. Over the chimney-piece in the drawing-room looking into Park-street, was a bas-relief in terracotta of a marriage ceremony, modelled by Mr. Nollekens from the one over the dining-room door. This performance was highly esteemed by Mr. Townley, who always spake of Mr. Nollekens as the first Sculptor of his day. The drawing-room, commanding a most beautiful view of the Park, contained principally the following heads and busts:—Decebatus, Marcus Aurelius, Hadrian, Trajan, Hercules, Antinous, and Adonis; but, of all others, that of Isis upon the Lotus was considered by artists to be one of the most perfect and beautiful specimens of sculpture. It was purchased of Prince Laurenzano of Naples, in 1772. This bust of Isis, which Mr. Nollekens considered to be a portrait of the sculptor's model, was so much admired by him, that he always had a copy of it in marble purposely for sale: the last one was sold, after the collection was purchased by Government, to John Townley, Esq. for one hundred guineas, who was delighted to see so exquisite a copy placed in the situation which the original had graced for so many years.

The same room also contained a Child asleep, a figure of Diana seated, and a Lion's head with horns. Of this last specimen, I have heard Mr. Chantrey speak in rapturous terms, particularly as to the animated manner in which the artist had used the drill in finishing the mane; for this tool, when judiciously introduced in hair, certainly gives wonderful vigour and depth of touch, as may be seen in the numerous portraits of persons of the highest rank and talent produced by Chantrey, whose busts alone have secured him unrivalled fame. The library was highly interesting; it was lighted from above, and was in every respect an excellent room for study. The Marbles in it were not so numerous as those in the dining-parlour, but they consisted of some choice specimens. Among the busts, were those of Antoninus Pius, Titan, Caracalla's wife Plautilla, Lucius Verus, and the celebrated one of Homer, which has been so repeatedly and admirably engraven.[1] Here were also the heads of Adonis, and that beautiful one of a Child with its locks uncut over its right ear; together with the exquisite little statue of Angerona, which is now called a Venus, and numbered 22 in the Gallery of the British Museum. Mr. Nollekens renewed the arms of this figure, for which restoration I stood when his pupil.

The Dilettanti Society, as well as other learned men, with whom Mr. Townley had lived in the most

[1] Mr. Townley was so enamoured with his favourite busts of Isis, Pericles, and Homer, the most perfect specimens of ancient art, that he employed the hand of Skelton, Sharpe's favourite pupil, to engrave them upon a small plate, which he used as his visiting card. This elegant performance, always considered a great rarity, was left only at the houses of particular persons, so that an impression of it is now greatly coveted by the collectors of such *bijoux*.

cheerful and instructive intercourse, were deprived of their accustomed pleasures by his death, which took place in the bedchamber on the second floor looking over the Park, on the 3rd of January, 1805.[1] In this room also died his uncle, John Townley, Esq. a highly respected gentleman, who had for many years been an eminent collector of Hollar's works, of English portraits for the illustration of Granger's Biographical History of England, and of rare and valuable books; for the reception of which he had fitted up the dining and drawing-rooms facing the Park, with accommodating galleries all round. The house is now inhabited by his son, Peregrine Edward Townley, Esq. a Family-Trustee of the British Museum.

This house, which was purchased by Mr. Townley in that state denominated by builders 'a shell', was finished according to his own taste; but the ground upon which it stands, as well as that of several adjoining mansions, belongs to Christ's Hospital. The late Royal Cock-pit, which afforded Hogarth an excellent

[1] Of all Mr. Townley's friends, I am perfectly convinced that no one respected him more than Mr. Christie, the Auctioneer, and a member of the Dilettanti Society; for whose learning and classical acquirements Mr. Townley had the highest esteem, and to whom he always gave up the keys of his cabinets whenever he visited him. Mr. Townley was buried at Burnley, near Townley Hall, in Lancashire; and so much was he beloved by the country people far and near, that, as his hearse passed, the sides of the road were crowded, and the windows of the town filled, the spectators being all silent and uncovered.

Mr. Townley's bust in the first room of the Gallery of Antiquities, in the British Museum, is considered a pretty good likeness; though the lower part of the face is certainly too full. Mr. Nollekens carved it after Mr. Townley's death, from a mask which he took from his face. Another bust by Nollekens, though by no means so good either in art or likeness, has been bequeathed to the same national Institution, by the late Richard Payne Knight, Esq.

scene for his humour, remained a next-door noisy nuisance to Mr. Townley for many years. It is a curious fact, that of this print of the Cock-pit by Hogarth, as well as those of the Gates of Calais, and Southwark Fair, I have never seen, read, nor heard of an etching, nor of any impression whatever, with a variation from the state in which they were published.

This is the more extraordinary, as they are all highly-finished plates, and the artist must have required many proofs of them in their progress before he could have been satisfied with their effect; particularly in that of Southwark Fair, which, in my opinion, is not only the deepest studied as to composition and light and shade, but the most elaborately finished, and perhaps the most innocently entertaining of all his works. For great as Hogarth was in his display of every variety of character, I should never think of exhibiting a portfolio of his prints to the youthful inquirer; nor can I agree that the man who was so accustomed to visit, so fond of delineating, and who gave up so much of his time to the vices of the most abandoned classes, was in truth a 'moral teacher of mankind'. My father knew Hogarth well, and I have often heard him declare, that he revelled in the company of the drunken and profligate: Churchill, Wilkes, Hayman, &c. were among his constant companions. Dr. John Hoadly, though in my opinion it reflected no credit on him, delighted in his company; but he did not approve of all the prints produced by him, particularly that of the first state of 'Enthusiasm Displayed', which had Mr. Garrick or Dr. Johnson seen, they could never for a moment have entertained their high esteem of so irreligious a character.

CHAPTER X

Mr. Nollekens's intelligence whilst abroad.—Prints of Marc-Antonio.—Distinction of draperies and flesh in Sculpture.—Dutch-tables, and improvement in English taste.—Difficulties attendant on the lighting of pieces of sculpture.—Ignorance of persons employed to erect and repair them.—Huge blocks of marble used by modern Sculptors.—Fatal consequences of piecing the stone.—Works of a mender of Antiques.—Anecdote of Mr. Whitbread.—Coquetry, death, and funeral of Angelica Kauffmann.—Death and epitaph of Miss Welch.—Mr. Nollekens's visits to the Opera.—Instances of his economy and ignorance.—Dog-Jennings.

It is reasonable to expect, in the course of repeated conversations with travellers, or with persons who have resided several years abroad, some little account of their particular pursuits and employments, as well as of their pleasures and amusements; but it is most extraordinary that Mr. Nollekens's observations on events which had taken place during his absence from England, never led him to speak of works of sculpture, unless he was questioned; and then his answers did not prove that he possessed any depth of knowledge of their history. Indeed, they amounted to little more than monosyllabic answers; though I am certain, if he had turned to his memorandum-books, in which there were numerous sketches of groups, statues, and busts, with their mutilations and measurements, he certainly could have afforded much information. But this power he did not possess; nor was he inclined to look them over until the later period of his life, when his mind, had it ever been qualified, would, according to the decay of nature, have been less capable to apply them to any use. During the long period of my knowledge of him, he never once attempted to descant upon the sublimity of thought, the grandeur of the composition, nor the energetic expression of the Laocoon, the Apollo Belvidere, the Farnese Hercules, the Niobe, the Venus de' Medici, nor the Diana of Ephesus. Nor did he ever appear to have an inclination to collect the rise, progress, and history of his Art. A Babylonian seal with him would have been a thing of no farther estimation than for its colour as a stone. A figure with its legs and feet closed together, was never noticed by him as the first attempt of Egyptian sculpture; nor was he aware, that the projection of one leg before the other, was their first step to action; nor that the arms of two seated figures, male and female, across each other's backs, was the first instance of grouping with the Egyptians. He knew very little as to the introduction of Grecian Art into Rome: though he was certainly pretty well informed as to the works of Michel Angelo and John di Bologna; yet at the same time, he expressed himself with as much pleasure when he saw Bernini's group in the coach-house of Sir Joshua Reynolds, as he possibly could with the productions of the two preceding great men. His usual communications to his friends were the number of miles from Rome to Loretto; the names of persons who walked together on a very hot day; that Mr. Dalton's conduct towards Mr. Strange, the Engraver, was shamefully cruel; that little Crone, the Landscape-draughtsman, who was employed to collect prints in Rome for Mr. Mangin, of Dublin, was much ridiculed by the natives on account of his deformity; or that such a Cardinal feigned a consumptive cough at the time of an election for a Pope. One curious anecdote, however, he frequently related when showing his prints; namely, that when he was at Rome, at the fair-time, the original plates, engraved by Marc-Antonio, were printed for the by-standers at a shilling an hour, the employer finding ink and paper; and that the eagerness with which these worn-out and repeatedly touched-up publications of Antonio Salamanca were collected, induced the visitors to cry out, 'The next shilling's worth is for me'; or, 'It is my turn now'. This will at once account for the great quantity of bad impressions from Marc-Antonio's plates which are now in existence.

Much has frequently been said by those persons who understand little of the matter, respecting the practice of modern Sculptors, as it regards the manner in which the texture of the respective materials they represent should be carved. They insist that no attempt to particularise any specific substance should be made; but that every description of drapery should be treated alike, whether linen, silk, or woollen: so that it be drapery, it is enough. Another states, that the silk drapery given by Roubiliac to the statue of Sir Isaac Newton, at Cambridge, is more often admired than the other parts of the figure; and this may probably be the case, as the ideas of those persons who praise the statue for its silk mantle, are confined to texture only. But surely it would have been highly improper if Roubiliac had given folds like those of linen or woollen, when he knew that he had to represent silk.

Chantrey's busts are valuable, in addition to their astonishing strength of natural character, for the fleshy manner in which he has treated them, which every real artist knows to be the most difficult part of the Sculptor's task. Surely the man of taste, after he has admired and spoken of the fleshiness of a figure, would not think of blaming the sculptor for attending to the manner in which he had carved the ermine of a king's robe, the lawn sleeves of a bishop's rochet, the silk riband of an order of knighthood, or the woollen coat of an admiral. Each of these articles should be precisely attended to, or they will not remind us of the things which they are intended to represent; and if the Sculptor were wholly inattentive to texture, many a lawyer would be deprived of his silk gown. Suppose the artist had to carve a Negro's woolly head, should the hair be as sleek and oily as his skin? In my opinion, unquestionably not; nor should the foam of the fiery steed be glossy like its coat. The flesh of that truly beautiful figure of Charity, by Westmacott, now in his studio, is powerfully and properly contrasted by the coarseness of the dowlas drapery, with which he has covered her limbs; and perhaps I cannot point out a more striking instance of the unequivocal influence of contrast, than that which is displayed in this figure.

Nollekens, great as he certainly was as a sculptor of busts, never produced that lively fleshiness which we see so pre-eminently attended to by the best English Sculptors of the present day; and yet he was fully aware of its beauty and high importance, for I have often heard him observe, when any one was looking at an antique head of a Faun, which was afterwards purchased at his sale by his Grace the Duke of Newcastle, that he never saw flesh better represented in marble, and that it was for that great excellence he bought it. But though texture of the mechanical materials is by no means to be neglected, it can be viewed by an intellectual person in a secondary light only; and it has often, of late years, given me great pleasure to observe that the same class of persons, who in my boyish days would admire a bleeding-heart-cherry painted upon a Pontipool tea-board, or a Tradescant-strawberry upon a Dutch table,[1] now attentively look,

[1] This description of table, the pride of our great-grandmothers, in which the brightest colours were most gorgeously displayed, was first imported from Holland into England in the reign of William and Mary. The top was nothing more than a large oval tea-tray, with a raised scalloped border round it, fixed upon a pillar, having a claw of three legs. They are now and then to be met with in our good old-fashioned family mansions, and brokers' shops.

They were formerly considered by our aunts Deborah to be such an ornament to a room, that in order to exhibit

and for a long time too, with the most awful respect at the majestic fragments of the Greek Sculptors' art, so gloriously displayed in the Elgin Gallery. These are, indeed, treasures, the merits of which, in my humble opinion, men of the first talent, however powerful might be their command of words, would find themselves at least inadequate to describe.

There is one truly lamentable disadvantage to which the works of our best Sculptors are frequently exposed, namely, the want of a good light, without which their labours cannot be viewed with that essential assistance which the painter's productions can in most instances procure.

The exquisitely-finished, and numerous beauties of a cabinet-picture, can at all times be appreciated by placing it in its proper light upon an easel, as the artist painted it, and intended it should be viewed; and a large picture may be hung in a gallery under a certain admission of light falling upon it, according to the arrangement and intention of the artist. For the old historical painters always considered very attentively the portion and power of light, as well as the precise time it would fall upon those parts of the walls to which their labours were destined; and they painted their pictures either brighter or darker, modestly low or powerfully strong, according to existing or adventitious circumstances. Sometimes, however, when they were unavoidably compelled to occupy a gloomy recess in a small chapel, illumined only by a borrowed or a reflected light, they first of all considered the angle of reflection under which their performances could be best seen, and then painted their picture so as to meet it. The Sculptor, on the contrary, unaided by colours, has perhaps either too much or too little

them to advantage, they were put up in the corner of a waiting-parlour for the admiration of country tenants, when they brought their rents, or sat waiting their turn for an order for coals in a severe winter.

light for his monument; and is often obliged to erect it where there is hardly any at all, because that part of the church belongs to the family, or they insist upon having it as near as possible to their pew, which has always gone with the mansion they reside in: thus enshrouding themselves in their own primitive importance in the parish, at the same time, perhaps, being totally ignorant of the effect of a master-piece of art, upon which they have expended a considerable sum; or not in any way evincing an interest for the fame of the artist employed, whose reputation has invited travellers to visit the church, which is often a great source of pleasure to the tourist. I remember that Flaxman, after he had put up his monument to the memory of Lord Mansfield, in Westminster Abbey, applied to the Dean for permission to cover a small portion of a window with a grey colour, in order to shut out an unpleasant glare of light; but the Dean, to the great mortification of the Sculptor, would not comply with the request. Nollekens seldom knew, nor indeed did any of the English Sculptors of former days care, in what part of a country church their monuments were to be placed: they received the measurements of the space they were to occupy from the family, who had them from the carpenter, who was not at all times very correct, without any notice of the aspect, or stating whether the space were over or under a window, or against a pier, or near the altar, receiving a vertical light, or a diagonal one; and upon this carelessly-measured order, the Sculptor proceeded, never dreaming that his work was to be placed close to the vestry-door in a dark corner. Then, too, when it was up, the plasterer was to adorn it with a *neat jet-black border, of a foot in width!* so that it should match ostentatiously with a monument on the opposite side, in an equally forlorn situation, belonging to a family with whom the relatives of the last deceased had been for ages inveterately at variance; whilst, to crown the whole of this unhappy injury to Art, the putting up was generally intrusted to a mason, who, upon his return to London, was rarely questioned as to where it was erected, or as to *how it looked!*

To the praise of the artists, and the improved taste of their employers of the present day, there is very little of that monumental jobbing now permitted; the aspect and situation are first seen and considered, accurate measurements are then made, and the Sculptor either sends his own experienced assistants from London to erect it, or superintends it himself. And here I consider it my duty to state, notwithstanding what I have said of a late Dean of Westminster, that even the country clergy of the present day, from their more general knowledge of works of art, are, with very few exceptions, both willing and desirous of affording the Sculptor every possible assistance in their power, either by shutting out obtrusive light, or admitting a greater flood of it, where the artist may consider it beneficial. I have also infinite pleasure in being able to state, that our present Sculptors of eminence will not submit to the directions of the *ignorant* employer, to the deterioration of their productions, however powerful his station in life may be. It would be as well if our dressers for theatrical representations would be as honestly firm, and not attend to the ridiculous gew-gaw directions of an obstinate manager; we should then stand a good chance of seeing the true costume of *place* and *period*, instead of being obliged to sit out a play grossly defective in almost every scene.

Of the mode of producing a figure by what Nollekens called manœuvring the marble, and making it up of bits, our modern Sculptors so completely disapprove, that they have even worked nearly the whole of the groups of their monuments, erected in St. Paul's Cathedral, out of one piece of marble; and so immense are the blocks now imported into England for works of sculpture, that at this moment Mr. Chantrey has one weighing many tons, for which he paid about the sum of six hundred pounds. Flaxman's last, and truly grand work, of St. Michael overpowering Satan, which he executed for the Earl of Egremont's noble gallery of modern sculpture at Petworth, is likewise of one block; and this is also the universal practice with all the other eminent Sculptors. Westmacott's charming group of Venus and Cupid, which he is now executing for the same liberal nobleman, is from one block; and Rossi's truly vigorous and masterly figure of the Boxer, just finished for the same gallery, is likewise cut out of one piece, as well as Bailey's animated statue of Earl St. Vincent, executed by order of Government.

And here I must earnestly request the reader, who may not at present be acquainted with the names of other Sculptors, not to suppose for a moment that I confine these remarks to the members of the Royal Academy. I should then consider myself unworthy of the esteem of many young artists, whose works are shining ornaments to their country, and who must ultimately fill the honourable seats of the present members; but as there are tares amongst the wheat, I considered it better to confine myself to those individuals only who have been acknowledged by so honourable a body as the Royal Academy; fully trusting that the time will arrive, when I shall more extensively have it in my power to hand down a list of the productions of some of them, with as much pleasure and impartiality as I have those who at present so deservedly flourish under the distinguished appellation of Royal Academicians.

To return to the subject, however, I should observe, that the disadvantages of piecing the marble are often obvious, even to the most common observer; as may be seen in many instances, where either the cramps have burst or given way, or, from their not having been properly covered with resin, the iron has so corroded the marble, as entirely to disfigure some of our finest works of Art. Another great objection which may be adduced to the joining of marble, is, that where the joints are made in preponderating parts, it usually happens that they give way, fall, and are broken: and even this is not all; for sometimes, when such an accident happens at a great distance from the capital, the seat of most of our eminent artists, the common mason of the district is called in to *re-set the head or a broken limb!*—a fellow, perhaps, who, with all the kindred and impenetrable hardness of his own granite, as soon as he is admitted into your presence, puts his mallet-hand to his side in readiness to pull out his two-foot rule, which he is always sure to open at a right-angle, before he answers or even hears the question; and then, immediately after rubbing the back of his right ear, and most accurately measuring the fractured parts, hits upon a plan of cutting out the mutilations, by taking about *three inches* from the arm of the statue! The very thoughts of such masonic masters of the craft, paint to my imagination the sort of fellow he must have been, who put the left-hand glove upon the right-hand of the effigy of Guy Faux, in Hogarth's humorously-entertaining print, illustrative of Hudibras, called the 'Burning of the Rumps'.

However, should any of my readers exclaim with Osric, 'A hit! a very palpable hit!' I could, in compassion to those who blindly employ these masonic followers of Praxiteles, relate several things equally good of a wealthy man of some family, who turns his back upon all modern sculpture, in consequence of his having been at Athens; and because he has become the *happy possessor* of some of the *worst fragments of the antique in this kingdom*, employs a mere mason to put them together, and is perfectly satisfied, though a right foot has been most ingeniously placed upon a left leg! Indeed, so fond is he of the antique, that I have known him to order his bungler to match a head with the best body he could find in the mass of his dearly-acquired treasures, and then to carve new limbs to match out of those that were too large for other purposes, so that he might have precisely the same stone. He is well acquainted with the quarries whence the marble of such and such a figure was taken, and is also quite perfect in recollecting the names of ancient marbles.

Mr. Nollekens informed me that the late Mr. Samuel Whitbread bought two fragments of antique statues of him for 200*l.* and that the man sent by Mr. Whitbread to pack them up for the country, used screws instead of nails. 'Why,' said Mr. Nollekens, 'do you use screws, when nails would answer every purpose?'—'Lord! Sir,' exclaimed the carpenter, 'I used screws to all the cases for the Piccadilly leaden-figures!' The fact was this: a man in the Borough had purchased the greater number of Cheere's leaden-figures at the auction in Piccadilly. Mr. Whitbread bought nearly the whole of him, and had them put up and sent to his pleasure-grounds, with as much caution as if they had been looking-glasses of the greatest dimensions for his drawing-room.

The reader will probably recollect the manner in which Angelica Kauffmann was imposed upon by a gentleman's servant, who married her under the name of Count Horn, and the way in which his treachery was discovered; as related in the early part of the present volume. Angelica, however, was universally considered as a coquette, so that we cannot deeply sympathize in her disappointment; and as a proof how justly she deserved that character, I shall give an anecdote which I have often heard Mr. Nollekens relate. When Angelica was at Rome, previously to her marriage, she was ridiculously fond of displaying her person, and being admired; for which purpose she one evening took her station in one of the most conspicuous boxes of the Theatre, accompanied by

Nathaniel Dance and another artist, both of whom, as well as many others, were desperately enamoured of her. Angelica, perhaps, might have recollected the remonstrance of Mrs. Peachum, where she says,

Oh, Polly! you might have toy'd and kiss'd:
By keeping men off you keep them on:

However, while she was standing between her two beaux, and finding an arm of each most lovingly embracing her waist, she contrived, whilst her arms were folded before her on the front of the box over which she was leaning, to squeeze the hand of both, so that each lover concluded himself beyond all doubt the man of her choice.

On page 20 of Mr. Prince Hoare's 'Academic Annals for 1808', is recorded the following communication which was made to the members of the Royal Academy.

'*December 23d.*—In the General Assembly, the President declared the decease of Angelica Kauffmann Zucchi, one of the Members of the Academy.'[1]

---

[1] The account of the loss of this distinguished artist was received in a letter from Dr. Borsi, of Rome, who, after relating the circumstances of her illness and death, which happened on the 5th of November previous, proceeds to describe her obsequies, celebrated in the Church of S. Andrea de' Frati, under the direction of the Sculptor Canova, and others of her friends. 'The church,' says Dr. Borsi, 'was decorated in the manner customary on the interment of those of noble family. At ten in the morning, the corpse was accompanied to the church by two very numerous fraternities, fifty Capuchins, and fifty priests. The bier was carried by some of the brotherhood, and the four corners of the pall were supported by four young ladies, dressed suitably to the occasion. The four tassels were held by the four principal members of the Academy of St. Luke; these were followed by the rest of the Academicians and other virtuosi, each one with a large wax taper lighted in his hand. Two pictures, painted by the deceased, completed the procession.'

After the death of the footman who had married Angelica, and to whom she had allowed a separate maintenance, she became the wife of Zucchi, the Painter, but continued to go by the name of Angelica Kauffmann.

Mrs. Nollekens, at this time, received a most severe and unexpected shock by the death of her sister, Miss Welch, with whom she had always lived in ties of the fondest love, paying the strictest respect to every observation or wish she uttered, according to the early advice given her by their mutual friend, Doctor Samuel Johnson, who generally spoke of Miss Welch as Miss Nancy. She died at Bath, and was buried in the Abbey of that City, where an inscription was erected as follows:

'Sacred to the Memory of Mrs. Anne Welch,
of Aylesbury, in the County of Bucks,
Daughter of Saunders Welch, Esq.

'Admired by her friends, beloved by her acquaintance, blessed with distinguished abilities, she was so improved by the knowledge of various languages and science, that elegance of diction, beauty of sentiment, the majesty of wisdom, and the grace of persuasion, ever hung upon her lips. The bonds of life being gradually dissolved, she winged her flight from this world in expectation of a better, on the 15th of January, 1810.

'Her afflicted and affectionate sister, Maria Nollekens, in full assurance of their happy re-union, caused this monument to be erected.'[1]

I am at present ignorant of the name of the author of the above inscription; but allowing Mrs. Nollekens to have breathed only half the feelings it sets forth, we shall be giving that lady credit for great forbearance; as her cousin, Mr. Woodcock, has informed me, that she was much chagrined upon finding that her sister's

[1] For this copy of Miss Welch's inscription I am obliged to my amiable friend Mrs. Gwillim.

house at Aylesbury, with its furniture, had been, but a short time before her death, willed to another person.

I have spoken of the partiality of Nollekens for the Italian Opera, at which place of amusement he used to exhibit himself in his sword and bag in the pit, to hear Grassini sing; though, at the same time, he was so ignorant of music, that he could not have discovered any difference between the major and minor keys. The portion of the performance which *really* attracted him was, I doubt not, the agile movements of the female dancers in the ballet. He was at that time so well known at the Opera-house, that several of the military, who had an eye to his property, would attend him, though in their full uniform, to the door to see him safe into a hackney-coach, an expense he indulged in only when it rained hard. If, however, the reader be surprised at this, what will he say when he is informed, that on the following morning he was sometimes seen disputing with the cobbler, his opposite neighbour, about the charge of two-pence; and refusing to pay Crispin's demand, unless he put three or four more sparables in the heels of the shoes which he had mended twice before!

One day, Mr. Northcote the Academician, the best and favourite pupil of Sir Joshua Reynolds, had just reached his door in Argyle-street, when Nollekens, who was looking up at the house, put the following question to him: 'Why don't you have your house painted, Northcote? why it's as dirty as Jem Barry's was in Castle-street. I wonder Beverly would let him live in it!' Now Nollekens had no right to exult over his brother artist in this way; for he had given his own door a coat of paint, and his front passage a white-wash, only the *day before*, and they had been for years in the most filthy state possible.

Miss Welch brought down upon herself his eternal hatred, by kindly venturing to improve him in his spelling. She was a friendly and benevolent woman; and I am indebted to her and the amiable Mrs. Barker for many acts of kindness during the time I was labouring under a tremendous loss by fire. One evening, when I was drinking tea with her at her lodgings, No. 69, in Newman-street, she showed me a little book in which she had put down Mr. Nollekens's way of spelling words in 1780, with the manner in which they should be written. I copied a few of them with her permission, which, I must say, she gave me with some reluctance, notwithstanding she disliked Nollekens most cordially, though they were both Catholics. The following instances may serve as specimens: 'yousual, scenceble, obligin, modle, wery, gentilman, promist, sarvices, desier, Inglish, perscription, hardently, jenerly, moust, devower, Jellis, Retier, sarved, themselfs, could *for* cold, clargeman, facis, cupple, foure, sun *for* son, boath sexis, daly, horsis, ladie, cheif, talkin, tould, shee, sarch, paing, ould mades, racis, yoummer in his face, palas, oke, lemman, are-bolloon, sammon, chimisters *for* chymists, yoke *for* yolk, grownd,' &c. &c. Let me, however, entreat my readers to believe that I detest the character of a critic of words, and that my only motive for touching upon Mr. Nollekens's ignorance in the year 1780, is to induce them to believe, that when he made so many codicils above forty years afterwards, he did not know the true meaning of many words that we now and then find in testamentary writings. A curious specimen or two will be given in a future page of this work, of his ignorance of the true meaning of words pronounced by him, even at a moment when most persons believed him to be perfectly sane.

Towards the close of one of the hottest days in summer, as Mr. Nollekens was returning from the bench placed in front of the Queen's-head and Artichoke as a seat for those persons whose dress did not appear to entitle them to accommodation withinside the house, he asked his man, Dodimy, what charitable actions he had done lately? 'Charity, Sir! bless you! it's a long time since you gave any.'—'Well, then,' said his master, 'take the twopence out of your waistcoat-pocket, that you had in change from the ale, to that poor fellow walking there.' 'What! to that little man in the brown coat?' 'Yes, Sir, to that little man in the brown coat.' 'Lord bless you! that's Dog-Jennings!'[1]—*Nollekens*. 'What! my old friend, Noel Jennings? What the devil does he do on this side of the water, in Marybone-fields? Does he look this way?'—'No, Sir,' was the reply.—'Ah! well then, walk on this side; don't let him see me. Why Mrs. Palmer left him a good piece of the pigeon-pie last Sunday, when she made a day of it. I paid the coach for both of us; and Jennings, according to custom, produced a bottle of champagne.'—'I know, Sir,' rejoined Dodimy, 'I heard Mrs. Nollekens tell Mary all about it; and, I can tell you, Mistress don't half like such ramblings.'

[1] This eccentric gentleman, who was a person of high taste and considerable family fortune, received the above name from his having brought into England an antique sculpture of a dog, with several other fine pieces of Art, which were sold by auction by the elder Christie. The Dog brought one thousand guineas, and was purchased by Mr. Duncombe, of Yorkshire; but a mould of it belongs to Sarti, the Figure-maker, a cast from which makes a most noble appearance in a gentleman's hall.

CHAPTER XI

The Elgin Marbles brought to England.—Inquiries on them by a Committee of the House of Commons, with answers by Nollekens, Flaxman, Westmacott, Chantrey, Rossi, Sir Thomas Lawrence, and President West.—Remarks on them by a Riding-master.—Contrast of the manners of Nollekens and Flaxman.—Collection of medals made by the latter.—Old medals of Italy, and those by Pisano.—English medals by T. Simon.—French medals of Andrieu.—Coins collected by Mr. Nollekens.—His loss by robbery.—His prints, gems, and casts in plaster.—Art not hereditary.

WHEN Lord Elgin's Marbles arrived in England, his Lordship invited all persons of taste to view them at his house, the corner of Park-lane, in Piccadilly, now the town-residence of His Royal Highness the Duke of Gloucester. They were shortly afterwards moved to the side premises of Burlington-house, where they remained until a temporary gallery could be prepared for them in the British Museum by Government, which had purchased them for the use of the public and the advancement of Art. During the time these Marbles were Lord Elgin's property, Mr. Nollekens, accompanied by his constant companion, Joseph Bonomi,—a truly amiable youth, to whom from his birth he had intended to be a benefactor,—paid them many visits; and indeed at that time, not only all the great artists, but every lover of the Arts, were readily admitted. The students of the Royal Academy, and even Flaxman, the Phidias of our times, and the venerable President West, drew from them for weeks together.

As the mention of these Marbles may bring to my readers the recollection of events which some of them may have nearly forgotten, I shall now introduce Mr. Nollekens's Answers to the Committee of the House of

Commons, contrasted with those of Flaxman; together with a few of those of Sir Thomas Lawrence and other great men of the highest eminence in our country, who were called upon for their opinion as to the excellence of those wonderful works of Art.

Chairman of the Committee.—'Mr. Nollekens, are you well acquainted with the collection of Marbles brought to England by Lord Elgin?'—'I am.'

'What is your opinion of those Marbles, as to the excellency of the work?'—'They are very fine,—the finest things that ever came to this country.'

'In what class do you place them, as compared with the finest Marbles which you have seen formerly in Italy?'—'I compare them to the finest of Italy.'

'Which of those of my Lord Elgin's do you hold in the highest estimation?'—'I hold the Theseus and the Neptune to be two of the finest things;—finer than any thing in this country.'

'In what class do you place the bas-reliefs?'—'They are very fine,—among the first class of bas-relief work.'

'Do you think that the bas-reliefs of the Centaurs are in the finest class of Art?'—'I do think so.'

'Do you think the bas-relief of the frieze, representing the Procession, also in the first class of the art?'—'In the first class of the art.'

'Do you conceive those two sets to be of or about the same date?'—'I cannot determine upon that.'

'Have you ever looked at this collection, with a view to the value of it?'—'No, I have not.'

'Can you form any sort of estimate of the value of it?'—'I cannot say any thing about the value.'

'Do you think it very desirable, as a national object, that this collection should become public property?'—'Undoubtedly.'

'Can you form any judgment as to the date of those works, comparing them with other works that you have seen in Italy?'—'I suppose they are about as old; but they may be older or later.'

'To which of the works you have seen in Italy do you think the Theseus bears the greatest resemblance?'—'I compare that to the Apollo Belvidere and Laocoon.'

'Do you think the Theseus of as fine sculpture as the Apollo?'—'I do.'

'Do you think it has more or less of ideal beauty than the Apollo?'—'I cannot say it has more than the Apollo.'

'Has it as much?'—'I think it has as much.'

'Do you think that the Theseus is a closer copy of fine nature than the Apollo?'—'No; I do not say it is a finer copy of nature than the Apollo.'

'Is there not a distinction among artists, between a close imitation of nature, and ideal beauty?'—'I look upon them as ideal beauty, and closeness of study from nature.'

'You were asked just now if you could form any estimate of the value of this collection; can you put any value upon them, comparatively with the Townley Marbles?'—'I reckon them very much higher than the Townley Marbles for beauty.'

'Suppose the Townley Marbles to be valued at 20,000*l*., what might you estimate these at?'—'They are quite a different thing; I think the one is all completely finished and mended up, and these are real fragments as they have been found, and it would cost a great deal of time and expense to put them in order.'

'For the use of artists, will they not answer every purpose in their present state?'—'Yes, perfectly; I would not have them touched.'

'Have you seen the Greek Marbles lately brought to the Museum?'—'I have.'

'How do you rank those in comparison with these?'—'Those are very clever, but not like those of Lord Elgin's.'

'Then you consider them very inferior?'—'No; I consider them inferior to Lord Elgin's,—not very inferior, though they may be called inferior.'

'Were you ever in Greece yourself?'—'No, never farther than Rome and Naples.'

'When you studied in Italy, had you many opportunities of seeing remains of Grecian Art?'—'I saw all the fine things to be seen at Rome, both in painting and sculpture.'

'Do you remember a piece of bas-relief representing Bacchus and Icarus, in the Townley Collection?'—'I recollect all those things; I used to spend my Sundays there with Mr. Townley.'

'Do you happen to recollect particularly that piece?'—'No, I do not recollect it among the great quantity of things.'

'Have you formed any idea of the value of these objects in the light of acquisitions to individuals, as objects of decoration, if sold individually?'—'I cannot put a value upon them; they are by far the finest things that ever came to this country.'

'Do you mean by that, that you consider them so valuable, that you cannot put a value upon them?'—'No, I do not know: as to fine things, they are not to be got every day.'

'Do you consider part of the value of the Townley Collection to have depended upon the cost and labour incurred in restoring them?'—'As for restoring them, that must have cost a great deal of money; I know Mr. Townley was there for years about them.'

'Have the Elgin Collection gained in general estimation and utility since they have been more known and studied?'—'Yes.'

John Flaxman, Esq., R. A., called in, and examined.

'Are you well acquainted with the Elgin Collection of Marbles?'—'Yes, I have seen them frequently, and I have drawn from them; and I have made such inquiries as I thought necessary concerning them respecting my art.'

'In what class do you hold them, as compared with the first works of Art, which you have seen before?'—'The Elgin Marbles are mostly basso-relievos, and the finest works of Art I have seen. Those in the Pope's Museum, and the other galleries of Italy, were the Laocoon, the Apollo Belvidere; and the other most celebrated works of antiquity were groups and statues. These differ in the respect that they are chiefly basso-relievos, and fragments of statuary. With respect to their excellence, they are the most excellent of their kind that I have seen; and I have every reason to believe that they were executed by Phidias, and those employed under him, or the general design of them given by him at the time the temple was built; as we are informed, that he was the artist principally employed by Pericles, and his principal scholars, mentioned by Pliny, Alcamenes, and about four others immediately under him; to which he adds a catalogue of seven or eight others, who followed in order; and he mentions their succeeding Phidias in the course of twenty years. I believe they are the works of those artists; and in this respect they are superior to almost any works of antiquity, excepting the Laocoon and Torso Farnese; because they are known to have been executed by the artists whose names are recorded by the ancient authors. With respect to the beauty of the basso-relievos, they are as perfect nature as it is possible to put into the compass of the marble in which they are executed, and that of the most elegant kind. There is one statue also, which is called a Hercules, or Theseus, of the first order of merit. The fragments are finely executed; but I do not, in my own estimation, think their merit is as great.'

'What fragments do you speak of?'—'Several fragments of women; the groups without their heads.'

'You do not mean the Metopes?'—'No; those statues which were in the east and west pediments originally.'

'In what estimation do you hold the Theseus, as compared with the Apollo Belvidere and the Laocoon?'—'If you would permit me to compare it with a fragment I will mention, I should estimate it before the Torso Belvidere.'

'As compared with the Apollo Bevidere, in what rank do you hold the Theseus?'—'For two reasons I cannot at this moment very correctly compare them in my own mind. In the first place, the Apollo Belvidere is a divinity of a higher order than Hercules, and therefore I cannot so well compare the two. I compared the Hercules with a Hercules before, to make the comparison more just. In the next place, the Theseus is not only on the surface corroded by the weather; but the head is in that impaired state, that I can scarcely give an opinion upon it; and the limbs are mutilated. To answer the question, I should prefer the Apollo Belvidere certainly, though I believe it is only a copy.'

'Does the Apollo Belvidere partake more of ideal beauty than the Theseus?'—'In my mind, it does decidedly; I have not the least question of it.'

'Do you think that increases its value?'—'Yes, very highly. The highest efforts of art in that class have always been the most difficult to succeed in, both among ancients and moderns, if they have succeeded in it.'

'Supposing the state of the Theseus to be perfect, would you value it more as a work of art than the Apollo?'—'No; I should value the Apollo for the ideal beauty, before any male statue I know.'

'Although you think it a copy?'—'I am sure it is a copy; the other is an original, and by a first-rate artist.'

'The Committee is very anxious to know the reason you have in stating so decidedly your opinion, that the Apollo is a copy.'—'There are many reasons; and I am afraid it would be troublesome to the Committee to go through them. The general appearance of the hair and the mantle of the Apollo Belvidere, is in the style more of bronze than of marble; and there is mentioned in the Pope's Museum (Pio Clementino) by the Chevalier Visconti, who illustrated that Museum, that there was a statue in Athens, I do not know whether it was in the city or some particular temple, or whether the place is mentioned, an Apollo Alexicacos, a driver away of evil, in bronze, by Calamis, erected on account of a plague that had been in Athens; from the representations of this statue in basso-relievos with a bow, it is believed that this figure might be a copy of that. One reason I have given is, that the execution of the hair and clock resembles bronze. But another thing convinces me of its being a copy. I had a conversation with Visconti and Canova on the spot; and my particular reason is this:—a cloak hangs over the left arm, which in bronze it was easy to execute, so that the folds on one side should answer to the folds on the other; the cloak is single, and therefore it is requisite that the folds on one side should answer to the folds on the other; there is no duplication of drapery: in bronze that was easy to execute, but in marble it was not; therefore, I presume, the copyist preferred copying the folds in front;—but the folds did not answer to each other on one side and the other: those on the back appear to have been calculated for strength in the marble, and those in front to represent the bronze, from which I apprehend they were copied. There is another reason; which is, that the most celebrated figure of antiquity is mentioned by Pliny and its sculptor, the Venus of Cnidus by Praxiteles; and he mentions it in a remarkable manner, for he says, the works of Praxiteles in the Ceramicus, not only excel those of all other sculptors, but his own; and this Venus excels all that he ever did. Now, it seems inconceivable that so fine a statue as the Apollo could have been executed without its name being brought down to us, either by Pliny or Pausanias, if it had been esteemed the first statue in the world.'

'Do you think it of great consequence to the progress of Art in Britain, that this collection should become the property of the public?'—'Of the greatest importance, I think; and I always have thought so as an individual.'

'Do you conceive practically, that any improvement has taken place in the state of the Arts in this country since this collection has been open to the public?'—'Within these last twenty years, I think, Sculpture has improved in a very great degree, and I believe my opinion is not singular; but unless I was to take time to reflect upon the several causes, of which that has been the consequence, I cannot pretend to answer the question: I think works of such prime importance could not remain in the country, without improving the public taste and the taste of the artists.'

'In what class do you hold the Metopes as compared with the Frieze?'—'I should think, from a parity of reasoning adopted between the Metopes and the flat basso-relievos, with that adopted between the Apollo Belvidere and the Theseus, or Hercules, that the Metopes are preferable to the flat basso-relievos, inasmuch as the heroic style is preferable to that of common nature.'

'Should you have judged the Metopes to be of higher antiquity, if you had seen them, not knowing from what temple they were brought?'—'I should certainly have taken them to be of the age to which they are attributed, the age of Phidias.'

'What characteristic mark do you observe of high antiquity, as compared with the other works of antiquity?'—'In the first place, I observe a particular classification of the parts of the body; and I have adverted to the medical writer of that age, Hippocrates, and find that the distinctions of the body, when they have been taken from the finest nature, in the highest state of exercise, and in the best condition, in all respects, which might be expected from those who possessed great personal beauty and cultivated habits of living, most likely to produce it, and who were accustomed to see it frequently in public exercises—this classification, which they appeared to prefer, is conformable to the distinctions in the statues. It is well known, that in the writings of Hippocrates, a great deal of attention is paid to the economy of the human body and its interior parts, but that its exteriors are not described as our modern anatomists describe them, but in a simple manner by a general classification of parts and muscles. What I would particularly say on the subject is this: Hippocrates describes the edges of the ribs as forming a semicircle at the bottom of the upper thorax; he describes with some accuracy, the meeting and form of the upper part of the scapula and acromion with the collar-bone: that part is particularly marked in these figures;—he describes the knee-pan as a single bone; and that was their manner of making the knee in the statues of that time;—and, if I remember right, he also describes the upper part of the basin-bone, which is particularly marked in the antique statues. In a few words, the form of the body has a classification of a simple kind in a few parts, such as I find in the ancient anatomists, and such as are common in the outlines of the painted Greek vases. Besides, as far as I can judge from our documents of antiquity,—the painted Greek vases, for example, those that come nearer to the time in which these Marbles are believed to be produced, are conceived in the same character, and drawn in the same manner.'

'Did not that classification continue much later than the time of Pericles?'—'Yes, it did continue later, but it became more complicated, and in some cases more geometrical.'

'Does the anatomy of these figures agree with the anatomy of the Laocoon, or of the Torso Farnese?'—'They agree most with the Torso Farnese. I cannot judge very accurately of that at this time, for it was about to be removed from Rome at the time I was there, and it is very much broken. In respect to the Laocoon, I believe it to be a very posterior work, done after a time when considerable discoveries had been made in anatomy in the Alexandrian school; which I think had been communicated not only among physicians, but among artists all over Greece; and in the Laocoon the divisions are much more numerous.'

'Do you observe any considerable difference in the conformation of the horses, between the Metopes and the Procession?'—'It is to be recollected, both in the Metopes and the Procession, that different hands have been employed upon them; so that it is difficult, unless I had them before me, to give a distinct opinion, particularly as the horses in the Metopes have not horses' heads: I do not think I can give a very decided opinion upon it, but in general the character appears to me very much the same.'

'Should you have judged the Metopes and the Frieze to be of the same age, if they had not come from the same temple?'—'Yes, undoubtedly I should.'

'Have you ever looked at this collection, with a view to its value in money?'—'I never have; but I conceive that the value in money must be very considerable, judging only from the quantity of sculpture in it: the question never occurred to me before this morning, but it appears to me that there is a quantity of labour equal to three or four of the greatest public monuments that have lately been erected; and I think it is said either in Chandler's Inscriptions, or in Stuart's Athens, that the temple cost a sum equal to 500,000*l*.'

'Have you seen the Greek Marbles lately deposited in the British Museum?'—'Yes.'

'In what class do you place those, as compared with the basso-relievos of Lord Elgin's Collection?'—'With respect to the excellence of workmanship, the Metopes and the basso-relievos of the Procession are very superior to those in the Museum, though the composition of the others is exquisite.'

'Which do you think the greatest antiquity?'—'Lord Elgin's; the others I take to be nearly twenty years later.'

'In what rate do you class these Marbles, as compared with Mr. Townley's Collection?'—'I should value them more, as being the ascertained works of the first artists of that celebrated age; the greater part of Mr. Townley's Marbles, with some few exceptions, are perhaps copies, or only acknowledged inferior works.'

'Do you reckon Lord Elgin's Marbles of greater value as never having been touched by any modern hand.'—'Yes.'

'In what class do you hold the draped figures, of which there are large fragments?'—'They are fine specimens of execution; but, in other respects, I do not esteem them very highly, excepting the Iris, and a fragment of the Victory.'

'Do you consider those to be of the same antiquity?'—'I do.'

'Be pleased to account for the difference in their appearance?'—'I think Sculpture at that time made a great stride. Phidias, having had the advantage of studying painting, first gave a great freedom to his designs; that freedom he was able to execute, or have executed, with great ease in small and flat works; but as the proportions of the particular drawings of the figures were not so well understood generally as they were a few years afterwards, there are some disproportions and inaccuracies in the larger figures; the necessary consequences of executing great works, when the principles of an art are not established.'

'Do you recollect two figures that are sitting together with the arms over each other?'—'Yes.'

'Is your low estimation of the draped figures applicable to those?'—'My opinion may be incorrect, and it may be more so by not having the figures before me; but I meant my observation to apply to all the draped figures.'

'Were the proportions of those statues calculated to have their effect at a particular distance?'—'I believe not; I do not believe the art had arrived at that nicety.'

'You have remarked probably those parts, particularly of the Neptune and some of the Metopes, that are in high perfection, from having been preserved from the weather?'—'I have remarked those that are in the best condition.'

'Did you ever see any statue higher finished than those parts, or that could convey an idea of high finish more completely to an artist?'—'I set out with saying, that the execution is admirable.'

'In those particular parts, have not you observed as high a finish as in any statue that ever you saw?'—'Yes; and, in some places, a very useless finish, in my opinion.'

'Do you think the Theseus and the Neptune of equal merit, or is one superior to the other?'—'Chevalier Canova, when I conversed with him on the same subject, seemed to think they were equal; I think the Ilissus is very inferior.'

'You think the Ilissus is inferior to the Theseus?'—'Extremely inferior; and I am convinced, if I had had an opportunity of considering it with Chevalier Canova, he would have thought so too.'

'Can you inform the Committee, whether the climate of England is likely to have a different effect upon the statues, from the climate from which they were brought, and whether it would be possible, by keeping them under cover, to prevent the effect of the climate?'—'Entirely.'

'You know the bas-relief, in the Townley Collection, of Bacchus and Icarus?'—'Yes.'

'What do you consider the workmanship of that, comparatively with any of Lord Elgin's bas-reliefs.'—'Very inferior.'

Richard Westmacott, Esq., R. A., called in, and examined.

'Are you well acquainted with the Elgin Marbles?'—'Yes.'

'In what class of art do you rate them?'—'I rate them of the first class of art.'

'In what rate should you place the Theseus and the River God, as compared with the Apollo Belvidere and Laocoon?'—'Infinitely superior to the Apollo Belvidere.'

'Which do you prefer; the Theseus or the River God?'—'They are both so excellent, that I cannot readily determine; I should say the back of the Theseus was the finest thing in the world; and that the anatomical skill displayed in front of the Ilissus, is not surpassed by any work of art.'

Francis Chantrey, Esq., called in, and examined.

'Are you well acquainted with the Elgin Marbles?'—'I have frequently visited them.'

'In what class, as to excellence of art, do you place them?'—'Unquestionably, in the first.'

'Have you ever looked at this collection, with a view towards its value in money?'—'I really do not know what to compare them with.'

'Do you think it of great importance to the art of sculpture, that this collection should become the property of the public?'—'I think it of the greatest importance, in a national point of view.'

Charles Rossi, Esq., R. A., called in, and examined.

'Are you well acquainted with the Elgin Marbles?'—'Yes.'

'In what class of art do you reckon them?'—'The finest that I have ever seen.'

'Do you reckon the Frieze of the Procession in the highest class of art?'—'Yes; they are in a superior style; I should say they were jewels.'

Sir Thomas Lawrence, Knt., R. A., called in, and examined.

'Are you well acquainted with the Elgin Marbles?'—'Yes, I am.'

'In what class of art do you consider them?'—'In the very highest.'

'In your own particular line of art, do you consider them of high importance as forming a national school?'—'In a line of art which I have very seldom practised, but which it is still my wish to do, I consider that they would; namely, Historical-painting.'

'Do you conceive any of them to be of a higher class than the Apollo Belvidere?'—'I do; because I consider that there is in them an union of fine composition, and very grand form, with a more true and natural expression of the effect of action upon the human frame than there is in the Apollo, or in any of the other most celebrated statues.'

'You have stated, that you thought these Marbles had great truth and imitation of nature; do you consider that that adds to their value?'—'It considerably adds to it, because I consider them as united with grand form. There is in them that variety that is produced in the human form by the alternate action and repose of the muscles, that strikes one particularly. I have myself a very good collection of the best casts from the antique statues, and was struck with that difference in them, in returning from the Elgin Marbles to my own house.'

Questions sent to the President of the Royal Academy, his health not permitting him to attend the Committee; with his Answers thereto.

'Are you well acquainted with the Elgin Collection?'—'I am; having drawn the most distinguished of them, the size of the original marbles.'

'In what class of art do you rank the best of these Marbles?'—'In the first of dignified art, brought out of nature upon uncertain truths, and not on mechanical principles, to form systematic characters and systematic art.'

'Do they appear to you the work of the same artists?'—'One mind pervades the whole, but not one hand has executed them.'

'As compared with the Apollo Belvidere, the Torso of the Belvidere, and the Laocoon, how do you estimate the Theseus or Hercules, and the River God or Ilissus?'—'The Apollo of the Belvidere, the Torso, and the Laocoon, are systematic art; the Theseus and the Ilissus stand supreme in art.'

'Can you compare, in money value, Lord Elgin's

Marbles, or any part of them, with the money value of the Phygalian, or Townley Collection?'—'I judge of the Elgin Marbles, from their purity and pre-eminence in art over all others I have ever seen, and from their truth and intellectual power; and I give them the preference to the Phygalian and Townley Collection, most of which is systematic art.'[1]

It was highly amusing to notice the glaring contrast of the two Sculptors, Nollekens and Flaxman, whenever they came in contact in a fashionable party, which I own was rarely the case. The former, upon these occasions, who was never known to expatiate upon Art, generally took out his pocket-book, and, in order to make himself agreeable, presented his recipes, perhaps for an inveterate sore throat or a virulent scorbutic humour, to some elegant woman with as much alacrity as Dr. Bossy, of Covent-garden fame, formerly did to the wife of a Fulham or a Mortlake

[1] The generality of my readers will be pleased with the following anecdote, and it must come home to every good rider when he mounts a horse:—Shortly after the Elgin Marbles were thrown open to the public indiscriminately, a gentlemanly-looking person was observed to stand in the middle of the gallery on one spot for upwards of an hour, changing his attitude only by turning himself round; at last he left the room, but in the course of two hours he again took his former station, attended by about a dozen young gentlemen; and there to them he made nearly the following observations:—'See, gentlemen, look at the riders all round the room,' alluding to the Friezes; 'see how they sit; see with what ease and elegance they ride; I never saw such men in my life; they have no saddles, no stirrups, they must have leaped upon their horses in a grand style. You will do well to study the position of these noble fellows; stay here this morning instead of riding with me, and I am sure you will seat yourselves better to-morrow.' I need hardly tell the reader that this person was a riding-master, and that after he had been so astonished at the sight of the sculptor's riders, he brought all his pupils, to whom he was that morning to have given lessons at his riding-school.

market-gardener. The latter, however, like a true descendant of Phidias, was modestly discoursing with a select circle upon the exquisite productions of Greece; at the same time, assuring his auditors, that every motion of the body of a well-proportioned, unaffected person, gave sufficient opportunities for the selection of similar attitudes of equal grace; that he considered himself frequently indebted to the simple and unadorned charity-girl for the best of his attitudes; and that these he had often collected during his walks in the streets, when the innocent objects themselves had been wholly ignorant of his admiration of their positions. I have also often heard him declare, that the most successful of his figures displayed in his Illustrations of Homer, Aeschylus, and Dante, were procured from similarly natural and unsophisticated sources. Flaxman, like Rubens, took infinite delight in his collection of Italian medals; the best of which he fortunately procured during his residence at Rome. They were mostly of the Fifteenth century, and were always estimated by him as the richest treasures in Art that he possibly could possess; and, perhaps, no man of his refined erudition felt or expressed greater pleasure than he did, when he conversed with any person possessed of sufficient feeling justly to appreciate their superior merits. Mr. Samuel Henning, a young artist of promising abilities as a medallist, asked Flaxman's permission to take an impression of one or two of these specimens: upon which the Sculptor, with his usual urbanity, not only instantly complied, but allowed him to mould a selection which he himself kindly made for him, and which he considered as the most interesting and beautiful of his collection. These consisted of Don Inigo de Davalos, the face of which person is of low relief, and the features are expressive of a man of great depth of thought and a superior mind; Benedictus Depastis, a medal which was a great favourite with Flaxman, though I have frequently seen him laugh at the collops of fat at the back of the neck; Leo Baptista, Albertus, Victorinus Feltrensis Summus, Sigismondus Pandulfus, Cardinal de Malatestis, Sanctæ Romanæ Ecclesiæ Cardin. Generalis, the hair of which head differs materially from the preceding medals, it being singularly cut in a precise straight line over the forehead.

Few persons are aware of the superior excellencies of these Italian medals, which exceed all others in point of natural character, the beautiful productions of Thomas Simon excepted. Many of them were executed under the glorious auspices of Leo X. after the designs of Michel Angelo, Cellini, Raffaelle, Julio Romano, &c. and possess as much fleshiness as Chantrey's busts; and the artist will, I am sure, be pleased, when he is informed, that casts of several of them may be obtained of Mr. Samuel Henning, at a price accommodated to the limited resources of the economical student. Vasari, in his valuable work, mentions the names of the following medallists who flourished in his time, viz. Miseldone, Mathei de Pastis, Sperandei, and Villore; and we find that Vittore Pisano, a Painter of Verona, was highly celebrated as the chief restorer of this branch of art: his medals, as well as those of his contemporaries, were first modelled in wax, and then cast; and a catalogue of his medallic productions is given by Vasari. In the British Museum, there is a brass medal of Pisano, executed by himself, which is considered as a rarity by collectors, it being one of those which were carefully worked up with the tool after they were cast. It displays rather a reserved set of features, short and close together, the nose of which inclines to that character commonly called the snub. His cap, which is an upright one with many folds, reminded me of that sort usually worn, when I was a boy, by the old glass-grinders of the Seven-Dials. I also remember seeing Smollett's man Strap, when he was a bookbinder, living near Chelsea

Old Church, in a similar one: he was afterwards, for several years before his death, Keeper of the lodge of Buckingham-terrace, Strand, near Inigo Jones's watergate; a truly correct engraving of which is given in Campbell's Vitruvius. In my opinion, the productions of Pisano,[1] are by far the most spirited, as must unquestionably be the case whenever a Painter executes a beloved task with his own hand. The medals by him are equal to pictures, as they display a fine breadth and a true character of Nature, excellencies which a mere mechanical and perpetual copyist can never arrive at. How far more refreshing it is to a person possessing a moderate share of discernment, to see an etching by Vandyke, with all its foul bitings, where the markings are firm and square, than an engraving by Vosterman or Bolswert, where every delineation is rounded comparatively to a dull, inanimate smoothness! How delighted too is the eye of taste with an old impression from the uncontaminated needles of Claude, Swaneveldt, Karel Du Jardin, or Rembrandt! How the fretful, weak, and laboured engravings by French artists in the Poullein, the Praslin, and the Choiseul Collections, sink under the comparison, when opposed to such treasures, delivered at once from the Painter's mind and by his own hand! So likewise it is with the works of Simon our own countryman, engraved during the Usurpation: that artist drew well; and his reliefs, which are low and broad, appear more like a fine chiaro-'scuro painting, than sculptured productions. His manner of treating the hair is beautiful, and perhaps superior to that of every other medallist; and nothing can surpass, in that particular, the specimens of his talent displayed in the head of Cromwell on the largest of the two Dunbar medals, and also that of Thomas Wriothesley

[1] I do not find Pisano mentioned in any of the Dictionaries of Painters, though I concluded Fuseli would have noticed him.

Earl of Southampton. This silver medal, which exhibits the Earl in a cap, is considered one of great rarity; but the one in gold, which was purchased of Mr. Young, by the late Barry Roberts, Esq. for the sum of twenty guineas, now in the British Museum, is looked upon as unique, not only on account of its being the only one known in that metal, but also from its variation from those in silver; the cap having been cut down so as to exhibit the hair without one, which the artist has managed in a most tasteful manner. In the gold impression, 'Tho. Simon' is cut under the projection of the shoulder, which is not the case with those in silver. Of this medal with the cap, there is also a bad copy, an impression of which may also be seen in the British Museum. It is a curious fact that, upon comparing the above medal with the circular one of Oliver Cromwell, inscribed 'Oliverus. Dei. Gra: Reipub: Angliæ. Sco: Et. Hib: &. Protector. Tho. Simon F.'—the lower parts of the faces are so like each other, that they would answer for either person.

I am well aware that there are numerous collectors who prefer dies engraven in France, and particularly the medallions and medals struck in favour of Napoleon, many of which unquestionably possess great merit, and are worthy of high admiration; but, in my opinion, none of them are equal in mind to those of Italy, produced under Leo X., nor do they in more than one instance, in point of taste, approach the productions of our own countryman, Thomas Simon.

The one I allude to, is that which was struck of Buonaparte, to commemorate the famous battle of Marengo. In the first state of the die, I certainly esteem this medal as the most beautiful performance of Andrieu. I was not aware of the superior excellence of this medal in its first stage of publication, until an old and worthy friend put me in possession of impressions in two states, in which the head differs widely, and which is, I believe, the only portion of that medal wherein an alteration has been made. At the time that the battle was fought, Buonaparte was a thin man, and consequently the extraordinary markings of his features were particularly visible, and, I conclude, accurately attended to by the medallist. For instance, the eye, by not being surrounded by much flesh, is keen and penetrating; the nose and lips are thin; and, indeed, the whole of his countenance appears steadfastly determined upon prosecuting his intentions. In the second state of this medal, the head and neck are so considerably enlarged, that every feature is rounded by an increase of flesh, as well as of years. In this state of corpulence, Napoleon's medals were more generally collected by his adherents, as well as by those who had cabinets for the reception of such works of Art; and it is supposed that Andrieu, in order that this Marengo medal of Buonaparte should be more like him when Emperor Napoleon, altered the head as we find it in its second state. He unfortunately, however, suffered the name of Buonaparte to remain, never caring for the periodical truth of physiognomy; and a distance of a few years made no difference to him. If an Englishman had been guilty of such violation of truth, what would have been said of him? and this is a more glaring instance of anachronism, as Andrieu has placed the countenance of his experienced and fattened hero upon his youthful shoulders, before he had been bloated by successful ambition, or had gone through half his depredations.

Mr. Nollekens, during his residence abroad, accumulated numerous coins, mostly the currency of the countries which he passed through; not with a view to their increasing in value, or for their particular merit, but with the usual idea of a miser who is fearful of a change in affairs, or what is more commonly called a revolution in the country, and who fully relies upon the intrinsic value of gold and silver. He probably never dreamed of the great loss sustained by hoarding up foreign money, which seldom produces more than its weight. Had he sold his coins, and put the amount out to interest, he would have increased the principal in the course of sixty years to at least ten times its original value, and thereby have saved himself many years' vexation for the loss of all; which he actually suffered in consequence of thieves breaking into his house and stealing all those pieces of gold and silver, together with Mr. Welch's silver cruet-stand, and other articles to a considerable amount. The depredators having entered the house at the back-window on the staircase, went at once to the place where the above articles were deposited, in the very next room to that in which Mr. and Mrs. Nollekens were asleep, and let themselves out at the street-door, without any one of the family being aware of their visit till the next morning. The window was then discovered to be open, and the ladder by which they had ascended from the yard, left to show the way by which they had gained admittance. It is a curious fact, that in a dirty book which they had dropped on their way out, bank notes were found to a considerable amount by the person who restored them to Mr. Nollekens; who, whenever this robbery was mentioned, which there was every reason to believe had been committed by persons connected with one of the numerous women who stood for his Venuses, observed that 'The rascals took away all my gold and silver coins, and left me all the copper ones.' These midnight moneyers also carried off to their melting-pot, after throwing away the rags in which they were folded, a few English silver medals of little value beyond their metallic gravity: fortunately there were no brass sand-moulded Pisanos in danger in Mortimer-street, such treasures being securely deposited in the choice cabinets of Flaxman.

Mr. Nollekens now and then amused himself and a

friend or two with his prints, but seldom spoke of the beauties of ancient bronzes; and as for expatiating upon the boldness and vigour of a Roman medal, that with him was quite out of the question. It is true that he had a collection of gems, impressions mostly taken from the antique, though certainly made with very little discrimination as to their superior excellence in point of art, in comparison with those by his contemporaries Burch, Merchant, and Tassie; for he would be as highly pleased with an inferior imitation of an antique, as with an original of the choicest excellence. In placing the various subjects in boxes, he never attended to any kind of classification whatever, since it was the same thing to him whether they were sacred or profane, and a figure of Eve or a Susannah was placed with that of a Lucretia or a Leda. His heads, though they were certainly kept by themselves, could boast of no better arrangement; as that of Hannibal was placed next to one of Flora. This mode of jumbling of eminent characters together, reminded me of Lingo the school-master, who, in 'The Agreeable Surprise', asks Cowslip the dairy-maid, if she had ever heard of Homer, Hercules, or Wat Tyler.

His assemblage of plaster-casts from the antique, had experienced very little augmentation since his departure from Rome, where he had purchased most of them at a trifling rate from the boys of Lucca, who at that time exhibited them for sale at fairs. His studio certainly could not boast of a vestibule of statues as large as life,—a most gratifying sight to the Sculptor's visitors so beautifully displayed in the Galleries of Chantrey and Westmacott;—but on the contrary, Nollekens's walls were principally covered with heads, arms, legs, hands, and feet, moulded from some of the most celebrated specimens abroad, together with a few casts of bas-reliefs of figures, and here and there a piece of foliage from the Vatican; all which were hung up without the least reference whatever to each other.

He paid but little attention to the productions of the ancients; though, indeed, I have seen him finish up the feet of his female figures from those of the statue of the Venus de Medicis; the English women, his constant models, having very bad toes in consequence of their abominable habit of wearing small and pointed shoes. My worthy friend, Joseph Bonomi, was sure to incur his displeasure whenever he discovered him studying the antique; and Nollekens would often chide him for not trusting more to Nature. I am, however, perfectly convinced, that if Nollekens had looked with more love towards the antique, his Venuses would have been considerably benefited, particularly in their ankles, which in many instances are too thick, and certainly remind me of Fuseli's observation, that 'they were Goltzïus's legs'.

We seldom find hereditary succession in Art, nor can I recollect a single instance in which the son of an eminent Painter or Sculptor has equalled the talent of his father: neither have I been able to discover, in the works of any pupil, merit equal to that of his great master; and I believe that it will be found, that the artists of the highest genius have sprung from the lowest schools, or have arisen to the pinnacle of fame by their own strength of mind and persevering application.

I do not mean here to insert an extended list of the bright living instances of a Lawrence, or a Jackson, a Wilkie, a Chantrey, a Westmacott, a Rossi, a Howard, a Turner, a Callcott, an Arnald, a Stothard, a Collins, &c. in support of my position, but shall principally confine my assertion to other eminent men who have already quitted this world; commencing with some of foreign countries, and concluding with those of England. Michel-Angelo Buonarroti, during the time he was with his master Domenico Ghirlandaio, corrected one of that artist's drawings to the astonishment of all the schools. The sublime Raffaelle soon excelled his master Pietro Perugino; and Antonio Correggio owed all his wonderful powers to nature, his master, Francesco Bianchi, being but of slender talent. The instructor of the inimitable Claude Lorraine, Agostino Tassi, merely taught him the method of preparing his colours; whilst Claude's famous contemporary, Nicolo Poussin, had for his masters Ferdinand Elle and L'Allement, who were both men of feeble abilities. How much did Sir Peter Paul Rubens surpass his preceptors, Tobias Verhaecht, Adam Van Oort, and Octavio Van Veen! how wonderfully did Rembrandt exceed his tutors Zwanenburg, Lastman, and Pinas! Albert Cuyp's pictures eminently stand before those of his father; and how far superior are the pictures of our own Dobson, to the productions of the English artists who preceded him, for his master was nothing more than a stationer and a picture-dealer! The immortal Hogarth was the apprentice of Ellis Gamble, a Silversmith, who employed him to engrave arms and shop-bills; and that exquisite Landscape-painter, Richard Wilson, courted Nature alone, under every variety of aërial tint, and his finest pictures display all her sparkling sunny freshness after a summer's shower. Thomas Gainsborough was another of Nature's pupils; and it might be said of him, as it has been said of Shakspeare, that he 'warbled his native wood-notes wild'. The portraits of Sir Joshua Reynolds's master, Thomas Hudson, would hardly be admitted into our present minor exhibitions; and the pictures painted by the instructor of the late venerable President West, Raffaelle Mengs, sink exceedingly low when they are mentioned with the works of his pupil. It will also be recollected, that Zoffany was originally only a decorater of clock-dials. Our three most eminent engravers, too, have never been equalled in any part of the globe; though William Woollett's master, Tinney, was so insignificant an artist, that Strutt, in his Biographical Dictionary, has not thought proper to give the least account of him; Sir Robert Strange's tutor was Cooper,[1] an obscure engraver in Scotland; and William Sharp, who has immortalized himself in his production from Sir Joshua Reynolds's portrait of John Hunter, was originally an engraver of the letters upon pewter-pots, dog-collars, door-plates, visiting-cards, &c.; and he assured me, that the only difference he ever had with William Byrne, the Landscape-engraver, was respecting the quantity of door-plates they had engraved, Sharp insisting upon his claim to the greatest number by some hundreds.

[1] Cooper was the father of Richard, the Drawing-master, who lately died at Eltham. The errors into which Mr. Strutt has fallen respecting the two Coopers, will, I doubt not, be entirely rectified by Mr. Ottley, in his Dictionary of Engravers; a work which, in the expectation of every one who is acquainted with that gentleman's great accuracy and most extensive knowledge of the subject, will supersede all others hitherto published.

CHAPTER XII

Mrs. Nollekens's new drawing-room.—Caleb Whitefoord's attentions to Nollekens.—Cross-readings.—Goldsmith's 'Retaliation'.—Whitefoord's letter to his nephew.—Mrs. Nollekens, her servant, and her acquaintances.—Her death and funeral.—Subsequent conduct of Mr. Nollekens.—Mrs. Lloyd and Mrs. Paradice.—A Garrick play-bill.—Mrs. Lloyd's Will.—Her death.—Eccentricities of Mr. Nollekens.—Mr. Barnard's Italian drawings.—Jernigan's lottery-medal.—Nollekens and his sitters.—George the Third's wig.—The Sculptor's family.—Bat. Pidgeon's Shop.

UPON the demise of Miss Welch,[1] Mrs. Nollekens, her sister, who had been most grievously disappointed in the bequest of her household furniture, to the great astonishment of her friends, and particularly of her husband, purchased articles perfectly new, in order to improve her drawing-room; which had remained for years as it was originally fitted up, increasing in nothing but dirt. So great was the change for the better, that for some time she only allowed her friends to take a peep in at the door now and then, while she held it what is often called *ajar*. Nor could she think of permitting even her set visitors to stay the evening in that room, as the *stupid servant* had forgotten to light a fire in it; so that, after they had been shown up, they were unavoidably obliged to be entertained, if it might be allowed that her parties were ever entertained, in the parlour with Nolly, where there had been a comfortable fire constantly kept up during the whole of the

[1] The late Mrs. Lloyd, R. A. informed Mrs. Nichols, her confidential domestic, that Miss Welch, after her father's death, whilst she was abroad, frequently travelled as a man, with sword and bag, attended by a man-servant only.

inclement season. In the summer, in order to let in a little fresh air, the sashes were thrown up, either to enable her to appear blowing the chaff from her canary bird's trough, or watering a delicate sprig or two of myrtle, which had been kindly presented to her by Mr. Whitefoord, whose sharp little eyes had been for some years so closely fixed upon No. 9, Mortimer-street, that he never suffered a week to pass without inviting them by some small present to recollect his kind remembrance of them, and by way of a pretty good instance of his tender anxiety for the continuance of his dear Nolly's health. By way of proving my assertion, I here insert a copy of an endearing epistle shown to me by Nollekens. This 'wine merchant' and *excellent connoisseur in old pictures*, had more prudence in sending his presents to a man enormously rich, than to a fellow-creature whose frame was shivering for the want of a trifle to procure him a basin of broth, and a night's lodging.

DEAR NOLLY,

Here is a fleecy hosiery shirt for you—put it on immediately, and also the breastplate. They will keep you warm and comfortable during the cold weather—keep you free from rheumatism, and prolong your life.

I intended to have delivered this myself, but I have not been out to-day.

Yours sincerely,
C. WHITEFOORD.

Wednesday evening.

At this time, Caleb was so constant a guardian of Nollekens's knocker, that no one ventured to cope with his wit on that Sculptor's threshold; for, like Goldsmith's goose,[1] he stoutly kept up his right to the pond's side.

'The pond, she said, was her's, and she would maintain her right in it, and support her honour, while she

[1] See Goldsmith's 'Essay on the Irresolution of Youth'.

had a bill to hiss, or a wing to flutter. In this manner she drove away ducks, pigs, and chickens;—nay, even the insidious cat was seen to scamper.'

Advanced on the journey of life as Nollekens was, little did this 'Cross-reader' imagine that the road he was treading was straiter for him, and that an earlier period was fixed for his own departure from what most persons are scrambling for—the good things of this life, as they are called by the worldly traveller. Whitefoord left us; and by his death, though Nollekens lost his primest of wits, his high reputation as a stockholder gained him a host of flatterers, for he was immediately and constantly assailed by foxes from all quarters; and one considered himself sure of the prey, by inviting him to take a peep at a jackdaw which perched every morning upon a pretty almond-tree in full blossom, near to which he himself lay, at a short distance from the Metropolis.

Whitefoord, who never ventured abroad but with a full determination to be noticed, dressed himself foppishly, particularly so in some instances. It is true he did not, upon trivial occasions, sport the strawberry embroidery of Cosway, yet he was considered extravagantly dashing in a sparkling black button, which for many years he continued to display within a loop upon a rosette on his three-cornered hat, which he was sure to take off whenever he considered *bowing politically essential*. The wig worn by him for years when he was at the summit of notoriety, had five curls on each side, and he was one of the last gentlemen who wore the true Garrick-cut.[1]

So delighted was Mr. Whitefoord with his celebrated 'cross-readings', that he liberally distributed among his friends specimens of some of the most whim-

[1] This peculiar wig, with five curls on each side, was brought into fashion by David Garrick, and its cut is precisely engraven by Sherwin, in his portrait of the Actor done for Davies's Memoirs.

sical, which he had been at the expense of printing upon small single sheets. As one of these trifles, which are now considered rarities, was preserved by my father, I am enabled to treat the reader with a selection of a dozen of its specimens, which may be considered, by those who are not fond of long digressions, quite enough.

Yesterday Dr. Pretyman preached at St. James's—
And perform'd it with ease in less than sixteen minutes.

The sword of state was carried—
Before Sir John Fielding, and committed to Newgate.

There was a numerous and brilliant Court—
A down-look, and a cast with one eye.

Several changes are talked of at Court—
Consisting of 9050 triple bob-majors.

Removed to Marybone, for the benefit of the air—
The City and Liberties of Westminster.

We hear a treaty of marriage is concluded—
For 50*l*. a-side, between the noted Dyer, and the famous Naylor.

Dr. Salamander will, by her Majesty's command, undertake a voyage round—
The head-dress of the present month.

Sunday night, many noble families were alarmed—
By the constable of the watch, who apprehended them at cards.

He has just opened an house for inoculation—
N.B.—Be careful you have the right sort.

Wanted, a genteel place under Government—
It is of great use to those who speak in public.

Wanted, to take care of an elderly gentlewoman—
An active young man just come from the country.

Notice is hereby given—
And no notice taken.

An assertion has been credited by many persons, that Goldsmith was not the author of the Postscript now printed with his poem entitled 'Retaliation', but that it was written by Caleb Whitefoord, whom it celebrates, and who now and then endeavoured to imitate his manner. It may be true that the lines were conveyed to the editor of the fifth edition by one of their mutual friends, and that they were not produced before the Doctor's death; but certainly the length of praise bestowed upon Whitefoord in the Postscript, has been considered unconscionably long as well as uncommonly great, especially for a man whose qualifications could never rank him with Burke or Reynolds. The author of 'Retaliation', however, thought proper to confine his praise of those immortal men, to a considerably less number than *eighteen lines*.

The late Charles Smith, Painter to the Great Mogul, favoured me, through my worthy friend Thomas Gilliland, Esq.[1] with a letter which he received from his uncle, Caleb Whitefoord, who was particularly anxious to witness his nephew's advancement; and as it is in some instances connected with the Arts, I shall here introduce a copy of it, leaving out two or three paragraphs of a private family nature.

DEAR CHARLES,

I have intended to write to you for for several days past, but have delayed it in expectation of a frank, which I have got at last.

I received your Nymph with the Infant Bacchus and a Satyr, which I think a very pretty picture. I also asked some Royal Academicians to view it, viz. Northcote, Cosway, &c. who approved of it much: it is well composed, and beautifully coloured; but the hangmen at the Exhibition have not hung it in a conspicuous situation; it is placed in the ante-room, and pretty high; but they have done the same with two very pretty pictures of the President

[1] This gentleman is author of the celebrated pamphlet of 'Diamond cut Diamond', and, I believe, about sixteen or seventeen others in defence and support of the English government.

himself, so you must not complain.——I have been proceeding in my canvass for the Associateship, and have great hopes of success: indeed it is a thing I have much at heart, for I wish much to see you a Royal Academician. Sir Joshua's pictures are *not* to be sold *this* year; but, in a few days Sir Thomas Dundas's collection is to come under Greenwood's hammer. What a pity it is that we are not rich!

I am now completing the arrangement of the Octagon-room;[1] but my Correggio is too fine to hang up. It is put into a handsome mahogany case, and kept under lock and key.

Mr. Barry has been to see it, and declares it to be the most capital picture he had ever beheld; and I brought it at a public sale for 9*l*. 9*s*.

I am, with compliments to Sir John,[2]
Dear Charles, yours, &c.
C. WHITEFOORD.

Since your worship has been gone, I have taken mightily to the young kitten: she is a very clever kit-cat, and I have taken some pains about her education; she skips about like a monkey, and sits up like a Christian.

---

1 This Octagon-room, with an upper light, one of a suite in the Adelphi, built purposely for him by his friend Adam, was considered by Mr. Christie of so excellent a shape for the exhibition of pictures, that he adopted it when he fitted up his great room in King-street, St. James's-square; so that all pictures consigned to him for public sale are sure of receiving an equally good light. The advantage derived from the octagonal shape is, that pictures are not continued up to the corners, as they most commonly are in a square room, where it is impossible to stand to view them to that advantage under which they are seen when the corners of a square are brought out to form the octagon.

2 Sir John Macpherson, who had been Governor of Bengal, and to whom Charles Smith dedicated a musical entertainment in two acts, entitled 'A Trip to Bengal'; to which a portrait of the author is prefixed, engraved by S. W. Reynolds, from a picture painted by himself. This entertainment, consisting of fifty-two pages, was printed, in 1802, for J. Ridgway, and Black and Parry, London. At the end is a Glossary of Hindoostanee words used in the work.

In closing these notices of Mrs. Nollekens, I must not forget to mention her servant, Mary Fairy. Her features, though tolerably handsome, were not equal to her figure; her arms were excellent; but it is pretty well known that her master was rather afraid of her; since she scolded him as well as Mrs. Nollekens, and indeed was frequently so rude to his visitors, that her conduct appeared more like an overbearing mistress of a mansion than a dependent. Mr. Joseph, an Associate of the Royal Academy, when painting the portrait of the Hon. Mr. Perceval from Mr. Nollekens's mask, taken from that gentleman's face after death, happened once to mention Mary Fairy in the presence of Mrs. Nollekens, who with her precision of emphasis said, 'Yes, Sir; she is Mr. Nollekens's Venus, Sir.' Mrs. Nollekens was at this time recollecting, with tears in her eyes, that she had herself in former days been flattered with that appellation from no less a character than the Marquis of Rockingham, who observed to Mr. Nollekens, soon after his marriage, 'Ah, Nollekens, we now see where you get your Venuses.'

One morning, when a fifer and drummer were row-de-dowing to a newly-married couple at the Sun and Horse-shoe at the opposite house to Nollekens's, she observed that her father Mr. Welch used to say that fifing-boys were first introduced in the army by the Culloden Duke of Cumberland.[1]

Mrs. Nollekens's female acquaintances were not all equally well or wisely selected; some of them having been opera-singers, and others servants to their husbands, or in some instances worse. Upon this egregious want of common decorum, her late steady, amiable, and universally-respected friend, Mrs. Carter, would now and then rate her roundly; particularly when she perceived her to pay increasing attention to

[1] I do not recollect an earlier representation of a fifing-boy than that introduced by Hogarth in his picture of the March to Finchley.

ladies for whom the world never cared, nor even spoke till after their marriage. 'You can clearly see,' she observed one day during a sale of choice china at Christie's, 'that duck-footed woman, your "dear friend", as you have just been pleased to call her, is not at all noticed by the wives of those gentlemen to whom her husband is known. They all shun her as they would a wife who had been made over to her husband with what her former possessor considered a *handsome consideration*. Indeed, my old friend, you should at all events be a little more cautious in your epithets, or you will at last, like her, pass unnoticed.' The truth was, that Mrs. Carter began to perceive, that whenever persons of rank noticed Mrs. Nollekens, it was only with the distant condescension of 'I hope Mr. Nollekens is well?'

Having given the reader a sufficient number of anecdotes concerning the manners and peculiarities of Mrs. Nollekens, the Pekuah[1] of Doctor Johnson's Rasselas, who will always retain a lasting seat among my most pleasant recollections, I come now to speak of her death; long previously to which, her emaciated frame had existed without the use of its limbs. She was at length relieved from her sufferings in the drawing-room of her husband's house, No. 9, Mortimer-street, on the 17th of August, 1817, in the seventy-fourth year of her age, and was interred in the public vault under Paddington church, on the 25th of the same month. The funeral was handsome. There

[1] A short time before Mrs. Nollekens's death, a gentleman, in looking round Nollekens's studio, inquired after her health, observing that he had not seen her for some time. 'Oh!' answered the artist, 'she's bad, very bad; she's now in bed. There's a mould of her spine down in that corner; see how crooked it is.' Little did Pekuah think, when her elegantly-formed figure was attired in her wedding-dress, that her admiring husband would one day display a cast of her deformed spine.

were eleven mourners; namely, Mr. Nollekens, and Mr. Peck of the Temple, (one of his two cousins,) Mr. Woodcock, (one of Mrs. Nollekens's cousins,) Mr. John Taylor, (Frank Hayman's only surviving pupil,) Mr. Joseph Bonomi, (Mr. Nollekens's pupil,) Mr. Gahagan, (one of his principal carvers,) &c.

Mrs. Nollekens, who was fond of using lofty sentences, even upon the most trifling occasions, in her Will styled her husband 'The sun of my life'. Upon this expression, a literary man, who at that time was slightly known to Mr. Nollekens, passed many compliments; though, as a reader, he might have known that the idea was borrowed from old Fuller, who says, when speaking of a female who had been kind to him in sickness, 'She was the medicine of my life.'

Upon the death of Mrs. Nollekens, her husband, who had received the condolence of Mrs. Zoffany, Mrs. Lloyd, and other steady old friends, conducted himself with all possible dolefulness and customary propriety, pacing his room up and down with his hands in his pockets, and for a time, I really believe, felt the want of her company, deplorable as it had been for the last three years. However, many ladies stoutly maintain an opinion, that very few gentlemen die of grief for their departed wives; and that short and not very distant removals to a lively prospect where new faces may be seen, generally bring about a change in the worldly affairs of men. And, as if he had been for too long a time what is usually denominated 'hen-pecked', Mr. Nollekens soon sported two mould-candles instead of one; took wine oftener; sat up later; laid in bed longer; and would, though he made no change whatever in his coarse manner of feeding, frequently ask his morning visitor to dine with him: and I have been informed that the late Rev. Thomas Kerrich, Principal Librarian of the University Library of Cambridge, to my very great astonishment, had stomach enough to partake of one of his repasts. As for my part, his viands were so dirtily cooked with half-melted butter, mountains high of flour, and his habits of eating so filthy, that he never could prevail upon me to sicken myself at any one of his feasts.

He continued now and then to amuse himself with his modelling-clay, and frequently gave tea and other entertainments to some one of his old models, who generally left his house a bank-note or two richer than they arrived. Indeed, so stupidly childish was he at times, that one of his Venuses, who had grown old in her practices, coaxed him out of ten pounds to enable her to make him a plum-pudding; and he grew so luxuriantly brilliant in his ideas of morning pleasures, that he would frequently, on a Sunday particularly, order a hackney-coach to be sent for, and take Taylor, Bonomi, Goblet, and sometimes his neighbour, the publican's wife from the 'Sun and Horse-shoe', a ride out of town of about ten or twelve miles before dinner. Now and then, however, in consequence of his neglecting his former cautious custom of bargaining for the fare before he started, he had a dispute with the coachman, on his return, as to the exact distance, to the no small amusement of Bronze and his brawny old Scotch nurse, a woman whose blotchy skin and dirty habits even Nollekens declared to be most obnoxious to his feelings, and wretchedly nasty in her mode of dressing his victuals.

I must freely declare, that, in some respects, Nollekens, aged as he was, attempted to practise the usual method of renovation of some of that species of widowers, who have not the least inclination whatever to follow their wives too hastily. Mrs. Nollekens had left him with his handsome maid, who became possessed of her mistress's wardrobe, which she quickly sold and cut up to her advantage. Her common name of Mary soon received the adjunct of Pretty from her kind master himself, who seldom took the liberty of addressing her without it. As it soon appeared, however, that 'pretty Mary', who had an eye to her master's disengaged hand, took upon herself mightily, and used her master rather roughly, she was one day very properly, though unceremoniously, put out of the house, before her schemes were brought to perfection.

I must not, however, quit Mrs. Nollekens without mentioning some circumstances of her survivor, Mrs. Lloyd. She now and then gave the retort-courteous to Mrs. Paradice, a woman she detested, and who once allowed her passion to overpower her good sense, of which in general she had a pretty good share; which overflowing of her gall took place at Mrs. Nollekens's table, when Doctor Johnson was present. Mrs. Paradice's figure was so neat and small, that Mrs. Lloyd called her a sylph. 'Better to be so,' rejoined Mrs. P. 'than to be as dull-looking and blind as a mole.'—'Mole as I am,' said Mrs. Lloyd, 'I never added to the weight of Paul Jodrell's phaeton.'—'Fie! fie! my dears,' exclaimed the Doctor, 'no sparring; off with your mufflers, and fight it fairly out!' At this time, Miss Welch, who communicated this anecdote to me, frowned at Mrs. Nollekens for suffering her house to be made the seat of discord; and that lady particularly requested Mrs. Paradice, for whom she entertained no high respect, to suspend the altercation, adding that such remarks were not altogether lady-like. Mrs. Lloyd, though she was pretty honest in what she at any time said, continued to bear no ill-will towards her little antagonist, as will appear by the following extract of a letter which she wrote to Mr. West in 1805.

'I am glad that our old acquaintance, Mrs. Paradice, got safe to America. Although she and I used to say uncivil things sometimes to each other, I should have been sorry any harm had happened to her, as I think she has many worthy qualities; in consideration of which, when she is out of my sight I like her very well, and can think of her with commiseration.'

Mrs. Lloyd was so near-sighted, that her nose, when she was painting, was within an inch of the canvas; and it is astonishing, with such an infirmity, about which Mrs. Paradice exposed herself by ignorantly comparing her to a mole, that she could display such harmony in her performances. Her pictures of flowers, for which she was so deservedly famed, possess a tasteful elegance of composition, a clearness of colouring, and, in most instances, exquisite finishing. She was remarkably choice in the colour she used, preferring ultramarine upon all occasions, wherever blue was required. My worthy friend, Mr. Sharp, the Painter of 'The King, God bless him!' purchased Mrs. Lloyd's colour-box, in which he found a curious colour twisted up in one of Garrick's playbills, which, with his usual good-nature, he gave to me. This bill is valuable for more points than one; as the play which it announced was to be performed on the 7th of May, for the benefit of the poor debtors in the Marshalsea Prison: and as it has been considered a great curiosity by many of the numerous play-bill collectors to whom it has been shown, I shall here insert a copy of it.

FOR THE BENEFIT OF THE PRISONERS

Confined for Debt in the Marshalsea Prison, Southwark.

(Being their first application of this kind.)

THEATRE ROYAL, in *Drury-Lane*,

On *Monday* next, being the 7th of *May*,

Will be presented a Comedy, called,

THE PROVOKED WIFE

The part of Sir John Brute, to be performed by Mr. GARRICK.

Constant, by Mr. Havard.
Heartfree, by Mr. Palmer.
Col. Bully (with proper Songs), by Mr. Beard.
Razor, by Mr. Yates.
Lord Rake, by Mr. Blakes.

Lady Fanciful, by Mrs. CLIVE.
Belinda, by Mrs. Willoughby,
Mademoiselle, by Mrs. Green.
And the part of *Lady Brute*, to be performed by
Mrs. PRITCHARD.

With Dancing,
By Mons. Grandchamps, Mad. Auretti, Mr. Mathews, &c.

To which will be added a Farce, called,
DUKE AND NO DUKE.

The part of *Trappolin* to be performed
by Mr. WOODWARD.

Boxes 5*s*. Pit 3*s*. First Gallery 2*s*. Upper Gallery 1*s*.

Tickets to be had at the *Marshalsea Prison, Southwark*, and of Mr. Hobson, at the Stage-door, of whom places may be taken.

On *Tuesday* next, *Love's Last Shift*. For the Benefit of Mr. *Dunbar*, Mr. *Jones*, Mr. *Atkinson*, Mr. *Prichard*, and Mr. *Bride*.

Mrs. Mary Lloyd leaving a Will which she wrote herself, and in which appear the names both of Mr. and Mrs. Nollekens, Mrs. Benjamin West, with her usual kindness, has enabled me to lay the following copy before the reader.

'Written in the year one thousand eight hundred and one.

'This is the last Will and Testament of me, Mary Lloyd, widow of the late Hugh Lloyd, Esq. I am now residing in John-street, in the Parish of St. Pancras, in the County of Middlesex. First, I direct that all my just debts, funeral expenses, and the charges of the Probate of this my Will, shall be paid by my Executors hereinafter named. I give and bequeath unto Joseph Nollekens, Esq. of Mortimer-street, and Joseph Moser, Esq. of Princes-street, Spitalfields, and the survivor, and the executors, administrators, or assigns of such survivor, all my money in the public funds called the Long Annuities, upon trust that they the said Joseph Nollekens and the said Joseph Moser, or the survivor of them, or the executors, administrators, or assigns of such survivor of them, shall and do, during the natural life of my cousin Elizabeth Graham, the wife of John Graham, pay and apply out of the interest or dividends in the Long Annuities, forty pounds every year to her use; and I direct that the said Elizabeth Graham shall receive the dividends herself at the Bank; and I direct that the said Elizabeth receive the forty pounds a year, free and clear of and from all tax, charge, and deductions whatever; and after the decease of the aforesaid Elizabeth Graham, I direct that the eight hundred pounds, from which the dividends of forty pounds were paid, shall be divided amongst the children of the said Elizabeth in equal shares, if she should not make a will; but if she should make a will in favour of any child or children, the eight hundred pounds, after her decease, shall be divided according to such will; but the money must not be willed by the said Elizabeth Graham to any person or persons except her children, unless she should survive them all; in that case, she may give the eight hundred pounds to whom she pleases after her decease; and I direct that the said Elizabeth Graham shall not make over to any one person or persons the beforenamed dividends of forty pounds per year, but always receive the interest herself of the eight hundred pounds. I give and bequeath to my dear friend Mary Nollekens, the wife of Joseph Nollekens, fifty pounds, to be transferred to her out of the Long Annuities. I give and bequeath to Juliet Moser, the wife of Joseph Moser, fifty pounds, to be transferred to her out of the Long Annuities. I give and bequeath to John Graham, husband of Elizabeth Graham, fifty pounds, to be transferred to him out of the Long Annuities. I give and bequeath to Conradt Habbick, of Schafhausen, the nephew of my father George Michel Moser, twenty guineas; if he should be dead, the money to be divided among my executors. I give and bequeath to my cousin Rachel Schewier, the wife of Jacques Schewier, late residing at Neuwied, twenty guineas. If the said Rachel Schewier should be dead, I direct the twenty guineas to be paid to her son; if he should be dead, I give it to my executors. I give and bequeath to Elizabeth West, wife of Benjamin West, Esq. fifty pounds, to be transferred to her out of the Long Annuities. I give and bequeath to George Panbury the Elder, twenty guineas. I give my silver teapot, and my silver caddy, and silver milk-ewer, to Charlotte Harward, the wife of Charles Harward, Esq. with my best wishes for her prosperity. I give and bequeath to Maria Cosway, the wife of Richard Cosway, twenty guineas for a ring. I desire that my drawings, prints, and books of prints, may be divided between Benjamin West, Esq. and Joseph Nollekens, Esq. and that they may make them into two parcels, and draw lots for them. I desire that Richard Cosway, Esq. may choose any three pictures he pleases. I give to Francis Ellis, daughter of Hugh Ellis, Esq. of Carnarvon, my ring with my late husband's hair; it is set round with diamonds; and twenty guineas. To the servant who lives with me at the time of my death I give ten pounds.

'The residue of my fortune of every kind I give to my cousin Joseph Moser, Esq.

'As I have written the above with my own hand, I am informed a witness is not required; and I do constitute, nominate, and appoint the aforesaid Joseph Nollekens and Joseph Moser executors of this my last will.

'MARY LLOYD.
22d Aug. 1801.

'I request to be buried in the same grave with my late husband Hugh Lloyd, Esq. if I should die in this country.

'MARY LLOYD.'[1]

Mrs. Lloyd, who was much respected by the Royal Family, was visited by the late Queen Charlotte; and had also the honour to receive the following letter from her Royal Highness the Princess Elizabeth:—

MY DEAR MRS. LLOYD,

To show you that though out of sight you are not out of mind, I send you a very quiet, sober-coloured gown, to show you that you have a sincere and old friend in

ELIZA.[2]

Jan. 20th.

Mrs. Lloyd died at ten o'clock on Sunday morning, May 2nd, 1819; in the front second-floor room of her lodgings, No. 21, Upper Thornhaugh-street, Totten-

---

[1] Mrs. Lloyd, when Miss Moser, obtained the following premiums from the Society of Arts:—

In 1758, for a drawing, 5*l* 5*s*.
In 1759, for a ditto 5*l*. 5*s*.

[2] The original is in the possession of Mrs. Nichols, who kindly permitted me to copy it.

ham-court-road; and was buried on the 10th of the same month at Kensington, in the grave of her husband, according to her request.

Mr. Nollekens was not very particular as to the material he used to render his skin clean. Whenever he had been modelling, a small bit of clay commonly answered the purpose, and after shaving, the barber's cloth, upon which a variety of customers had already wiped themselves, was considered both convenient and economical.

He took snuff, but seldom used his handkerchief; and the custom of the common drovers was too often practised by him to need the assistance of that truly cleanly article necessary upon all occasions. By long experience he was convinced that employing the common shoe-cleaner was by far the cheapest mode, for that by standing over him when he was putting on the blacking to the brush, he had a penny-worth for his halfpenny; so that when he wanted to go out two days running, the quantity of blacking enabled him, with a little moisture applied to his own shiner, to make them do. He chewed tobacco, it mattered not to him whether shag or pig-tail; and for the most part his supply was gratuitous by his sawyer or his polisher, who both kept in his good opinion by continuing the habit of chewing it, and they both were equally eager to allow their polished-iron box to shine in the sun whenever he came to converse with them, either upon the clearness or softness of the stone upon which they were engaged.

Snuff was a luxury he at all times expected to find in the studio, and was highly pleased that the generality of its takers preferred rappee; and also that they confined their custom to the same shop, Simpson's in Princes-street, as the varieties of manufacture were apt to render his nose sore. But it was very remarkable, that at one time when he was an extensive snuff-taker, he would put up with an early pinch of

Scotch from a North Briton, who industriously made seven days in the week by attending an hour earlier, and staying an hour later than the rest of his workmen. Nollekens certainly kept a box, but then it was very often in his other coat-pocket, an apology frequently made when he partook of that refreshment at the expense of another.

If any one of his labourers found a feather, and tied it to the string of the oil-bottle, to enable Nollekens to oil the locks, bars, bolts, and hinges of the doors, without wasting the oil upon a worn-out quill, he was delighted beyond measure. The man who put it there was sure to be questioned as to the place he found it in; and if he happened to say Oxford-market, Nollekens exulted upon reflecting that he stood some chance of having his sixpennyworth for the money the butchers exacted of him for exhibiting to him their house of snow.

Nollekens had no wish to visit those gardens of Damascus at Kensington, shaded by lofty trees and adorned by fragrant shrubs, under whose refreshing shades he might have enjoyed the cooling breezes from the waters. The place in which he most delighted was Primrose-hill, where he was to be seen in the summer season, either fagging up or running down its heated declivities, almost destitute of even bramble or brier. Often have I been nearly scorched to death when walking with him, as he invariably gave preference to the sunny side of the street; while his dog Cerberus, by way of a treat, walked in the shade.

John Barnard, Esq. nicknamed Jacky Barnard, who was very fond of showing his collection of Italian drawings, expressed surprise that Mr. Nollekens did not pay a sufficient attention to them. 'Yes, I do,' replied he; 'but I saw many of them at Jenkins's at Rome, while the man was making them for my friend Crone, the Artist, one of your agents.' This so offended Mr. Barnard, who piqued himself upon his judgment, that he scratched Nollekens out of his will.

Walking with Mr. Nollekens to see Mr. Grignon's pictures, consigned to him from Rome by his brother Charles, just as we were going up to his door, No. 10, Great Russell-street, Covent-garden, Mr. Nollekens regretted that he had left home without putting the Jernigan medal into his pocket, as Mr. Grignon had promised to give him some account of it.

What information Mr. Nollekens obtained, I know not; but I find that in one of Mr. Grignon's interesting letters to me, upon my Covent-garden collections, he mentions it in the following words:

'Henry Jernigan was a Silversmith and Roman Catholic banker, residing in London, and had offices in Jermyn-street and Great Russell-street, and in the house in which I now reside. He had a lottery for jewellery, which he could not dispose of,[1] and to those persons who were unfortunate, he presented medals. The number of his tickets amounted to 30,000, at seven or ten shillings each.'

Jernigan died October 8, 1761, was buried in the churchyard of St. Paul, Covent-garden, and upon his tombstone are the following lines by Aaron Hill:

All that *accomplished body* lends mankind,
From earth receiving, he *to earth* resign'd.
All that e'er graced a soul, from *Heaven* he drew,
And took back with him, as an angel's due.

'You must sometimes be much annoyed,' observed a lady, addressing herself to Mr. Nollekens, 'by the ridiculous remarks made by your sitters and their flattering friends, after you have produced a good likeness.'—'No, Ma'am, I never allow any body to fret me. I tell 'em all, "If you don't like it, don't take it."' This may be done by an artist who is, what is usually termed 'tiled in'; but the dependent man is sometimes known to submit to observations, as the witty Northcote has stated, even from 'nursery maids, both wet and dry'.[2]

[1] A large cistern of silver was the grand prize.

[2] This observation occurs in a paper addressed to Prince

Notwithstanding the professed independence of Nollekens, however, he not unfrequently has been known to appear to comply with the wishes of his employers, who in most instances consider they have an unequivocal right to maintain their ignorant opinions for articles bespoken by them, and for which they are to give cheques; and so they certainly have, if they confine their observations to their household furniture. But I must declare, that persons of real taste and good sense are at all times better pleased with a work of art, that has emanated entirely from the mind of a talented man, who has deeply studied his subject. Nollekens, I was about to observe, at times, like many other Sculptors, played off the old practice, by pretending to cut away whenever the employer pronounced a lip too pouting, an eye too crow-footed, or a brow too severe.[1]

Nollekens observed one morning, after he had attended Sir Joshua's Lecture at the Royal Academy the preceding evening, that he believed all the deformed students in the Academy had assembled together upon one spot, while waiting the opening of the Lecture-room, since he had noticed Ryley, Flaxman, the two Edwards's, Crone, and Feary.

Whenever Nollekens was asked, in the presence of his wife, if he had any family, she would answer, pointing to his figures, 'A very great family, Sir; all these are Mr. Nollekens's children; and as they behave so well, and never make a noise, they shall be his repre-

Hoare, dated June 20, 1807, in an entertaining work edited by that gentleman, entitled 'The Artist'.

[1] This deception of cutting away is effected by the help of a little stone-dust, which the sculptor allows to fall gradually from his hand every time he strikes his chisel or moves his rasp, until the *critic* cries, 'Stop! stop! don't cut away too much, that will do admirably well. Now, don't you see, my dear Sir, how wonderfully that has improved it?' See Duppa's Life of Michel Angelo Buonarroti.

sentatives,' at the same time making a most formal curtsey to Mr. Nollekens.

He seldom wrote long letters: Lady Newborough was one of the most favoured of his friends. To her he wrote long epistles; and so '*unbosomed himself*', as he called it, by offering his advice about her domestic concerns, that she was pleased, when she wrote in reply, to call him her father.

At the commencement of the French Revolution, when such immense numbers of Priests threw themselves upon the hospitality of this country, Nollekens was highly indignant at the great quantity of bread they consumed. 'Why, do you know, now,' said he, 'there's one of 'em living next door but one to me, that eats two whole quartern loaves a-day to his own share! and I am sure the fellow's body could not be bigger, if he was to eat up his blanket.'

Whenever Nollekens crossed the water, he always carried the money the waterman was to have for his fare, in his mouth: he kept it between his teeth, not in imitation of Egyptian mummies, whose mouths held a piece of gold to pay old Charon his fare, but in order that he might not, in getting out of the boat, lose his money by taking more out than he wanted.

He never suffered his tenants to remain long after their rents were due, without reminding them how matters stood; and when he applied by letters, he stated that a quarter's rent was due on the 10th of November last, for which he requested payment to be made on or before Thursday next, by twelve o'clock at noon, having occasion for a sum of money. Of late years, however, in consequence of his having so many houses, he employed an agent to collect for him, so that, at all events, his bodily fatigue was lessened.

Mr. Browne,[1] one of Nolleken's old friends, after

[1] The late Mr. Browne was father to George Howe Browne, Esq. the highly-respected Secretary to the Westminster Fire-Office.

having received repeated invitations to 'step in and take pot-luck with him,' one day took him at his word. The Sculptor apologized for his entertainment, by saying, that as it was Friday, Mrs. Nollekens had proposed to take fish with him, so that they had bought a few sprats, of which he was wiping some in a dish, whilst she was turning others on the gridiron.

One day, when Mr. Nollekens was walking in Cavendish-square, attended by his man Dodimy, he desired him to take up some sop which a boy had just thrown out of a beer-pot, observing that it would make a nice dinner for his dog Cerberus. 'Lord, Sir! I take it up!' exclaimed Dodimy, 'what! in the sight of your friends, Lord Besborough and Lord Brownlow? See Sir, there's Mr. Shee looking down at you. No, Sir, I would not do it, if you were even to *scratch me*!'[1]

As I have given so many instances of the meanness of the wealthy Sculptor, I should feel very considerable regret, if I omitted to record any act of his, which bears the least appearance of liberality; and it gives me pleasure to say, that I have been assured by Mr. Turner, the Royal Academician, that when he solicited Mr. Nollekens for his subscription to 'The Artists' Fund', he enquired how much he wanted from him; 'Only a guinea,' was the answer; upon which the Sculptor immediately opened a table-drawer, and gave Mr. Turner *thirty guineas*, saying, 'There, take that.' Mr. Bailey, the Royal Academician, was also equally surprised, when he applied to him on behalf of 'The Artists' Society', to which he is a subscriber.—And yet this man was continually exercising his thoughts to devise the cheapest meal he could pos-

[1] Whenever Dodimy displeased his master, he commonly threatened to *scratch him*, meaning out of his will, which he finally did, and gave his intended annuity of 30*l*. to his principal assistant, Mr. Goblet, *as the long promised provision for himself and family!*

sibly take; and has been seen disputing with a half-starved and slip-shod cobbler, because he refused to put a few more nails in his shoes, having entered into an agreement to pay him the sum of twopence for their mending!

As a piece of topographical gossip relative to an old house, the fame of which has been perpetuated in 'The Spectator', I shall close the present chapter with the following information touching the renowned shop of 'Bat Pidgeon'.

Mr. Nollekens informed me, that his mother took her children to have their hair cut at the 'Three Pigeons', in the Strand; and having heard my friend Mr. Sheldrake state that that shop had been the one formerly kept by the famous Bat Pigeon, I begged of him to favour me with what he knew about it, and the following letter is the result of my enquiry:—

January 18th, 1823.

DEAR SIR,

I WELL remember Bat Pidgeon's house in the Strand; it was nearly opposite Norfolk-street. It bore a sign of three Pigeons, underneath which was written 'Bat Pidgeon'; beneath which was another inscription, 'late Bat Pidgeon'.

Since our conversation, I have examined the spot; the original brickwork of the house is there, but the shop front has been modernized. The house is now numbered 277, and is inhabited by Mr. Wilson, manufacturer of ornamental hair, &c. I talked with Mr. Wilson, who has no knowledge of his ancestors, if I may so call them, but said he well knows that his house bore the sign of 'The Three Pigeons'. I remember them and the inscriptions many years of my early life, long after the year 1770, but I cannot recollect the names of Bat's successors.

I enclose Mr. Wilson's card, which will lead you to the house.

I am, dear Sir,
Yours sincerely,
T. SHELDRAKE.

J. T. Smith, Esq.

CHAPTER XIII

Mr. Nollekens's Confessor.—Description of the Sculptor's house, paintings, &c.—His indifference towards religion, and sacred subjects in Art.—Decoration of churches, and exhibition of Westminster Abbey.—Mr. Nollekens and Sir William Staines.—Anecdotes of Biaggio Rebecca.—The Pond family.—Anthony Pasquin.—Canal excursions.—Mrs. Lobb and living models.—Mr. Nollekens's visit to the British Museum.—Recollections of his manners, &c.—Eccentricity in persons of eminent talent.—The advantages of greatness.—Mr. Nollekens and his patrons and visitors.

Mr. Nollekens was in possession of a set of those extremely rare engravings, from the Aretin subjects, so often mentioned by print-collectors; but it so happened, as he was glancing at them one day, that his Confessor came in, who insisted upon their being put into the fire, before he would give him absolution. I once saw them; and he lent them to Cosway, to make tracings from them. However, this loan Cosway stoutly denied, which when Nollekens heard, he exclaimed, 'He's a d—d liar! that every body knows; and I know this, that I could hardly get them back again out of his hands.' Upon Nollekens being asked how he, as an artist, could make up his mind to burn them, he answered, 'The priest made me do it:' and he was now and then seen to shed tears for what he called his folly. He was frequently questioned thus: 'Where did you get them, Sir? whose were they?' His answer was, 'I brought them all the way from Rome.'

The rigid economy and eccentricity of Mr. Nollekens were scarcely more remarkable in his person and manners, than in his dwelling; of which I shall now give the reader a short description. The kitchen was paved with odd bits of stone, close to the dust-hole, which was infested with rats; the drains had long been choked up; and the windows were glazed with glass of a smoky greenish hue, having all the cracked panes carefully puttied. The shelves contained only a bare change of dishes and plates, knives and forks just enough, and those odd ones, the handles of which had undergone a 'sea-change', from a gay pea-green tint, to the yellow tone visible in an overgrown cucumber. No Flanders-brick was ever used to them; a piece of true English was preferred, and brought to Bronze from Marylebone-fields by her master; nor was the sink often stopped with tea-leaves, since they were carefully saved to sprinkle the best carpet, to lay the dust, before it was swept. The remainder of the furniture consisted of a flat-candlestick, with a saveall; but, for snuffers, Bronze used her scissors, or indeed, upon most occasions, her fingers. Of the dining and sitting-parlour, the description will be familiar to many of the most elegant, witty, and noble characters of the country, who have been sitters for their busts to Mr. Nollekens.

That which we will call the dining, sitting, and sitter's parlour, was the corner room, which had two windows looking south, the entrance to it being on the right-hand in the passage from the street-door in Mortimer-street. The visitors will recollect, that over the chimney-piece there was a three-quarter portrait of the Sculptor himself, with a modelling-tool in his hand, leaning with his right elbow upon the bust of the Hon. Charles James Fox, the execution of which brought him both reputation and profit.

The Artist's modelling-stool was placed near the street-door window, and the sitter's chair nearer the door; whilst facing the window, there were several small models of Venus upon the chimney-piece, over which, and under his own portrait, hung three miniatures, one being of Sir Joshua Reynolds, by Edridge, taken from the picture in the club-room in the Thatched-house Tavern, St. James's-street. The other two were of Mrs. Nollekens and Miss Welch, painted by Smart, all of which were presented by the artists. Between the chimney and the corner window, hung two beautiful impressions, one of Michel Angelo's Last Judgment, by Martin Rota, and the other, Raffaelle's St. Cecilia, by Marc-Antonio, both from the Blackburn Collection. On the closet-door was suspended a beautiful picture of flowers, by Deheim, which had been the property of Miss Moser, and for which Mr. Nollekens said he gave her forty guineas; and nearer the window hung a drawing of Cupid and Psyche, by Tresham, with another portrait of Nollekens, drawn by Smart. This drawing is now in the possession of Mr. Taylor, to whom Mr. Nollekens had formerly promised it. For many years, two pieces of old green canvas were festooned at the lower parts of the windows for blinds; but of late, a pretty good glass was placed against the pier. On the west side of the parlour, from the window to the north of the room, hung Mr. Taylor's drawing of Mr. Pitt's statue, in a black frame, which almost destroyed its effect; and over it were two pictures, one of Nymphs, by 'Old Nollekens', the other was of a dog, by Stubbs. Under these, appeared the print of Three Marys, after Carracci; and close in the corner by the window, upon a bracket, was placed a small copy of Raffaelle's model of Jonah; whilst between the door and the north end was a small picture with sheep, by Bourgeois: and at the north end, also upon a bracket, stood a small copy of Michel Angelo's figure of Moses.[1] On the north side of the room hung two landscapes, drawn and presented by Gainsborough; two drawings by Zoffany, also presentations; a drawing, by Mr. Taylor, of Mr. Nollekens's monument to the memory of Mrs. Howard, of Corby, and a drawing from Cipriani, were sus-

[1] Casts of the magnificent originals of these statues are now exhibiting by Mr. Day, in the Egyptian-hall, Piccadilly.

pended against the door. Near these were a picture of flowers, by Mrs. Lloyd, and a portrait of Mr. Welch, by Brompton; beside which, hung Barry's picture of the Origin of Music. On each side of the chimney was a drawing by Paul Sandby; and close to the fire-place, though rather out of sight, hung two bits of slate dangling upon a nail, on which Mr. and Mrs. Nollekens kept their separate memoranda of the day's expenditure; for they kept distinct accounts against each other, as to letters, porters employed, or things purchased for the house, &c. Near the corner window was a closet, in which were placed candles—though, as for soap, Bronze declared the house had never known any for forty years,—and a few preserves, pickles, or other little presents from persons who had great expectations. Caleb Whitefoord's wine also found a safe depository in this closet, together with an uncut loaf, or a bit of fresh-butter, a little scalded milk, a paper containing the academic nutmegs, fragments of string, and old screws and nails, which were picked up as things that might be wanted some time or other.

The drawing-room contained a three-quarter portrait of Mrs. Nollekens, as Innocence with a Dove, painted by her friend Angelica Kauffmann; on the chimney-piece were several models, particularly the one of Mercury,[1] for which I was standing, when Mr. Taylor smelt the leg of pork. There were also three landscapes, by Wilson, two of which had been painted for Mr. Welch, and came to Mrs. Nollekens at the death of her sister; a picture by West; four friezes by Bartolozzi, after Cipriani; and a drawing by Clarisseau, which hung against the door. This room was decorated with some of the furniture of Mrs. Nollekens's mother. Mr. Welch's library, which also descended to Mrs. Nollekens, was closely locked up in a

[1] This was promised me by Mr. Nollekens; however, I purchased it at the sale of his property.

small back-room, where she had deposited eleven hundred guineas. They were accumulated after the one and two pound notes were issued; for Mrs. Nollekens, not trusting in the safety of paper currency, prevailed upon most of her tenants to pay her in gold; which request she walked all the way to Mr. Alderman Combe's brewhouse to make, as to the payment of a house rented of her by that firm in Drury-lane. These guineas she would look over pretty often, and weigh in her hands against each other, partly from the enjoyment she felt in counting her wealth, and partly to discover if any one had been deceiving her with coin short of weight. Her feeling of delight in this occupation is not unhappily expressed in the following lines:

> As these alternate poising in each hand,
> He cries, 'This doth—no—no—this weigheth most
> By half a grain or so; and half a grain
> Of gold is something worth:—I'd buy me scales,
> But scales cost *money*; so, I *must* do without 'em.'

I very much fear that Mr. Nollekens had no innate love of religion, nor ever dedicated much time to devotion. He was a Roman Catholic, because his father had died in that faith; but his attendance at Warwick-street Chapel, and subsequently at the one in Sutton-street, Soho-square, was confined, I am sorry to say, to fine Sunday mornings: his regard to Christianity, on a rainy day, never extended beyond his own threshold; nor was he, according to Bronze's assertion, ever known to be in private meditation. He now and then, however, according to the custom of an observant Catholic, received visits from a Priest, who confessed him, and gave him absolution. He was never known to give money to benefit the Roman Church; but at times he has certainly been seen to extend his charity to a mendicant at the door of the chapel; who cunningly moved him by soliciting alms in the name of Saint Francis, the favourite Saint of Antwerp, the native city of his father.

In the course of my long acquaintance with his pursuits in Art, I never saw a single model by his hand of Our Saviour, the Virgin Mary, nor even St. Francis; nor do I believe, during his long practice, that he has once erected a monument to which the cross has been attached: no doubt he would have been employed by many of the Catholic profession, had he applied to them; though perhaps it was owing to his careless inattention to his duty, that those of his own persuasion did not employ him. Whenever Mr. Nollekens spake of the Bible, he did not appear to have a general knowledge of its contents, nor do I recollect his selecting a subject for the exercise of his art from Holy Writ: and even farther, I never once heard him observe, that such and such a subject would model well. How different, on the contrary, was the pious mind of Flaxman; for though he was passionately fond of Homer, and other authors never noticed by Nollekens, he was never more delighted than when he was engaged upon sacred subjects, as witness his noble designs from the Lord's Prayer: for how sweetly, and, I was going to say, in how heavenly a manner he has treated them! I will venture to assert boldly in the face of the unbeliever who may laugh at this page, that if our churches were decorated with sculptured subjects taken from the best and oldest book in the world, their religious sentiments would be much more strongly excited when in a place of public worship, than by the filthy exhibition of General Monk's cap, the shoe-buckles worn by Lord Nelson, or a favourite 'Poll Parrot' of the deceased lady, 'modelled', as the show-men of the Abbey are pleased to tell the gaping visitors, 'as naturally as life!'

I sincerely hope, however, that a time will come, when Westminster Abbey, and all other buildings dedicated to sacred purposes, will be cleared of such mummery, and laid open to the free inspection of the public, who may walk about such noble edifices, and see the works of ancient and modern art, without being invited to pay for the exhibition of wax-work and models of churches which have nothing whatever to do with the edifice itself: indeed, the former were better destroyed, and the models presented to the Society of Arts. I will also ask the inquiring reader, whether it be fair that the public should be obliged to pay for a sight of these monuments, which the Government has so liberally erected to perpetuate the memory of those to whom they have been inscribed? I speak as an artist; my present theme being principally upon works of the Sculptors of them. The doors should be opened for certain hours daily, so that the public might see how extensively liberal, particularly of late years, the nation has been in voting monuments to the memory of men of departed genius; and more especially to those military and naval victors who have so nobly shed their blood, and fallen in their country's service.

To view the Abbey of Westminster, unincumbered of its waxen effigies, would be a gratification for many a morning; and the servants, instead of expecting a few pence for their own pockets, might still be employed to walk about to see that no mischief was done to the treasures of that venerable structure.[1] Surely it would be far better, were a man to be thus healthfully exercised, than to shut him up in a small recess at the entrance of Poet's Corner, where now the contribution is demanded, and where he closes upon the visitor, as a pair of snuffers top the wick of a candle; and as if the money-taking business, according to the custom of a playhouse, was to be looked after first. Now I will venture to say, that a regular citizen never calls upon

[1] I must, however, add, that I should like to see the curious old iron-work put up again, which inclosed the most ancient monuments in the Abbey.

any one for payment before sight; nor do the servants of the very few high families, which still suffer their domestics to take money, expect to receive what the visitors choose to give them, before they are attended back to the portal. Again, I will ask this question, how far is the London investigator of religious structure to go before he meets with any thing to be compared with such a specimen of sacred architecture as Westminster Abbey, mutilated and metamorphosed as it has been? St. Alban's Abbey, I believe, is the nearest to the Metropolis.

When Mr. Nollekens once had occasion to visit the Church of St. Giles, Cripplegate, he asked me to walk with him; and as we entered Jewin-street, we met Sir William Staines, who informed him of his having been chosen Mayor, and that he should send him a ticket for the civic dinner. *Nollekens*. 'Dinner! bless your heart, I'd rather dine at home; you citizens make such a noise, and I get my clothes spoiled. You've seen me in my *Pourpre du Pape*, and do you know, that at our last Academy dinner, a stupid fool *spilt the butter-boat* upon it? Have you any *comforts* in your pocket? I've got such a cold! Now, pray tell me, will they let you smoke your pipe in the mayor's coach?' —*Staines*. 'Bless you! I don't mean to attempt such a thing; but when I'm in my private carriage they can't hinder me; then if they offer it, I'll take them up!— Have you bought any stone lately? I've some very close Yorkshire.'—*Nollekens*. 'No, I don't want any. —*Staines*. 'Well, then, you won't dine on my day?'— *Nollekens*. 'No; but I suppose my friends Sir William Beechey and Sir Francis Bourgeois will be there. Well, good bye; I am going into the church.'—*Staines*. 'What, into *our* church? stay, I'll save you a shilling. I'll ring the bell for Mrs. Richardson, the Sexton's wife. Oh! here she comes. We want to go into the church-yard; I want to show my wife's tomb-stone to Mr. Nollekens and his friend.'—*Mrs. Richardson*. 'Do you know, Sir William, there's a corner off?'—'Ay, I am very sorry for it; I had the largest I could get for money, and, as I am a dealer in stone, you see, I had a little pride about me on that occasion.'—*Nollekens.* 'What a thick one it is!—why did you waste so much stone?'—*Staines.* 'That's the reason, I was determined to have the thickest for its size that ever came to London; it measures nine feet eight inches in length, by seven feet three inches and three-quarters in width.'

I was present one morning when Mr. West was sitting to Nollekens, for the bust which the British Institution had honoured him by ordering for their gallery, when, among other anecdotes, the President related the following of Biagio Rebecca, an artist principally employed in painting staircases and ceilings with allegorical subjects in arabesque decorations, formerly much in fashion in England; Mortimer, Cipriani, Angelica Kauffmann, Zucchi, Hamilton, and many other eminent artists being often engaged upon such works. King George III. had commanded Rebecca to adorn some of the royal apartments at Windsor, during which employment his Majesty, with his usual affability, would frequently converse with him; but in such conversations the artist, who was not a little conceited of his talents, attempted to conduct himself in the presence of his Majesty, as Verrio did before King Charles II., being so silly as to believe that his conduct would be laughed at by the condescending Monarch. In this, however, the impudent Rebecca was mistaken; for whenever he was guilty of the slightest impropriety of that kind, the King never failed to mention it to Mr. West. One day, at Windsor, after Rebecca had received a considerable sum of money, he proposed to share the expense of a post-chaise to London with Mr. West; and just as they had reached Hounslow Heath, the King, who was returning to Windsor, looked into their chaise. The next time Mr. West was in the Royal presence, the

King asked him who the foreign nobleman was that he had in the chaise with him the last time they met on Hounslow Heath. Mr. West declared Rebecca was his only companion. 'Oh, no,' observed his Majesty, 'it was a person of distinction.' Mr. West, upon inquiry, found out that Rebecca, who expected to meet the King, and knew his Majesty to be near-sighted, had the impudence to fix a paper star on his coat, which he had cut out for the purpose of attracting the King's notice, supposing that he would certainly laugh at it as a jest.—Rebecca, being fully aware of the great fondness people in general have for money, would, in whatever company he was, pass his jokes, purposely to amuse the frivolous part of them; and the following trick in particular he was sure to practise. He had prepared a drawing in imitation of a half-crown piece, which he would unobservedly place upon the floor, and then laugh immoderately at the eagerness with which even a gentleman in full dress, with his sword and bag, would sometimes run and scuffle to pick it up.

One day I was standing with Mr. Nollekens at his gate in Titchfield-street, when a man with full staring eyes accosted him with, 'Well, Mr. Nollekens, how do you do? you don't remember me; but you recollect my grandfather, Arthur Pond.'—'Oh, yes, very well; he used to christen old drawings for Hudson: ay, I have often seen him when I was a boy.'—'The same,' observed the stranger; 'my name's John, commonly Jack; his son, my father, was a livery-stable keeper,[1] and so Anthony Pasquin[2] always called me "*Horse*

[1] This Stable-keeper was the compiler of the 'Racing Calendar'.

[2] Many persons know that Anthony Pasquin's real name was Williams, but I believe very few are aware that he had been articled to learn the art of engraving of Matt. Darley, of the Strand, the famous caricaturist. A particular friend of mine has a set of coat buttons, upon every one of which

Pond".' Of this man's sister, there is a mezzotinto head, nearly as large as nature, drawn and engraved from the life, by John Spilsbury, and published by him, Dec. 1, 1766, then living in Russell-court, Covent-garden. This female has been celebrated by Dr. Johnson, in his Idler, as the lady who rode a thousand miles in a thousand hours. I have a portrait of her in her grey hairs, which I drew when I was studying the various expressions of insane people in Bethlehem Hospital, of which institution she was an unfortunate inmate. An Engraver of the name of Smith, published, in 1787, a quarto portrait of the above John Pond, who being notorious for nothing but getting drunk, it did not sell; but in order to make it answer his purpose, he, to the great annoyance of Doctor Wolcot, erased the name of John Pond, and substituted that of Peter Pindar, without making the least alteration in the features or person, when in a few days he distributed impressions in the shop windows all over the town, and many a portrait-collector has *enriched* his book with it, as the true and lively effigy of the man who cared not whose character he traduced.

I ought to have noticed in a former page, that when it was customary for so much company to visit Uxbridge by the barges drawn by horses gaily decked out with ribands, Mr. and Mrs. Nollekens, with all the gaiety of youthful extravagance, embarked on board, and actually dined out on that gala-day at their own expense. The sights they saw on this memorable aquatic excursion afforded them mutual conversation for several weeks; and Mrs. Nollekens actually tired her friends with letters upon their canal adventures

Anthony engraved a boat, as the badge of a member of a club, entitled 'The Sons of Neptune'; consisting of youths who strictly observed the Lord Mayor's rules of Swan-Upping, for the enjoyment of the scenery of the banks of Old Father Thames, confining the stretch of their oars from Wapping Old Stairs to the Bush at Staines.

from Paddington to Uxbridge, and from Uxbridge to Paddington. In these epistles, she most poetically expatiated upon the clearness of the water, the fragrance of the flowers, the nut-brown tints of the wavy corn, and the ruddy and healthful complexions of the cottagers' children, who waited anxiously to see the vessel approach their native shores. The only fatigue was the hasty walk from Mortimer-street to Paddington, and the loitering return from Paddington, to Mortimer-street; where, soon after their arrival, they refreshed themselves with an additional cup of tea, and for that evening indulged in going to bed before sun-set.[1]

One May morning, during Mrs. Nollekens's absence from town, Mrs. Lobb, an elderly lady, in a green calash, from the sign of the 'Fan', in Dyot-street, St. Giles's, was announced by Kit Finney, the mason's son, as wishing to see Mr. Nollekens. 'Tell her to come in,' said Nollekens, concluding that she had brought him a fresh subject for a model, just arrived from the country; but upon that lady's entering the studio, she vociferated before all his people, 'I am determined to expose you! I am, you little grub!'—'Kit!' cried Nollekens, 'call the yard-bitch;' adding, with a clenched and extended fist, that 'if she

[1] The pleasures of a similar excursion induced the late venerable President West to paint a picture of the barge he went by, on the crowded deck of which he has introduced his own portrait, and also those of several of his friends who were that day on board. This pleasing and singular picture adorns the splendid Gallery of West's works, daily exhibiting at his late house in Newman-street.

These excursions to Uxbridge were, like many other fashionable entertainments, soon laid aside. Air-balloons were also formerly much sought after; but now on a summer's afternoon, if one be announced, few people will turn up their eyes to look at it. And steam-boats, which have engaged the thoughts of the aquatic travellers, are already talked of with indifference, since a steam stage-coach is about to start without horses.

kicked up any *bobbery* there, he would send Lloyd for Lefuse, the constable.'—'Ay, ay, honey!' exclaimed the dame, 'that won't do. It's all mighty fine talking in your own shop. I'll tell his worship Collins, in another place, what a scurvy way you behaved to young Bet Belmanno yesterday! Why the girl is hardly able to move a limb to-day. To think of keeping a young creature eight hours in that room, without a thread upon her, or a morsel of any thing to eat or a drop to drink, and then to give her only two shillings to bring home! Neither Mr. Fuseli nor Mr. Tresham would have served me so. How do you think I can live and pay the income-tax? Never let me catch you or your dog beating our rounds again; if you do, I'll have you both skinned and hung up in Rats' Castle.[1] —Who do you laugh at?' she continued, at the same time advancing towards him; 'I have a great mind to break all your *gashly* images about the head of your fine Miss, in her silks and satins;'—mistaking his lay-figure for a living model of the highest sort.—'I suppose, you pay my lady well enough, and pamper her besides?'

Nollekens perceiving Mrs. Lobb's rage to increase, for the first time, perhaps, drew his purse-strings willingly; and putting shilling after shilling into her hand, counted four and then stopped. 'No, no,' said she, 'if you don't give me t'other shilling, believe me, I don't budge an inch!'[2] This he did; and Kit, after closing the gates, received peremptory orders from his master to keep them locked for three or four days, at least, for fear of a second attack.

[1] 'Rats' Castle', a shattered house then standing on the east side of Dyot-street, and so called from the rat-catchers and canine snackers who inhabited it, and where they cleaned the skins of those unfortunate stray dogs who had suffered death the preceding night.

[2] Mrs. Lobb succeeded the notorious Dame Phillips, formerly of the sign of the Fan, in Orange-court.

Soon after I had the honour of being appointed Keeper of the Prints and Drawings in the British Museum, Mr. Nollekens, accompanied by Mr. Gibson and Mr. Bonomi, the Sculptors, came to visit me. Upon my being apprised of my old friend's arrival in the Gallery, I went to meet him, in order to see that he had a chair, as he was then very feeble. I remember, when he was seated in the middle of the Elgin-room, he put the following question to the late Mr. Combe, loud enough to be heard by every one present who approached to see him:—'Why did not you bring the Ægina Marbles with you? they are more clever than the Phygalian Marbles. How could you be so stupid as to miss them?' Mr. Combe, thinking to divert him from the subject, said, 'I thought you wore hair-powder, Sir? I continue to wear hair-powder, and always use the best I can get.' Mr. Nollekens, not hearing him, repeated nearly the same question in a louder voice—'I say! why did you let them go?' Fortunately for Mr. Combe, however, he was sent for, and so escaped a farther interrogation. Mr. Nollekens then walked up to No. 64, the fragment of a male figure, and exclaimed, 'There, you see —look at that shoulder and a part of the breast—look at the veins! The ancients *did* put veins to their gods, though my old friend, Gavin Hamilton, would have it they never did.'

When he was again descending to the Townley-gallery, he stopped at the first flight of steps, and taking hold of a button of my coat, desired me to go and stand there; adding, 'Now, you stand where Queen Charlotte *sot* when she came to see the Museum: she was very tired; they brought her a chair, and I stood upon the steps below.'

As we were passing along the gallery, he said, 'Ay, I remember seeing the tears fall down the cheeks of Mr. John Townley, when the Parliament said they would buy the Marbles. He didn't wish 'em to take 'em, and he said to me, "Mr. Nollekens, if Government don't take my nephew's Marbles, I'll send 'em down to Townley-hall, and make a grand show with 'em there." Poor man, I never shall forget how forlorn he looked.' When we arrived at the Terracotta-room, he exclaimed, looking up, 'How white these things are getting! now, I dare say, they put 'em into the wall with wet plaster; they should have put 'em in with what Mr. Townley used to call bitumen, and then they won't moulder. Well, make my compliments to Mr. Planta; I've remembered him, and so I have Combe, though he did let the Marbles slip through his fingers; and so I have you, Tom. Well, good-bye! this Museum will be a fine place very soon.' —'Ay, Sir,' observed I, 'suppose you were to leave us your fine heads of Commodus and Mercury;' to which he answered, 'Well, perhaps I may: Townley wanted *'em* very much, but I could not get my price —he sent to me about *'em* just before he died.'

To continue these recollections of Mr. Nollekens at this period, I shall present my readers with a few more anecdotes communicated to me by friends.

The late Mr. Garrard, the Associate of the Royal Academy, said to Nollekens, 'Well, they tell me I shall be elected an R. A.'—*Nollekens*. 'Indeed! why you've told me that these seven years.' When Garrard had taken his leave, a friend present observed, 'He's a sculptor as well as a painter.'—*Nollekens*. 'Yes, he paints better than he sculps; he's jack-of-all-trades; the rest we'll leave out.'

A lady, with her three daughters, once visited Mr. Nollekens, to show him the drawings of her youngest, who was a natural genius. Upon his looking at them, he advised her to have a regular drawing-master; 'And I can recommend you one,' added he; 'he only lives over the way, and his name is John Varley.' The lady asked him if he were a man of mind.—'Oh, yes,' said Nollekens, 'he's a clever fellow, one of our best:

I'll ring the bell, and send my maid for him; he'll soon tell you his mind;' so ignorant was our Sculptor of the lady's meaning.

Whenever he was in Chelsea with a friend, he was always pleased in pointing out the house in which his mother lived after her marriage with Williams, saying, that 'when he took leave of her at the street-door, upon his going to Rome, she said to him, 'There, Joey, take that; you may want it when you are abroad.' It was a housewife, containing needles, a bodkin, and thread; 'and, do you know,' added he, 'it was the most useful thing she could have given me, for it lasted all the time I was at Rome to mend my clothes with; ay, and I have got that very housewife by me now; and, do you know, I would not take any money for it.'

Desenfans, the famous dealer in old pictures, whose remains rest in a splendid mausoleum at Dulwich, erected after a design by Soane, was originally a dealer in Brussels lace, and a teacher of the French language. A lady, however, one of his pupils, possessed of five thousand pounds, fell so desperately in love with him, that she soon after married him. During their honeymoon, they, like most people in a similar situation, drove into the country for a little recreation, and there, at an auction, he purchased a few old pictures, which, on his return to London, he sold to such advantage, that he considered it his interest to follow up the trade. By great industry and a little taste, he at length amassed so considerable a sum, that he finally was enabled to form a much better collection, which he left to his *protegé* Sir Francis Bourgeois; who, at the suggestion of the late John Kemble, left it to Dulwich College, merely because that institution had been founded by an actor. I mention these particulars, because Nollekens told my worthy friend Arnald, that he and a friend went halves in purchasing a picture by Pordenone, for which he gave eleven pounds five shillings, and which they speedily sold to Desenfans for thirty pounds. In these brokering bargains Nollekens often showed considerable cunning, for he would, to my knowledge, seldom speculate without a partner.

I receive infinite pleasure whenever an opportunity presents itself, in which I can exhibit the conduct of my old friend Mr. Nollekens to advantage; and I must do him the justice to prove his attachment to modern Art, by mentioning the purchases which he made at various times, and which will clearly evince his general inclination towards his brother artists. He would certainly have more extensively indulged in these purchases, had not Mrs. Nollekens checked his liberality. I remember his giving ninety pounds for a small picture by West; and that he also purchased at Barry's auction the Origin of Music, a small specimen, but one of that artist's most interesting designs, and a remarkable good piece of colouring for him.[1]

Nollekens had likewise a fine collection of the engravings from Sir Joshua Reynolds's pictures, in which he took great delight, and was never better pleased than when he could add to their number. Some persons have said that many of them were presented to him by those mezzotinto engravers who were looking after Associates' places in the Academy; but be this as it might, I never knew him to ask an engraver for a print. He certainly accepted impressions from the owners of private plates; and the Earl of Essex, who is in possession of a choice collection of impressions after Sir Joshua, gave him one which had been engraved at the expense of his Lordship purposely to present to his friends.

It is very remarkable, that many of our eminent characters, and it possibly may be so with those of

[1] It was bought at Nollekens's sale by the Earl of Egremont, one of the many noblemen who upon all occasions contribute liberally to the encouragement of modern Art.

other nations, sometimes glaringly expose themselves, by descending to the most frivolous meannesses; particularly in preserving every insignificant article, which gratification as often excites astonishment in their friends, as it exposes them to the unreflecting remarks of their enemies, who illiberally report such anecdotes without making the least allowance for the odd compound of ingredients of which the human mind is in general composed.

As corroborations of these imbecilities, I shall venture to give four instances, the first two of which the reader will not so much wonder at, as they certainly are related of persons of weak intellect, though standing on eminent ground as artists; but he will be surprised at the two latter, as they relate to sensible men, who have shone in society, and of the first talents, perhaps, in their respective classes, which this country has produced.

Nollekens, who was born to shine as one of our brightest stars as a bust-modeller, whilst he was forming the beautiful bosom of Lady Charlemont, suddenly left her Ladyship to desire the helper in the yard not to give the dog more than half the paunch that day, observing that the rest would serve him to-morrow, as Mr. John Townley had given him the greatest part of a French roll that very morning.[1]

When Abraham Pether, the painter of the celebrated picture of the Harvest Moon, employed himself a whole day to make his wife a dust-shovel, he was so indiscreet, though he at that time stood in need of

[1] Nollekens, however, I firmly believe, had no idea whatever of making himself noticed by singularities. His actions were all of the simplest nature; and he cared not what he said or did before any one, however high might be their station in life. He so shocked the whole of a large party one night at Lady Beechey's, that several gentlemen complained of his conduct, to which Sir William could only reply, 'Why, it is Nollekens the Sculptor!'

purchasers, as to refuse the admittance of two gentlemen, who walked from London to Chelsea with the full determination to bespeak pictures of him. The Painter, however, after he had whistled through a dozen new tunes and smoked as many pipes, at length finished his task, and remarked to a friend, 'There! my boy! if you were to give half-a-crown for a dust-shovel, I will be bound to say you could not get a better.'[1]

It is reported of Sir Joshua Reynolds, that one day, when the Knight was looking about the house for old canvases, he found a mop-stick put up in the corner of the back-kitchen, and that he strictly charged Ralph to see to its preservation, in order that its value might be deducted when the next new mop was purchased. Who could imagine such a charge to proceed from the author of his noble Lectures, and the artist who painted the glorious pictures of Ugolino at Knowle; the Infant Hercules at Petersburgh; and Mrs. Siddons, as the Tragic Muse, at Lord Grosvenor's![2]

It has been asserted also that Pope, when engaged in writing some of his most elegant works, would leave off to cook lampreys, in a silver saucepan, over his own fire.[3]

Nollekens, who was at one time passionately fond of seeing the soldiers relieve guard, was accosted one Sunday morning, when bustling down the Haymarket

[1] Abraham Pether was one of those silly beings who endeavoured to gain popularity by being called eccentric; and amongst others, he often practised the following trick. He would knock at a friend's door, and, when the servant opened it, he was discovered striking a light to set fire to his pipe, and then when he had accomplished his task, he would walk in whiffing his tobacco.

[2] Sir Joshua Reynolds was an elegant man, and admired for the mildness of his manners.

[3] Pope piqued himself upon the high birth of those with whom he associated.

with his little *protégé* Joseph, towards the Parade, by a little girl, who supplicated him to ring an upper bell. 'Ring a bell, ring a bell, my pretty little maid, that I will;' but he could not accomplish it. A Life-guardsman, well knowing the advantage of a few inches, coming down the street, and seeing Nollekens on tip-toe, straining himself to enjoy his favourite amusement of bell-pulling, raised his arm at a right angle from his body, and pulled the bell with the greatest ease, to the great surprise of Nollekens, and the joy of the child, who had been squeezed by the crescent, tip-toe position of Nollekens against the door-post. This scene would be a good one for the spirited pencil of Cruikshank, and it might be called the Advantage of Greatness.

Mr. Nollekens, when modelling the bust of a lady of high fashion, requested her to lower her handkerchief in front; the lady objected, and observed, 'I am sure, Mr. Nollekens, you must be sufficiently acquainted with the general form; therefore, there can be no necessity for my complying with your wish:' upon which Nollekens muttered, that 'there was no bosom worth looking at beyond the age of eighteen.'

Lady Arden had once been waiting some time in the parlour for Mr. Nollekens, who had the decency to attempt an apology, by assuring her Ladyship, 'That he could not come up before, for that he had been down-stairs washing his feet;' farther adding, that they were 'now quite comfortable'.

Nollekens being once in expectation of a very high personage to visit his studio, was dressed to receive him; and after walking up and down the passage for nearly an hour, being deprived of the advantage of using his clay, for fear of spoiling his clothes, he at length heard the equipage arrive. According to his usual custom, he opened the street-door, and as the illustrious visitor alighted, he cried out, 'So, you're come at last! why, you are an hour beyond your time;

you would not have found me at home, if I had had any where to have gone to, I assure you!'

One day, when Lady Newborough, who was a great favourite with Mr. and Mrs. Nollekens, was invited to dinner, they sent, just before they were about to sit down, to Taylor to make up the party; Taylor's spirit, however, would not allow him to accept of so short a notice, and he preferred dining at home. The next day, Mrs. Nollekens expressed her sorrow that she had not the pleasure of his company, stating that they had a venison pasty which she could not eat, at the same time blabbing that the preceding week they had had a fine haunch, of which she was very fond, and, indeed, never tired.

When Tuppin, a carpenter, received orders for a packing-case, he was always obliged to state precisely what it would amount to, and then Mr. Nollekens would strengthen the bargain by insisting upon it being sent home well stuffed with shavings; but these he never suffered the servants to have at their mercy, they were locked up in a place called a wine-cellar, and given out by himself the night before they were wanted for morning use.

In some instances, however, Mr. Nollekens was, according to the old adage, 'Penny wise and pound foolish'; and this was particularly the case as to sweeping his chimneys, since he thought that many persons had them swept too often. However, after having been several times annoyed by the fire-engines and their regular attendants, the mob, he was determined to have them more frequently cleaned; though some of them, for the want of fires, yielded no soot. He nevertheless consoled himself for this increased expenditure, by discovering that such a practice kept up the fame of a consumption of coals; like one of the masters of Gil Blas, who always picked his teeth after the dinner-hour, to induce his neighbours to believe he had dined.

Mr. Nollekens once showed Mr. Gahagan a sketch in charcoal, which he had made of Mrs. Palmer attending her daughter, who had been ill for a considerable time: having drawn the young lady with a book in her hand which she had been reading. The Sculptor, however, smeared out the book, observing to Gahagan, 'She is getting better now; she shan't have a book.'

The most insignificant eatable offered to him by the poorest of his labourers, he would not only accept and eat, but was sure to make some observation upon it. I recollect a stone-polisher of the name of Lloyd giving him a cheesecake, and Nollekens, after asking him where he had bought it, observed, that the Kensington cheesecakes, and those made at Birch's in Cornhill, Mrs. Nollekens allowed to be the best. Whenever my friend Mr. John Renton, the Portrait-painter, presented a melon to Mr. Nollekens, he always observed, 'This I like, it puts me so much in mind of Rome.'

Mr. Deville, well-known for his fine phrenological collection of busts, &c. when a young man, was employed by Mr. Nollekens to make casts from moulds which required oil; upon which he produced a little, saying, 'There, you'll find that to be more than enough.' Deville, having poured it out into a shallow basin, declared it to be insufficient. 'I don't wonder at that,' replied Nollekens, snappishly; 'why did you not ask me for a wine-glass? you've wasted half of it on the broad bottom of the basin!'

CHAPTER XIV

Mr. Nollekens's insensibility to ancient Art, and liberality to modern Artists.—Stewart's picture of Washington.—Farther instances of Mr. Nollekens's eccentricities and manners.—His intended bequest to the Royal Academy.—Condescension of the Princess of Wales to him.—Bantering letters. Conduct of Sir F. Bourgeois.—Mr. Nollekens's man Dodimy.—Moses Kean.—Nollekens's summons to his tenants for rent.—His household economy and habits.—His custom when Visitor at the Royal Academy.—Caprice of his charities.—Lord Mansfield's benevolence.—Mr. Wivell.—Nollekens's love of newspapers, and memoranda of remarkable events.—Unfeeling treatment of his model.—Other anecdotes of his domestic arrangements, art, and liberality.—Frivolous presents, &c. sent him towards the close of his life.—Beauty of foliated ornaments in sculpture.—Inferiority of Architecture to Sculpture and Painting.

My friend Mr. Robertson, the justly-admired Miniature-painter, upon receiving an exquisitely beautiful picture by Raffaelle, consigned to him by Mr. Trumbold, invited Mr. Nollekens, among many other artists of eminence, to see it: but, with all its excellence, it appeared to make no impression upon him whatever; and the only observation he made upon leaving the house, was, 'Well, as you are pleased with it, I am glad you have got it.'

Insensible, however, as Nollekens generally was when looking at works of ancient Art, I must do him the justice to say, that in no instance, excepting when speaking of Flaxman, have I known him attempt to depreciate the productions of modern artists; on the contrary, I have frequently heard him say, when he has been solicited to model a bust, 'Go to Chantrey, he's the man for a bust! he'll make a good busto of you; I always recommend him.' I have also known him to give an artist, who could not afford to purchase it, a lump of stone, to enable him to execute an order, though at the same time I have seen him throw himself into a violent passion with a favourite cat, for biting the feather of an old pen, with which he had for many years oiled the hinges of his gates whenever they creaked. I can almost imagine I see him now standing before the cat, with the pen in his hand, actually showing her what mischief she had done; with as much gravity as a certain *stupid* Sheriff manifested when he was counting the horse-shoe nails, or chopping his finger instead of the stick in the Court of Exchequer, when he was sworn into office by the Lord Chief Baron.

Mr. Nollekens once called out across the street to me, on the opposite side of Hay-hill, 'Smith, Peter Coxe has just knocked down General Washington, Stewart's picture. Well, what do you think? it fetched a great deal more than any modern picture ever brought by auction before, for he has just sold it at Lord Lansdown's for 540*l.* 15*s.*! You know Stewart; he was born in America; he painted that fine portrait of Caleb Whitefoord: he's a very clever fellow: just as clever as Dance, I mean Sir Nathaniel Dance Holland.'

One evening, Bronze happening to place the tea-kettle over the fire, Nollekens immediately cried out, 'You careless devil! you don't care for the work you'll have in the morning to get it clean!'—and when she left the room he angrily muttered, 'Extravagant creature! burning out the kettle!'

Mr. Nollekens, when he dined out of late years, always over-ate himself, particularly with the pastry and dessert. However, he contrived to purloin a small quantity of sweetmeats from the table, which he carried to Bronze, saying, 'There, Betty, you see what I have brought you home; I don't forget you.'

When he was showing Mr. Rossi, the Academician, his design for a monument to the memory of the late

Mrs. Coke, of Norfolk, Mrs. Nollekens, being the latest up that morning, came into the room, and immediately walked up to her husband, and then, after making a stately curtsey, with her accustomed precision of pronunciation, said, 'Sir, your watch; my dear father never left his watch about.'

When Mr. Jackson was once making a drawing of a monument at the Sculptor's house, Nollekens came into the room and said, 'I'm afraid you're cold here.'—'I am, indeed,' said Jackson.—'Ay,' answered the Sculptor, 'I don't wonder at it; why, do you know, there has not been a fire in this room for these forty years!'

The same artist having asked him what he meant to exhibit at the Royal Academy, Nollekens answered, 'Oh, nothing; I be done now.'—'Well,' replied the Painter, 'but you should send something to add to our display of Sculpture:' but his reply was still a selfish one—'No; I be done.' For he had no idea of sending any thing simply for the advantage of the establishment, of which he was so old a member; although at one period of his life he told me that he had left, in one of his wills, the sum of 100,000*l.* to enable that highly respectable body to erect a new Academy.

Miss Gerrard, the daughter of the auctioneer, who received a legacy of 19*l.* 19*s.* after Mrs. Nollekens's death, frequently called to know how he did; and once, the Sculptor pressed her to dine with him, to which she at last consented. 'Well, then,' said he to his pupil, Joseph Bonomi, 'go and order a mackerel; stay, one won't be enough, you had better get two, and you shall dine with us!' It must here be observed, that his two servants were now on board-wages.

During the time Mr. Nollekens was modelling the bust of the Princess of Wales, at Blackheath, her Royal Highness, upon seeing his ear filled with powder, observed, 'Mr. Nollekens, your hair-dresser has left some powder in your ear, it will make you deaf;' and immediately leaving her chair, she took up a handkerchief, and actually wiped it away.

About this time he was courted by several legacy-hunters who were beating about the bush, and amusing trifles from various quarters were continually planted before him in his room. One brought him a tall and extended chimney campanula; and, to make it look taller, had it placed upon a table within a foot of his nose, so that he was obliged to throw his head back to survey it: and another brought the French Giant in a coach, when he was delighted to ecstasy to see him touch the ceiling. During this visit, Bonomi made a mould of his immense right hand.

Now and then Nollekens received letters that were written by way of hoax; one of which, I remember, in particular, was in the name of a very high personage, to know what he would charge for cutting a figure in porphyry, ten feet high. This application Mrs. Nollekens absolutely answered, addressing her letter to the nobleman in whose name it was written, which brought his Lordship the next day; when, to make amends for the trouble Mrs. Nollekens had taken in answering the silly writer's letter, he bespoke a bust of his lady.

For many years, every summer's morn, Mr. Nollekens was up with the rising sun. He began his work by watering his clay, when he modelled till eight o'clock, at which hour he generally breakfasted; and then, as he entered his studio, would observe to his workmen, that every man should earn his breakfast before he ate it.

It is occasionally proper to expose in public print the cruel manner in which some persons treat their nearest relatives; in order that other hardened offenders may repent of their conduct before it be too late. Such a person was the late Sir Francis Bourgeois, who left his property to Dulwich College, without leaving a farthing to his niece and her poor, innocent, and unoffending children. I recollect Mr. Nollekens once showing me a letter which he had received from Sir William Beechey; and, to the best of my recollection, the purport of it was, that the bearer of it was the niece of Sir Francis Bourgeois, who had been walking about the streets all night, with her children, for want of a lodging. Sir William applied to Mr. Nollekens to give her a trifle, directing his attention to her miserable looks and state of apparel. God forbid we should have other instances of such pride and cruelty!

A candle with Nollekens, as is generally the case with misers, was a serious article of consumption: indeed so much so, that he would frequently put it out, and, merely to save an inch or two, sit entirely in the dark, at times too when he was not in the least inclined to sleep. So keen was he in watching the use of that commodity, that whenever Bronze ventured into the yard with a light, he always scolded her for so shamefully flaring the candle. One evening, his man Dodimy, who then slept in the house, came home rather late, but quite sober enough to attempt to go up-stairs unheard without his shoes; but, as he was passing Nollekens's door, the immensely-increased shape of the key-hole shone upon the side of the room so brilliantly, that he cried out, 'Who's there?' 'It's only me, Sir,' answered Dodimy, 'I am going to bed.'—'Going to bed, you extravagant rascal! why don't you go to bed in the dark, you scoundrel?'—'It's my own candle,' replied Dodimy. 'Your own candle! well, then, mind you don't set fire to yourself. Well, how did you come on at Lord George Cavendish's? you have been cleaning bustos there these six days; I told you, Dodimy, things could not be done so soon; —no, things are not to be done in a hurry, Master Dodimy.'—'Lord bless you, Sir, I had some turtle-soup there to-day, and such ale!'—'Well, well, take care of yourself; I say things must not be done in a hurry.'

One day Dodimy opened the studio-door and cried out, 'Sir! Sir! here comes the Chelsea-pensioner to have his shoulders moulded for your busto of Mr. Perceval!'—'What,' said Nollekens, 'the man with his two wooden-legs and a crutch?'—'Yes, Sir,' answered Dodimy. 'Lord, Sir,' he has left off his crutch, and is swaggering on his buttocks, twirling a little switch, just as Moses Kean used to do.'

The late Moses Kean was a tailor, a stout-built man with black-bushy hair, and a wooden leg. He was always dressed in a dashing manner, in a scarlet coat, white satin waistcoat, black satin small-clothes, and a 'Scott's Liquid dye' blue silk-stocking; he had also a long-quartered shoe, with a large buckle covering his foot, a cocked hat and a ruffled shirt, and never went out without a switch or cane in his hand. He was a very extraordinary mimic, particularly in his imitations of Charles James Fox, which he gave occasionally at the Little Theatre in the Haymarket. Mr. Alefounder painted a whole-length portrait of him as large as life in the above dress, which was exhibited in the left-hand corner of the Ante-room at Somerset-House. There is also a whole-length etching of him, of a quarto size. Mr. Edmund Kean, the celebrated actor, owes his education to the above person, who was his uncle; and, when I was a boy, lived at No. 9, Little St. Martin's-lane.

Mr. Nollekens, in former days, when he was alive to the interest of money, before he suffered thousands of pounds to rest in his bankers' hands unemployed, would write to his tenants in the following style, in what he considered a lawyer's manner. '*Mr. Nollekens request Mr.* ——— *will pay him that quarter's rent, due the* 29*th, forthwith, without delay, on or before Thursday next, twelve o'clock at noon.*'

Nollekens's old coal-box was of a square shape; it had been a lawyer's wig-box, that had been sent with a barrister's wig to be modelled from. This box had been mended with bits of tin, which he had picked up of a morning near the dust-heaps in the fields; but his house contained neither coal hods nor scoops; nor any thing like the splendour of a certain created lord, who had his coronet painted upon his coal-scuttles.

Bronze, who, as the reader will recollect, was called 'Black Bet' by the Oxford-market butchers, would, in her master's dotage, put her arm round his neck and ask him how he did. 'What!' observed Nollekens, 'now you want some money—I've got none.'—'Why, Sir, how am I to buy things for your table, without it? You have enough of it, fresh and blooming, and all alive, at Chambers's.'—*Nollekens.* 'Can you dance?' —'Dance, Sir! to be sure I can. Give me the cat;' and then she jigged about with it, at which he would laugh heartily.

Nollekens often baited his rat-trap with an unusual quantity of cheese, thinking to catch all the vermin at once: never dreaming that when one was caught, the trap would shut the rest out, and that the solitary visitor would eat up the whole. Why the rats infested *his* house, Bronze declared she never could make out. Food they certainly had not; and an old rat might have said to Nollekens, when he was busy in setting his trap,

Fear not, old fellow! for your hoard;
I come to lodge, and not to board.

A lady of high fashion once brought her child to have her beautiful arm moulded. Mr. Nollekens, who, as usual upon such occasions, began with his gibberish to the child, 'What a pretty handy-dandy!' was requested by the lady not to utter such nonsense, but to proceed with his task; adding, that her child's nurse was a well-educated woman.

So determined was Nollekens upon all ocasions to have a pennyworth for *his* penny, that he has frequently been noticed, when Visitor at the Royal

Academy, to turn down the hour-glass whenever Charles, the model, got up to rest himself; in order that the students might not be deprived of one moment of the time for which the model was paid. However, one evening, in doing this, he let the glass fall and broke it. This, he observed, he would replace by one which he would bring from his studio, muttering, 'They don't make things so strong as they did when I was a boy.'

One day, Mrs. Nollekens, after a trifling brush with her husband, who had declined taking farther orders for the studio, rated him soundly for paying full wages to his man Dodimy, who had nothing to do but to sweep the yard and feed the dog. Nollekens, sidling up to Dodimy, in a whisper, told him not to mind her; for that he would raise his wages two shillings per week, purposely to spite her, that he would.

His acts of kindness, indeed, depended entirely on his momentary humour; for he had no fixed principle of generosity. In which he illustrated the remark of Mrs. Hannah More, in her 'Christian Morals', vol. I. page 187, where she says, 'We must not judge of our charity by single acts and particular instances, for they are not always good men who do good things; but by our general tendencies and propensities. We must strive after an uniformity in our charity, examine whether it be equable, steady, voluntary, and not a charity of times, and seasons, and humours.'

Mr. Nollekens was standing with the late Earl Mansfield, in his Lordship's farm-yard at Ken-wood, when a little girl came up to him and presented her mother's compliments to Farmer Mansfield, and she would be obliged to him for a jug of milk. 'Who is your mother, my little dear?' asked his Lordship. 'She's just come to live in that small house close by the road.' His Lordship, with his usual smile, called to one of the helpers, and desired him to fill the child's mug, and if he found the family deserving, never to refuse them milk. Although Nollekens was frequently heard to relate the above anecdote, yet he never felt the force of this noble example, as his contributions were generally capricious.

Mr. Wivell, who is now an artist of ability, was, before the dawn of his talent, a hair-dresser, and, as he himself relates, frequently shaved and dressed Mr. Nollekens, who took great notice of him, and from whom he now and then received some kindnesses. Mr. Wivell informs me that one day, when Mr. Nollekens was under his hand, or, as Rowlandson humorously styles it, 'a sufferer for decency', Wivell stated to him that some one had stepped into his shop and carried off a new hat which had just been sent home. The Sculptor, when the operation was over, took a one-pound note from his pocket-book, and giving it to him said, 'There, that will buy you another.'

Wivell was also with him one day when shirts were mentioned; 'How many do you wear in a week?' asked Nollekens. 'Two, Sir,' replied Wivell; 'and that's all my stock, for I wear one while the other is washed.'—'Poor Wivell!' whispered he, and then gave him a one-pound note. Nollekens's own stock only consisted of three.

Wivell was frequently invited to spend the evening with him to look over his prints. After going through those after Sir Joshua Reynolds, Mr. Wivell recommended him to throw out his duplicates; which he did, and then asked him to value them. 'Sir,' said he, upon looking them over, 'I think I could make two guineas of them.'—'What will you give me for them?' demanded Nollekens; 'Thirty shillings,' replied Wivell. 'Then,' said the Sculptor, 'I won't sell them; I'll give them to you.'

Having had some success, Mr. Wivell published, at his own expense, an engraving, in mezzotinto, from Sir William Beechey's portrait of his patron Nollekens; and did himself the pleasure of presenting him with a proof impression, also indulging in the like liberality to Mrs. Nollekens. This plate, however, did not sell; and the engraver lost twenty-five pounds in the undertaking. Some time after its publication, Mr. Nollekens informed the artist that he wanted an impression to give away, and after asking the price of a proof said, 'Well, I'll have a print.' Upon its delivery he asked the price of it. 'Seven shillings and sixpence, Sir, was the price I put upon it,' observed Wivell. 'Well, then, what will it be to me? you won't charge me that sum,' said Nollekens. 'Oh, Sir, pray give me what you please,' returned Wivell, who felt grateful for past favours. 'Well, then,' returned he, 'there's three shillings for you.'

He also relates that Mr. Nollekens frequently spoke of a man that he met in the fields, who would now and then, with all the gravity of an apothecary, inquire after the state of his *bowels*. 'At last,' said he, 'I found he wanted to borrow money of me.'

One morning, while he was under the razor, he told Wivell, that the day before, he had witnessed two scenes of the greatest contrast; the first was the inside of Newgate, where he had been to ask Mr. Alexander Davison how he did. The other was in one of the grand rooms in Carlton House, where he had been to see how the Prince was, and that there the tables were all set out with such grand plate for an entertainment, that he could not help exclaiming to himself 'What a difference!'

It was now and then amusing to hear Nollekens read the newspaper to his wife in his most audible voice, when she was unable to read it to him; a practice in which she indulged him from the period of her marriage till she became much affected by a paralytic seizure, which deprived her of that power. He gave up a considerable portion of the day for that description of mutual amusement; for so I may fairly state it to have been, as he was perfectly and equally satisfied with his own method of reading it; for he read the paper entirely through, beginning with the play-bills and ending with the Editor's address. His partner however, notwithstanding her serious affliction, was often led into a smile by his misnomers and bad pronunciation, which were at times most whimsically ridiculous.

Before he became the reader of these daily papers, he frequently amused himself by recording on the covers of letters what he considered curious daily events; and by looking over these scraps, he was not only pleased, but would endeavour to amuse his friends by now and then reading them aloud. As for works on Art, he cared for neither 'Shee's Rhymes', 'Flaxman's Homer', nor Blake's 'Songs of Innocence'.

The following memoranda were copied from the back of one of his charcoal sketches, and will at once convince the reader of the estimation in which he sometimes held his leisure moments.

'1803, May 23d.—Lady Newborough brought forth a second sun.—Sweep the parlour and kitchen chimneys.—Clean the cestern in the kitchen.—Lent Northcot the cable rope and the piece of hoke tre.

1805, Dec. 30.—Mrs. Whiteford brought to bed of a sun.

1806, Feb. 8th.—Died Mrs. Peck, in Marlbrough-street.

April 14th.—The Duke of Gloster came to my house.

June 28th.—The Duke and Duches of York came to my house.

July 7th.—His R. H. the Duke of Cumberland made me a visit.

July 19th.—Lord Wellesley began to set.

August 4th.—Sent to Lord Yarborough the head of Sir Isack Nuton.

1808, December 16th.—Sent Mr. Bignell, by order of Lady Jersey, Lord Jersey's head in a case.

1809, Jan. 12th.—Cast-off Mr. Pitt for Mr. Wilberforce, by order of Lord Muncaster.

April 11th.—The Dukes of York, Cumberland, and Cambridge made me a visit.'

Mr. Nollekens, when modelling the statue of Pitt, for the Senate House, Cambridge, threw his drapery over his man Dodimy, who after standing in an immovable position for the unconscionable space of two hours, had permission to come down and rest himself; but the poor fellow found himself so stiff, that he could not move. 'What!' exclaimed Nollekens, 'can't you move yourself, then you had better stop a bit.' I am sorry to say there are other artists who go on painting with as little compassion for their models.

Mr. Arminger has declared that, in eating, nothing could exceed the meanness of Mr. and Mrs. Nollekens; for whenever they had a present of a leveret, which they always called a hare, they contrived, by splitting it, to make it last for two dinners for four persons. The one half was roasted, and the other jugged.

Much has been said respecting those Sculptors who have employed painters to make designs for their monuments. How far such assertions are correct, at the present moment, I will not take upon myself to say; but this I know, that Sir Joshua made a sketch of his idea of what Mr. Nollekens's monument erected to the memory of the three captains should be, and which certainly was attended to by the Sculptor in his composition.

To the eternal honour of Mr. Nollekens, who was unquestionably a most curious compound of misery and affluence, it should be recorded, that he gave twenty-five pounds as his subscription to the widows and children of the brave soldiers, who were killed or wounded in the glorious Battle of Waterloo.

It is reported, that once when Nollekens was walking round the yard with a brother artist, he was questioned by him, why he kept so many small pieces of marble, to which Nollekens replied, 'They'll all come into use.'—'What's the use of this lump?' asked his friend. 'Oh! that will do for a small busto.'—'Why, it's only seven inches thick!'—'Ay; but then, you know, I shall model a busto for that piece with the head twisted, looking over the shoulder!'

About this time, it was highly amusing to witness the great variety of trifling presents and frivolous messages which he daily received. One person was particularly desirous to be informed where he liked his cheesecakes purchased; another, who ventured to buy stale tarts from a shop in his neighbourhood, sent his servant in a laced livery in the evening, to inquire whether his cook had made them to his taste; whilst a third continued constantly to ply him with the very best pig-tail tobacco, which he had most carefully cut in very small pieces purposely for him. A fourth truly kind friend, who was not inclined to spend money upon such speculations himself, endeavoured once more to persuade him to take a cockney ride in a hackney-coach to Kensington, to view the pretty almond-tree in perfect blossom, and to accept of a few gooseberries to carry home with him to make a tartlet for himself! A fifth sent him jellies, or sometimes a chicken, with gravy ready made, in a silver butter-boat; and a sixth regularly presented him with a change of large showy plants, to stand on the mahogany table, especially in his latter years, when he was a valetudinarian, so that he might see them from his bed. The sight of these plants certainly amused him, but as for the delightful odour they diffused, it mattered not to him, as his olfactories were not over-delicate; a carrion flower, or a marigold, being equally refreshing to him as a sprig of jessamine or mignonette. It is a very curious fact, that during seventy years' constant practice in his art, Nollekens was never known to hold up or to admire the elegance of a tendril, or even the leaf of a plant; nor to take casts of those simple and beautiful productions of Nature, the lily, the vine, the ivy, the olive-branch, the laurel, or the oak, which so often have been introduced in all ages and countries in monumental sculpture. This, however, is not the case with artists of the present day. Flaxman, whose mind was elegance itself, was never more delighted than in the accumulation of such examples, nor has any Sculptor displayed them with greater taste; and we find by the splendid and inestimable collection of foliated ornaments so liberally and tastefully displayed on the walls of the staircase and painting-rooms of Sir Thomas Lawrence, in his house in Russell-square, that the ancient Greeks and Romans carefully and extensively studied that luxuriant branch of their art, particularly in their architectural decorations. Thus far, too, Mr. Soane may be considered correct in his assertion, that the sculptor's art is the 'Lace-work of architecture'; but that gentleman surely never could mean to say that busts, figures in niches, and groups of historical composition, were ever meant to be so considered. Such a degradation, I believe, was never attempted. Indeed, it has been a matter of strong contention whether Sculpture should not take the precedence of Painting. Architecture should certainly be the last mentioned of the sister arts, whatever ideas some architects may entertain upon the subject. Men of true taste visit a mansion upon the report of its statues, busts, and pictures. The architecture of a house, unadorned by such productions of art, would not induce the general traveller to drive twenty miles out of his road, nor even five. How few allurements, indeed, would the Marquis of Lansdown's, Lord Pembroke's, Lord Egremont's, Lord Farnborough's, Sir Abraham Hume's, Mr. Peel's, and many other noble mansions have, if totally destitute of their fine collections of statues and pictures: and however delightful may be the society of the truly amiable brothers, Samuel and Henry Rogers, surely their visitors receive double pleasure in being surrounded not only with some of the finest specimens of ancient Art, but by the choicest works of Sir Joshua Reynolds, Wilson, Stothard, and other professors of the highest eminence and merit.

CHAPTER XV

Cause of Mr. Nollekens dismissing his Confessor.—Songs of his youthful days.—His bed.—Unquiet nights productive of charity.—Liberality to his domestics.—Coarseness of his food and manner of eating.—Inferiority of his wardrobe, and meanness of his domestic arrangements.—Character of his drawings and those of other Sculptors.—His Monumental designs and models.—Infirmity of his latter days, and death.—Attested copy of his Will and Codicils.

ONE rainy morning, Nollekens, after confession, invited his holy father to stay till the weather cleared up. The wet, however, continued till dinner was ready, and Nollekens felt obliged to ask the Priest to partake of a bird, one of the last of a present from his Grace the Duke of Newcastle. Down they sat; the reverend man helped his host to a wing, and then carved for himself, assuring Nollekens that he never indulged in much food; though he soon picked the rest of the bones. 'I have no pudding,' said Nollekens, 'but won't you have a glass of wine? Oh, you have got some ale.' However, Bronze brought in a bottle of wine; and on the remove, Nollekens, after taking a glass, went, as usual, to sleep. The priest, after enjoying himself, was desired by Nollekens, while removing the handkerchief from his head, to take another glass. 'Tank you, Sare, I have a finish de bottel.' 'The devil you have!' muttered Nollekens. 'Now, Sare,' continued his Reverence, 'ass de rain be ovare, I vil take my leaf.'—'Well, do so,' said Nollekens, who was not only determined to let him go without his coffee, but gave strict orders to Bronze not to let the old rascal in again. 'Why, do you know,' continued he, 'that he ate up all that large bird, for he only gave me one wing; and he swallowed all the ale; and out of a whole bottle of wine, I had only one glass!'

After this, being without a Confessor, Mrs. Holt, his kind attendant, read his prayers to him; but when she had gone through them, his feelings were so little affected by his religious duties, that he always made her conclude her labours by reading either 'Gay's Fables', or 'The Beggar's Opera'! at the latter of which, when she came to certain songs, he would laugh most heartily, saying, 'I used to sing them songs once; and it was when I was courting my *Polly*.'

I recollect that the bedstead upon which Mr. Nollekens slept of late years was four-posted; the curtains being yellow, orange, red, and black, and when first put up, they made a most gorgeous display: though he had for many years but one counterpane, of which he was so extremely choice, that he would not suffer it to be washed, but Mrs. Holt, being ashamed to see it, put on one of her own of a much superior quality. When he saw it upon the bed, he swore at her, and asked her why it had been washed? but upon her informing him that it was one of her own, he allowed it to remain, saying, 'Well, indeed, it does look very comfortable.'[1]

Mrs. Holt, to whom I am obliged for many particulars in this volume, who had by her amiable disposition and strict attention to cleanliness, rendered the last two years of Mr. Nollekens's life more comfortable than any period of his existence, informed me that when he could not rest in his bed, he would frequently endeavour to raise himself up, and call to her to know if she was asleep. Mrs. Holt, who rested upon a hard sofa by the side of his bed, would answer, 'I'm here, Sir; can I give you any thing?'—

[1] When this counterpane required washing, Mrs. Holt put on his own, at which he angrily cried out, 'I won't have it on, I always sleep better without one; I don't like a counterpane'; to which she answered, that 'The poorest creature in a workhouse had a rug on his bed, and that she would have it on.'

Nollekens. 'Sit up; I can't sleep: I can't rest. Is there any body that I know that wants a little money to do 'em good?'—*Mrs. Holt*. 'Yes, Sir, there is Mrs. ——.' —*Nollekens*. 'Well, in the morning I'll send her ten pounds.'—'That's a good old boy,' said she, patting him on the back, 'you will eat a better dinner for it to-morrow, and enjoy it.' And Mrs. Holt has added, that she never knew him to forget his promise.

With all his propensity for saving, he indulged for many years in the gratification of making his household domestics a present of a little sum of money on his birthday; and lately, upon this occasion, he became even more generous, by bestowing on them, to their great astonishment, ten and twenty pounds each.

A broad-necked gooseberry-bottle, leather-bunged, containing coffee, which had been purchased and ground full forty years, was brought out when he intended to give a particular friend a treat; but it was so dried to the sides of the bottle, that it was with difficulty he could scrape together enough for the purpose, and even when it *was* made, time had so altered its properties, from the top having been but half closed, that it was impossible to tell what it had originally been. He used to say, however, of this turbid mixture, 'Some people fine their coffee with the skin of a sole, but for my part, I think this is clear enough for any body!'

Mrs. Wilson, a most amiable lady, one of the daughters of Mr. Major, the late celebrated Engraver of the Stamp-Office, was once asked to stay and drink tea with him. As Mr. Nollekens was putting in more tea than he would for himself, he was stopped by Mrs. Wilson, who observed, that she was afraid he had misunderstood her, for she could not stay: on which he muttered, 'Oh! I'm glad you spoke,' and then returned half the tea out of the pot to the canister. I do not wonder that so elegant a woman as Mrs. Wilson declined his invitation, particularly at this time, when the paralytic seizures which he had undergone, rendered his society at some times insupportable; for, independent of his natural stupidity and ignorance in conversation, his bodily humours appeared in several parts of his person as well as his face, which was seldom free from scorbutic eruptions, particularly about his mouth. Indeed, poor man! his appearance and want of decent manners rendered it impossible for any one accustomed to tolerable society, to associate with him; and yet there were persons, whose servants would send such an object from their master's door, who actually sat down and partook of his boiled rabbit smothered with parsley and butter, even when he had thick napkins four times doubled under his chin. For my own part, I must say, I always declined accepting an invitation, though I have seen ladies arrive in their carriages, with an expectation of being remembered when next he made his Will; for it was pretty well known, that in the course of the last twenty-five years, he had made several, in some of which he had remembered all his old friends. However, I shall for the present drop this subject, and state to my readers the few amusements which he enjoyed at this period.

His principal attendant, Goblet, who at this time was empowered with the full control of the studio, stone-yard, and gate, cleared a space of ground which he formed into a small garden, purposely to be viewed from a window of an upper room, into which he and Mrs. Holt, and sometimes poor Bronze, guided the castored-chair with the man who had for years repeatedly promised to make them all happy for life. Of these three persons, Mr. Nollekens made the most free with Bronze; he listened to her silly nonsense with the full expectation of hearing what she had often said, and then would joke in his way in return; and though she was not over-cleanly in her domestic habits or person, he voraciously ate the food prepared by her hands. His attendant, Mrs. Holt, always cooked her own dinner; for lately, though Nollekens' savoury dish was sometimes relished by a crafty visitor, she declined eating with him, well knowing how negligent Bronze was as to the state of her culinary articles before she used them. Indeed, Bronze, in her grey-haired state, became addicted to drinking, and then Mrs. Holt would not allow her to dress any thing more for her master, but kindly cooked his dinner herself.

Perhaps there never was a Royal Academician, or even a servant of one, whose wardrobes were so scantily provided with change of dress as those of Mr. Nollekens and his old servant Bronze. He had but one night-cap, two shirts, and three pairs of stockings; two coats, one of them his *Pourpre de Pape*, one pair of smallclothes, and two waistcoats. His shoes had been repeatedly mended and nailed; they were two odd ones, and the best of his last two pair. This was the amount of his dress: indeed, so niggardly was he as to his clothes, that when Mrs. Holt took possession of his effects, she declared she would not live with him, unless he had a new coat and waistcoat. With this reasonable request he complied, saying nothing about any other part of his dress. Poor Bronze, who had to support herself upon what were called board-wages, had barely a change, and looked more like the wife of a chimney-sweeper that any other kind of human being. As for table linen, two small breakfast napkins and a large old tablecloth, a descendant in the family, which, when used, was always folded into four, was the whole of his stock; for he possessed no doileys; and Bronze declared to me that she had never seen such a thing as a jack-towel in the house, nor even the nail-holes where one had been. She always washed without soap: there were no hearth-stones nor black-lead dust for the stoves; nor a cake of whitening for the kitchen-grate; nor even a yard of oil-cloth to preserve the stones from grease, much less an old bit of bed-side carpet, to keep the bones of poor old Bronze free from rheumatism.

In this state, Mrs. Holt found things at No. 9, Mortimer-street, and in a worse condition did they appear when the secrets of the prison-house were laid open, as will be found after the insertion of Mr. Nollekens's Will in a future page of this volume.

Of late years he diverted himself with several sketch-books filled with outlines and measurements of busts, statues, groups, and basso-relievos, which he had most industriously and carefully made during his residence in Italy from numerous fragments, and several celebrated antiques in the Vatican, the Palaces, and Villas Bassano, Belvidere, Bologna, Borghese, Frascati, Giustiniani, Loretto, Mantua, Massani, Tivoli, &c.

These sketch-books, which are now mostly in the possession of Mrs. Palmer, may very justly be considered to contain some of his best drawings, and are beyond doubt most valuable memoranda. Of the interesting subjects delineated,—particularly as to their measurements, which in my belief are strictly accurate, —the outlines in my mind bear too visibly the cold hand of perseverance only, since they are not executed with any thing like the feeling with which Flaxman drew; and when compared with his Italian studies, also made from some of the same antiques, they fall far short of the mind visible in every thing Flaxman touched, even in his earliest years. However this may be, and feebly as Nollekens's copies were made, he unquestionably not only considerably outstripped his master Scheemakers, but, to do him only common justice, his strides were considered greatly beyond the usual extent of the abilities in drawing of the Sculptors of his early days; Rysbrack excepted, whose drawings, though certainly considerably mannered, possess a fertility of invention, and a spirit of style in their execution, seldom emanating from the hand of a Sculptor of modern times.[1] They are for the most part washed in bistre, and are frequently to be met with. Michel Angelo's productions as a draughtsman were divinely magnificent, and they are pre-eminently placed in all collections where they are to be found; he drew with the pen or charcoal, and also in red chalk, but most of his finest drawings are in black chalk, in which he seemed to delight, if we may judge from the exquisite manner in which many of them are finished.[2]

During Nollekens's juvenile practice, he received a few lessons in drawing from a Sculptor, now but little known, Michel Henry Spang, a Dane,[3] who drew the figure beautifully and with anatomical truth; a most essential component of the art, indispensably requisite for all those who would climb to the summit of Fame; but this invaluable acquirement was neglected by Nollekens, nor did he at any period of his life venture to carve a subject in which a knowledge of anatomy would have been extensively wanted: his naked figures were of the most simple class, being either a

[1] Painters, and indeed Engravers, at that time were much better draughtsmen than the Sculptors. There were Moser, Mortimer, Cipriani, West, Barry, Bartolozzi, Sherwin, Ryland, Strutt, Legat, and Grignon, who drew the figure well. Since their time we have been enabled to boast of Blake, Flaxman, Lawrence, Stothard, Burney, Ryley, Howard, Hilton, Etty, Briggs, and Morton, all faithful and constant delineators of form and muscular action.

[2] When I had the honour of viewing Sir Thomas Lawrence's princely collection of drawings by Michel Angelo and Raffaelle, their productions alone engaged my admiration from seven o'clock till past eleven. Jeremiah Harman, Esq. has also some most powerful drawings by Michel Angelo, which were brought into England by W. Y. Ottley, Esq.

[3] Spang, who produced that small anatomical figure so well known to every draughtsman who assiduously studies his art. He also designed and executed the figures on the pediment of Earl Spencer's house in the Green-park, and the decorations on the screen at the Admiralty.

young Bacchus, a Diana, or a Venus, with limbs sleek, plump, and round; but I never knew him, like Banks, to attempt the grandeur of a Jupiter, or even the strength of a gladiator. His monumental effigies, too, were always so draped and placid, that very little expression of muscle was exercised. Nollekens's large academical drawings, made when he was Visitor in the Royal Academy, were feebly executed, his men were destitute of animation, and his females often lame in the joints; their faces were usually finished-up at home from his wife, and in compliment to her, he generally contrived to give them little noses.

There were in the Academy at the time when Mr. Nollekens was visitor, three young Sculptors, who drew remarkably well, Flaxman, Proctor, and Deare; whose abilities were so much noticed by their fellow-students, that Nollekens gave up his practice of drawing for that of modelling the figure in basso-relievo, and many of his productions possessed great merit. Having throughout his long life had fewer vexations than most men, by reason of his natural imbecility, he was on all occasions industriously inclined to his art, and was never known to riot in dissipation; on the contrary, whenever he was not engaged in modelling, he employed himself, particularly in the evening, in making designs upon the backs of letters, and other scraps of paper, for every description of monument of the simple kind, such as a female weeping or entwining festoons of flowers over an urn, or a child with an inverted torch; and for one and the same monument I have known him make half a dozen or more trials.[1]

[1] Quantities of these sketches were purchased at his auction by Mrs. Palmer, who, having so many of his works, at one time had an idea of building a room for their reception; as I have been informed by Mr. Taylor, the pupil of Frank Hayman, who still continues an inquisitive and communicative man, notwithstanding his great age, which now and then screens him from the retort-courteous.

These sketches were often in pencil, or sometimes finished in Indian-ink, but many of his later ones were drawn only with charcoal; he kept them always at hand, to show a gentleman who had lost his wife, or a lady who had been deprived of her husband or child; and he has often been heard to say, when he has received an order for a monument, 'You see I take 'em when the tear's in the eye.'

The greatest pleasure our Sculptor ever received, was when modelling small figures in clay, either singly or in groups, which he had baked; and in consequence of his refusing to sell them, and giving very few away, they became so extremely numerous, that they not only afforded a great display of his industry, but considerable entertainment to his friends.

His talent in this way was esteemed superior to many things executed by him of a large size; and it would ill become me, after venturing to amuse my readers with my old master's weaknesses, if I were, by my silence upon these beautiful models, to deprive him of one particle of that share of praise to which he was so deservedly entitled for their composition and spirit; for though he was but a poor artist as a draughtsman, no one equalled him in his time as a modeller, particularly in his Venuses. There is in some of them, notwithstanding their want of that grace, which he might have derived from the antique, a luxuriant display of Nature's elegance, of which there was then no sculptor better able to make a selection. His models towards the decline of his practice, were not possessed of much variety of composition; and as for his attempts in his latter years, they very much resembled the productions of a dozing man. However, I will still do him the justice to own, that they were in some points natural, and to the last evinced a strong attachment to his branch of the art, although produced in his second childhood. As a proof of my assertion, Sir William Beechey has a little group possessing much merit, which Nollekens modelled from his design only a short time before his last attack; though he would then occasionally leave off, and give Bronze, his poor old servant, money to dance his favourite cat, 'Jenny Dawdle', round about the room to please him; and at which he would always laugh himself heartily into a fit of coughing, and continue to laugh and cough, with tears of pleasure trickling down his cheeks upon his bib, until Bronze declared the cat to be quite tired enough for that morning.[1]

In this state of imbecility, he continued to exist for a considerable time, under the kind superintendence of his housekeeper Mrs. Holt, who deserves the highest praise for the feeling manner in which she watched over him. As for his faithful servant poor Betty, whose name was dropped at the beginning of this work for that of Bronze, she was too old and feeble to do much; her hair had become grey in his service, and she was not altogether unlike the figure of the poor old soul so wretchedly employed in lighting the fire in the miser's room, represented by Hogarth in his first plate of the Rake's Progress. Goblet, his principal carver, who had slept in the house for some months, was at all times ready, night and day, to render him every assistance in his power, for which he had been induced to give up his own domestic comforts. His medical attendant was Sir Anthony Carlisle, who for a long time had visited him at all hours, and who was always with him at the shortest possible notice; and whose

[1] This cat, the favourite of her master, his constant companion at his breakfast and dinner-table, *being no longer praised and petted* by her master's visitors *after his death*, was kindly rescued from unthinking boys, or the stealers of cats for the sake of their skins, by Mrs. Holt, who took her to her home, which she had left to oblige Mr. Nollekens, where it now enjoys a warm-hearted fireside friend. As for the fate of poor Bronze, alas! a future page will declare it.

kind and skilful hand frequently relieved his sufferings, for he had been visited in the course of his life with three paralytic seizures.

Under these circumstances, Mr. Nollekens at length departed this life in the drawing-room on the first-floor, at the south-east corner of his house, April 23d, 1823, in the presence of Mrs. Holt and Mr. Goblet, who immediately sent to inform the three Executors; of which number he had, upon the death of my honoured friend the Rev. Edward Balme, chosen me to be one. I considered it my duty to attend the same day, when I found Sir William Beechey. The next day Mr. Douce met us; and the Will was read. Of this document the following is an attested copy, without the least animadversion:—

'This is the last Will and Testament of me, Joseph Nollekens, of Mortimer-street, in the Parish of St. Mary-le-bone, in the County of Middlesex, Esquire: I desire that my body be decently deposited in the vault under the parish church of Paddington, in the said County; and that there be not any scarfs given at my funeral, but that I be buried in a plain black coffin, without any gilt ornaments. And that all such just debts as I shall owe at the time of my decease, and my funeral and testamentary charges and expenses be paid and satisfied. I give to Mrs. Frances Burslem, of Michleover, in the County of Derby, the sum of two hundred pounds. I give to Mrs. Mary Lee, late the widow of my esteemed friend, Caleb Whitefoord, Esquire, deceased, the sum of one hundred pounds, to be paid into her own proper hands, for her sole and separate use, and for which her receipt alone (notwithstanding her coverture) shall be a sufficient discharge to my Executors hereinafter named. I give to Mr. Lee, the husband of the said Mary Lee, the sum of five hundred pounds, in trust for Maria Whiteford, Caleb Whiteford, Charles Whiteford, Harriet Whiteford, and John Whiteford, children of the said Mary Lee, by her said former husband, in equal shares, and to be paid them at their respective ages of twenty-one years; but if any, or either of them, shall happen to die before attaining that age, then as to the parts of him, her, or them, so dying, in trust for the survivors or survivor of them, equally between such survivors, if more than one; and the interest of their said several shares to be in the mean time paid or applied towards their respective maintenance or education. And I direct that the receipt of the said Mr. Lee shall be a sufficient discharge to my Executors for the same legacy. And that they shall not afterwards be liable to see to the application or disposition of the said legacy, or any part thereof, I give to the said Mr. Lee, the sum of one hundred pounds, as an acknowledgement for the trouble he will have in the execution of the aforesaid trust. I give to Mary Ann Bonomi, Agnes Bonomi, Justina Bonomi, Ignatius Bonomi, Joseph Bonomi, and Charles Bonomi, children of my late friend, Mrs. Rosa Bonomi, one hundred pounds each, to be paid them at their respective ages of twenty-one years; but if any, or either of them, shall happen to die before attaining that age, then I give the aforesaid legacy or legacies of him, her, or them, so dying, unto the survivors or survivor of them, equally between such survivors, if more than one. And I direct that the interest of their said several legacies may, if deemed necessary, be in the mean time paid or applied towards their respective maintenance or education. I give to my friend, Mrs. Mary Lloyd, widow of the late Captain Hugh Lloyd, one hundred pounds. I give to my friend, Sir William Beechey, two hundred pounds. I give to Mrs. Mary Zoffany, three hundred pounds. I give to Mrs. Green, widow of the late Valentine Green, one hundred pounds. I give to my worthy friend, Francis Douce, Esquire, the book of all my prints by Albert Durer, together with the print of the Triumphant Arch of the Emperor Maximilian; also the golden medallion which I obtained at Rome, in the year One Thousand Seven Hundred and Sixty-eight; but I request that he do, at his decease, leave and bequeath the said prints unto the British Museum. I give to my worthy friend, the Reverend Mr. Kerrick, one hundred pounds; and I desire that he the said Mr. Kerrick do select from my Prints of Reubens, twelve of them for his collection, and which twelve Prints I hereby bequeath to him. I give to my old friend, Benjamin West, Esquire, one hundred pounds, with the model of his bust. I give to my old friend, Richard Cosway, Esquire, one hundred pounds. I give to the Reverend Mr.

Wollaston, of South Weale, one hundred pounds, as a token of my regard for him. I give to my old friend, Mr. J. Taylor, of Cirencester-place, Mary-le-bone, one hundred pounds. I give and remit to my friend, Mrs. Elizabeth Rumsey, the principal and interest due from her to me, on her promissory note for one hundred pounds; and I direct that the said note be delivered up to her to be cancelled. I give to my esteemed friend, Mrs. Walford, one hundred pounds. I give to Mr. Charles Robertson, of Great Marlborough-street, fifty pounds, as a testimony of the regard I have for him. I give to Mrs. Byrne, widow of the late Mr. Byrne, Engraver, one hundred pounds. I give to Miss Susanna Devins, two hundred pounds. I give to the Reverend Doctor Charles Symmons, two hundred pounds. I give to Mr. John Woodcock, cousin of my late dear wife, three hundred pounds. I give to Mr. John Soilleux, of Notting-hill, Kensington, one hundred pounds. I give to Doctor Rudeman, of Bryanstone-street, fifty pounds. I give to Mrs. Mary Holt, fifty pounds. I give to Mrs. Gerrard, nineteen guineas. I give to Hancock, my Hair-dresser, nineteen guineas. I give to Mary Bailleux, now in Saint George's workhouse, forty pounds. I give to Mrs. Henshall, nineteen guineas. I give to Elizabeth Clements, my servant, nineteen guineas. I give to Mary Fearey, my late servant, all my wearing apparel, clothes, and body-linen. I give to Sebastian Gahagan, Alexander Goblet, and George Lupton, three of my workmen, one hundred pounds each, to be paid as soon as convenient after my decease; and to George Gahagan, another of my said workmen, twenty pounds, to be paid in like manner. I give to Louisa Goblet, daughter of the said Alexander Goblet, thirty pounds. I give to the said Mary Fearey, to Ann Clibbon, my late servant, and to Dodemy, (another of my workmen) an annuity of thirty pounds to each of them, for their respective lives, to be paid by equal half yearly payments, the first of such payments to be made at the end of six calendar months next after my decease. I give to the Trustees or Treasurer, for the time being, of the Saint Patrick Orphan Charity School, three hundred pounds for the benefit of the said school. I give to the Treasurer or Treasurers of the Middlesex Hospital, three hundred pounds for the benefit of the said hospital. I give to the Treasurer or Treasurers of the Parish Charity School of Saint Mary-le-bone, three hundred pounds for the benefit of the said school. I give to the Treasurer or Treasurers of the Society for the Relief of Persons imprisoned for Small Debts, three hundred pounds, for the purposes of the said society. I give to the Treasurer or Treasurers of the Meeting or Contribution for the Relief of distressed Seamen, held at the King's Head Tavern in the Poultry, nineteen guineas, to be applied for the purposes of the said meeting. I desire that my collection of virtu in antiques, marbles, busts, models, printed books, prints, and drawings, (except such books and prints as I have hereinbefore given) be sold by public auction; and that the said Alexander Goblet be employed to arrange, repair, and clean my said marbles, busts, and models, to fit them for sale, under the direction of my executors; and that he, the said Alexander Goblet, be paid for his trouble therein, at the rate of one guinea per day, during such time as he shall be so engaged, and which I suppose may be effected in three or four days; and I desire that my said antiques, marbles, busts, models, books, prints, and drawings, (except as aforesaid,) be sold by Mr. Christie, of Pall Mall. I give to the said Francis Douce, Esquire, and to the Reverend Edward Balme, the Executors of this my Will, five hundred pounds each, as an acknowledgement for their trouble. I give to Mrs. Sadler my leasehold house, situate and being No. 66, Great Portland-street, now in her occupation; and all my estate, term, and interest therein. I give to Mrs. Hawkins my leasehold house, situate in Edward-street, Manchester-square, now in her occupation; and all my estate, term, and interest therein. I give to Jasper Peck, Esquire, my four leasehold houses, situate in St. James's-street; my four other houses, situate in Edward-street, aforesaid; my two ground-rents of two houses, in the same street; my leasehold house in Margaret-street, Cavendish-square; and my two corner houses in Norton-street and Clipstone-street, and all my estate and interest therein respectively. And as to my property in the funds at the Bank of England, the monies to arise by the sales hereinbefore directed, the debts that shall be owing to me at my decease, and all other the residue of my estate and effects whatsoever, I give the same to Mr. Francis Russell Palmer, of Cumberland-place, New-road, and the said Francis Douce, and Mr. Edward Balme, equally to be divided between them. And I appoint the said

Francis Douce and Edward Balme, Executors of this my Will. And I declare that they, or either of them, or their respective Executors, shall not be charged or chargeable with, or answerable or accountable for any loss or damage that may happen of or to my estate and effects, or any part thereof, so as the same happens without their wilful neglect or default; and that they, or any, or either of them, shall not be answerable or accountable for the others or other of them, or for the receipts, payments, acts, neglects, or defaults of the others or other of them, but each of them only for himself, and his own receipts, payments, acts, neglects, and defaults. And that they my said Executors, and their respective Executors, shall and may, by, from, and out of my estate and effects, or any part thereof, deduct, retain, and reimburse himself and themselves respectively; all such costs, charges, and expenses as they shall respectively pay, sustain, or be put unto, in or about the execution of this my Will or relating thereto. And I do hereby revoke and make void all and every other will and wills by me at any time or times heretofore made, and do publish and declare this to be my last Will and Testament. In witness whereof, I have to this my last Will and Testament contained in three sheets of paper, set my hand and seal (that is to say) have set my hand to the first two sheets, and to this third and last sheet have set my hand and seal, this twenty-first day of March, in the year of our Lord one thousand eight hundred and eighteen.

JOSEPH NOLLEKENS, L.S.

Signed, sealed, published and declared by the said Joseph Nollekens the Testator, as and for his last Will and Testament in the presence of us who at his request in his presence, and in the presence of each other, have subscribed our names as witnesses thereto.

HENRY JEANNERET,
EDWARD CARY GROJAN, } Golden-square.

No. 1.

I give to Mrs. Harness of Stanmore in the County of Middlesex a Cousin of my late dear wife *Mary* Nollekens, three hundred pounds and I publish and declare this to be a Codicil to my foregoing Will witness my hand and seal this twenty seventh day of March one thousand eight hundred and eighteen.

JOSEPH NOLLEKENS, L.S.

Signed sealed and published by the said Joseph Nollekens in the presence of us

HENRY JEANNERET,
W. T. STUBBS.

No. 2.

I will and direct that the annuity of thirty pounds by my Will given to Mary Fearey therein named be increased to an annuity of fifty pounds and that the annuity of thirty pounds by my said Will given to Ann Clibbon therein also named be increased to an annuity of forty pounds which increased annuities I give to them respectively (in lieu of the said annuities given them by my said Will) and to be paid half yearly as in my said Will mentioned. I give to Mr. Henshall of Mortimer street Stone Mason (over and above the legacy by my said Will given to Mrs. Henshall his wife) the sum of one hundred pounds and I publish and declare this to be a further Codicil to my said Will, witness my hand and seal this twenty fourth day of June, one thousand eight hundred and eighteen.

JOSEPH NOLLEKENS, L.S.

Signed, sealed, and published, by the said Joseph Nollekens, in the presence of us,

HENRY JEANNERET,
EDW. CARY GROJAN.

No. 3.

Has a presant to Maria Verninck daughter of the Reverend Doctor and the Honorable Mrs. Verninck, of Camberwell who was the Goddaughter of my late dear wife Mrs. Nollekens and was in May last six years of age the sum of two hundred pounds Also, I have given to Sophia Baroness de Belmont the sum of two hundred pounds as a remembrance I had of her late worthy father God bless them boath. These are boath paid October the 29th, 1818.

JOSEPH NOLLEKENS.

I desire that Mr. Carlisle the Surgent be presented with a note of fifty pounds for his attendance on me.

No. 4.

It is my desier and request that my executors do make a presant of the sum of two hundred pounds to each of the daughters of Mr. John Woodcock cousens of my late dear wife Maria Nollekens, that they shall not be at the expence of the legacy duty *videlicet*, Mary Ann Woodcock and her sister Mrs. Cockell, wife of Mr. Cockell, Surgen, of Bronwick Terrace, Hackney Road this 20th day of November 1818.

JOSEPH NOLLEKENS.

(Witness)
WM. WINGFIELD,
George-street, Hanover-square.

No. 5.

I revoke the legacy or bequest in my foregoing Will contained of my property in the funds at the Bank of England the monies to arise by the sales in my said Will, directed the debts that shall be owing to me at my decease, and all other the residue of my estate and effects to Mr. Francis Russell Palmer, Mr. Francis Douce, and Mr. Edward Balme equally between them; and in lieu and stead thereof, I give and bequeath my said property in the funds at the Bank of England the said monies to arise by the aforesaid sales, the said debts that shall be owing to me at my decease and all other the said residue of my estate and effects whatsoever unto the said Francis Russell Palmer Francis Douse Edward Balme and the Reverend Mr. Kerrick in my said Will named equally to be divided between them the said Francis Russell Palmer Francis Douse Edward Balme and Mr. Kerrick And I publish and declare this to be a further Codicil to my said Will Witness my hand and seal this twenty-ninth day of January, One thousand eight hundred and nineteen.

JOSEPH NOLLEKENS, L.S.

Signed, sealed, and published by the said Joseph Nollekens in the presence of us,

HENRY JEANNERET.
W. T. STUBBS.

No. 6.

I do hereby revoke every legacy and bequest by my Will or Codicils given to or in favour of, Dodemy, and also the legacy of one hundred pounds to Alexander Goblet and instead of the said last legacy, I give to the said Alexander Goblet an annuity of thirty pounds for his life to commence from my decease, and to be payable half-yearly. Witness my hand and seal the fifteenth day of April, 1819.

JOSEPH NOLLEKENS, L.S.

(Witness)
HENRY JEANNERET.
JOSEPH BONOMI.

No. 7.

Mortimer street 27th September 1819.

It is my desire that my executors do give as a present from me to Mrs. Elizabeth Gee widow of No 4, King-street, Golden-square the sum of fifty pounds, as a token of my regard for her.

And it is my desire that my executors do give, in the same manner as above, the sum of fifty pounds to Mrs. Ray, the wife of Lieut. Ray as a token of my regard for her and her ffamily like of my friend Mr. Trumbold in America.

And it is my desire that twenty pounds shall be given to Mrs. Rouw the wife of Mr. Rouw the Modler for the regard I have for her, for her sole use and benefit, and the long slabb of marble in my yard shall be given to him for his own use. Also, that young Pastorini shall be given twenty pounds as a token of my regard for him.

And it is my request that in case of the demise of my hair dresser Hancock a legacy of twenty pounds shall be given to his daughter.

JOSEPH NOLLEKENS.

(Signed in the presence of me)
JOHN WORNINCK, D.D. &c.
Camberwell Grove.

No. 8.

Whereas, by a former memorandum I had directed that the marble in the yard and the working tools in the study should be equally divided and one-half of the same given to Mr. Alexander Goblet I do hereby revoke such former direction and instead thereof do hereby will and direct that the whole of the said marble and all the working tools in the study be delivered by my Executors to the said Alexander Goblet for his sole use and benefit in consideration of his care and attention to me.

And whereas in the aforesaid memorandum, I had directed that my books drawings and prints should be sold by Mr. King I do hereby direct that they be sold by Mr. Evans, of Pall Mall.

JOSEPH NOLLEKENS.

February the 7th, 1820.

No. 9.

It is my desier that I wish that my executors will give as a presant the sum of fifty guineas unto Henry Goblet for the servises he has done for me.

J. NOLLEKENS.

August 14th, 1820.

No. 10.

All the working tools in the shop I give to his father with the marble in the yard and the boards and utenserals for working the jack I lent to Lupto above a year ago he ought to return it I have paid and for what.—

J. NOLLEKENS.

This 14th of August, 1820.

No. 11.

This 28th day of January 1822.

Memorandum that in case of my death all the marble in the yard the tools in the shop Bankers mod tools for carving the rasp in the draw with and the draw in the parlour shall be the property of Alex. Goblet.

JOSEPH NOLLEKENS.

(Witness my hand.)
MARY HOLT.

No. 12.

Codicil to my Will.

It is my request that the legacy of fifty pounds per annum which I have left in my Will, besides my cloaths and body linen left to Mary Fiery, now Mrs. Edmonds, be revoked, and I give the said fifty pounds per annum to

Mary Holt for her life, together with my cloaths and body linen, for the care she has taken of me in my weak state of body. This is my desire, to which I set my hand and seal, this thirtieth day of July, Eighteen Hundred and Twenty-two.

JOSEPH NOLLEKENS, L.S.

(Witness)
A. H. CHAMBERS.
WM. GADSBY.

No. 13.

Since executing this Will, the Reverend Edward Balme, one of the Executors therein named, has departed this life, and I do therefore appoint as my Executors Sir William Beechy, Knight; Francis Douce, Esquire; and Thomas Smith, Esquire, of the British Museum, the joint Executors of this my Will; and I do now hereby give to the said Sir William Beechy the sum of one hundred pounds for his trouble, and to the said Thomas Smith one hundred pounds for his trouble; I do likewise hereby give and bequeath to Henry Francis Goblet, the son of Alexander Goblet, one hundred pounds, and to Mrs. Mary Holt the additional sum of one hundred pounds to what I may have already given her by this Will, which I do in all other respects hereby confirm; as witness my hand, this sixth day of December, One Thousand Eight Hundred and Twenty-two.

J. NOLLEKENS.

(Signed in the presence of us)
JOHN MEAKIN.
THOMAS MATTHEW.

No. 14.

It is my desire that my Executors pay to Mr. Peter Rouw, the Modeller, the sum of one hundred pounds. As witness my hand, this twenty-eighth day of December, One Thousand Eight Hundred and Twenty-two.

JOSEPH NOLLEKENS.

Died 23d April, 1823.

CHAPTER XVI

Funeral of Mr. Nollekens.—His wardrobe.—List of his intended bequests.—Professional anecdotes of him.—Modeling in full dress.—Taking casts from dead subjects.—His mask of Mr. Pitt.—Statue erected at Cambridge.—Mrs. Siddon's remarks on it.—Economy and profits of the Sculptor.—Bust of Lord Londonderry.—Economy in fuel.—Fuseli's opinion of Nollekens.—His bust of Mr. Coutts; anecdotes of its execution.—His collection of casts and models.—Wigs painted by Lely and Kneller.—Wycherley and Fielding wigs.—Old system of wig-stealing.—Mr. Nollekens's features of likeness in his busts.—His busts of Mr. Fox.

On the day of the funeral, May the 1st, 1823, at eleven o'clock, the hour proposed for the meeting of the carriages invited to attend it, only four appeared, namely, the Hon. Thomas Grenville's, Mr. Chambers', Mr. Palmer's; and last of all, that which the mob saluted as my Lord Mayor's. The cry was, 'Lord Mayor! Lord Mayor!'—'Lord Mayor!' rejoined the stately coachman, drawing on his sable glove; 'the Duke of Wellington's, if you please,—Lord Mayor, indeed!' and really the coach and dressings were truly splendid and worthy of so noble a Duke. The Rev. Thomas Kerrick, or, in true spelling, Kerrich, Principal Librarian to the University of Cambridge, did not appear. The mourners were all in waiting; and Mr. Douce arrived at twelve. The street-lamp-irons and windows were thronged to see 'The Miser's Funeral'; and all was now in silent motion. The first coach contained Francis Douce, Esq. an Executor, and one of the residuary-legatees. Sir William Beechey, also an Executor, but not a residuary-legatee, was obliged to attend his own interests in touching up his pictures in the Royal Academy-room, previous to the opening of the Exhibition. The second in the coach was the late Dr. Simmonds, of Chiswick, an old and steady friend to the deceased; the third was Russel Palmer, Esq. the son of Mrs. Palmer, an acquaintance of some standing with the deceased; and the fourth was myself, an Executor, but, like Sir William Beechey, no residuary-legatee. The other mourners were, Mr. Woodcock, a cousin of Mrs. Nollekens, to whom a small legacy had been left; Mr. Nelson Beechey, for his father; Mr. Christie, the auctioneer, the gentleman who sold part of the property; Raphael and Benjamin West, Esquires, sons of the late venerable President; the Rev. Stephen Weston; Mr. Jeanneret, who was sent for after Mr. Nollekens's death to read the will; Mr. Gahagan; Mr. Goblet, sen. and his son; Mr. Rouw, Mr. Taylor, and Mr. Soilleux.[1] Being now in a state of motion, the conversation between Dr. Simmonds and myself fell upon notices in the newspapers respecting the very extraordinary manner in which it was stated that Mr. Nollekens's money was to be distributed. As the coach in which I was, turned round Harley-street, I had a perfect view of the procession, and the crowd that followed the Duke of Wellington's carriage was immense; it was a new one, built for state occasions. By the time we got into the New Road, the concourse of people was beyond all conception; for it was May-day, and the chimney-sweepers in their trappings, and the Jacks-in-the-green, or Bunter's Garland, had all followed what they still looked upon as my Lord Mayor's coach. Indeed, so strongly was this believed by the drivers of the Paddington stages, whose horses were gaily decked

[1] Early on the day of the funeral, when Sir William Beechey and myself found that Mr. Peck, one of Mr. Nollekens's two nearest relations, had not been included in the list of those invited, we immediately directed Mr. Turner, the undertaker, to send a coach to the Temple for that gentleman, but it arrived too late for him to attend.

with ribbons of various dies, that they, out of respect or fear of the City Magistrate, fell back and slowly followed the Duke's coach.

By the time we had arrived at the Yorkshire Stingo, a crowd of milk-maids and inferior maid-servants, who had been dancing and drinking on the green all the morning, so choked up the turnpike, that for some time a stoppage took place. At last, the mob, finding it to be only a funeral, and that it was going to Paddington, the greater part of our company left us, to follow their accustomed gambols. On our arrival at the church-yard, Old Dodimy was waiting to see the last of his master, with whom had he remained, most likely he would have had the annuity of thirty pounds once bequeathed him; but since transferred to Lewis Goblet, Sculptor, as a reward for his long and faithful services. Before this time, however, Goblet was not noticed, though he had received many assurances from Mr. Nollekens that he had left him and his family comfortably in his will. When the funeral was over, Mr. Douce returned from the church-yard to his house in Kensington-square, and most of the other mourners returned to the house of the deceased, in order to hear the Will read. This I, as an Executor, firmly insisted upon, and it was accordingly read in the presence of many persons now living.

Some time was employed by two of the Executors and the three solicitors, in looking over Mr. Nollekens's property, before the Will was proved. At one of these meetings, Mr. Nollekens's wardrobe was inspected, when we found it to consist of his court-coat of *Pourpre de Pape*, in which he was married; his hat, sword, and bag; two shirts; two pairs of worsted stockings, one table-cloth, three sheets, and two pillow-cases, but all these were in such a state of decay, that, with other rags, Mrs. Holt informed me she could only procure *one pound five shillings* for her legacy. His smart green velvet-cap, one of the two kindly presented to him by a lady, Mrs. Holt presented to a friend.

During the investigation of his papers, I was in anxious expectation of finding a Will subsequent to the one produced, as he had been for years in the habit of signing many Wills, in all of which he assured me he had recollected me and my family. 'That you may depend upon, Tom,' were his words. In the year 1810, he showed me a list of the names of one hundred persons, to every one of whom he said he intended to leave one thousand pounds!

Of this list, which was in his own handwriting, he said I might make a copy to show to my wife; but I only drew out the names of those persons whom I knew; and as I never destroy any paper of the least moment, I am enabled to insert the following copy.

Mr. Arnald.
Sir William Beechey.
Lady Beechey.
Countess de Belmont.
Mr. Bone.
Mrs. Bone.
Joseph Bonomi.
Bonomi, Jun.
Mrs. Bonomi.
Miss Bonomi.
Agnes Bonomi.
Mr. Browne.
Mrs. Byrne.
Mr. Byrne.
Miss Byrne.
Mr. Carlisle.
Lady Chambers.[1]
Mr. Chambers.
Mrs. Chambers.
Miss Chambers.
Mr. Chantrey.
Mr. Christie.
Mr. Collins.
Mr. Colnaghi.
Mr. Combe.
Mr. Cosway.
Mrs. Cosway.
Mr. Peter Coxe.
Charles Cranmer.[2]
Mr. Dean.

[1] The wife of Sir Robert Chambers, Chief-Justice of India. Sir Robert and his lady are mentioned by Boswell, in his Life of Doctor Johnson. Lady Chambers is the daughter of the late Joseph Wilton, Esq. R. A.

[2] One of the early models at the Royal Academy, who sat to Angelica Kauffmann when she resided with her father in Golden-square.

Mr. Devall.
Mr. Farington.
Mrs. Fox.
Mr. Gahagan.
Mr. Gahagan, Jun.
Miss Gerrard.
Mr. Gregory.
Mr. Goblet.
Mrs. Goblet.
Henry Goblet.
Louisa Goblet.
Mr. Harness.
Mr. Adair Hawkins.
Mr. Henshall.
Mr. Howard.
Mr. Joseph.
Mr. Kenrick.
Mr. Knight, Jun.
Sir Thomas Lawrence.
Mr. Lonsdale.
Mrs. Lloyd.
Mr. Lupton.
Mr. Northcote.
Mrs. Palmer.
Mr. Palmer.
Mr. William Pether.
Mr. Panzetta.
Mr. Planta.
Mr. Poingnon.
Mr. Richards.
Mr. Rossi.
Mr. Rouw.
Mrs. Rouw.
Mr. N. Smith.
Mr. J. T. Smith.
Mrs. Smith.
N. J. Smith, Jun.
Jane Smith.
Johanna Smith.
Mr. Sharp.
Dr. Simmonds.
Mr. John Taylor.
Mr. Ward.
Mr. West.
Mrs. West.
Mrs. Wilson.
Mr. Wivell.
Mr. Woodcock.
Mrs. Zoffany.[1]

Having illustrated the peculiar manners of Mr. Nollekens in his ordinary life, I shall now introduce a few professional anecdotes of him as an artist, which will probably be not less amusing to the reader.

During the time an illustrious personage was sitting for his bust, he could not refrain from smiling at his friend, who stood behind Nollekens, at the truly ridi-

[1] Mr. Nollekens, who had been extremely intimate with Mr. Zoffany, when approaching his 80th year, offered his hand to his widow, who very civilly declined it, prudently observing, 'No, Sir, the world would then say, she has married him for his money.' Mrs. Zoffany, when she found poor Bronze had been set down in his Will for only 19*l.* 19*s.* very generously gave Mrs. Holt a guinea for her, long before she received her own legacy.

culous manner in which the artist had inconvenienced himself for the occasion. His powdered toupet,[1] which was stiffly pomatumed, stood pointedly erect; and he had, for the first time, put on a coat, to which the tailor had given an enormously high buckramed cape, so that, like Allscrip's, in 'The Heiress', his head appeared as if it were in the pillory. To look over this cape, Nollekens had for some time painfully exerted himself, by stretching his neck to its fullest possible extent; but, as he proceeded with his model, his body by degrees relaxed, and his head at last was so completely buried within the cape, that nothing but the pinnacle of his toupet was visible above it. This ridiculous exit of Nollekens's head so operated upon the risibility of the noble sitter, that, at last, he irresistibly indulged in a liberal fit of laughter, which so irritated the little Sculptor, who had for some time noticed their smiles, that, instead of good-temperedly finding fault with the tailor, he lost sight of propriety, and thrusting his thumb into the mouth of the model, impetuously exclaimed, with a treble wag of his head, '*If you laugh, I'll make a fool of ye!*'

Nollekens, after reading the death of any great person in the newspaper, generally ordered some plaster to be got ready, so that he might attend at a minute's notice. One day, when a lady who had sent for him desired him not to make so free with her dear husband's corpse, he observed, 'Oh, bless ye, you had better let me close his eyelids; for then, when I cast him in my mould, he'll look for all the world as if he was asleep. Why do you take on so? you do wrong to *prey* upon such a dismal prospect; do leave the room

[1] Mr. Nollekens, when at Rome, wore his long hair tied up in a club; when he arrived in England, he commenced wearing hair-powder, and continued the use of it till his hair became thin; he then, at the recommendation of Caleb Whitefoord, had it all cut off, and wore a natural wig without powder.

to me and my man; I am used to it, it makes no impression on me; I have got a good many noted down in my journal.'

Mr. Sebastian Gahagan, the Sculptor, Mr. Nollekens's assistant, attended him to cast the face of Lord Lake, after his decease; his Lordship's brother was then inconsolably pacing the room, but Mr. Nollekens shook him by the elbow, and applied to him for a little sweet-oil, a large basin, some water, and pen, ink, and paper.

The gentleman, astonished at his want of decency, referred him to the servant; and Nollekens, after he had taken the mask, muttered the following soliloquy: 'Now, let me see, I must begin to measure him; where's my callipers? I must take him from his chin to the upper pinnacle of his head; I'll put him down in ink; ay, that will do; now, I must have him from his nose to the back part of his skull; well, now let's take his shoulders; now for his neck; well, now I've got him all.'

On Mr. Nollekens's return from Putney Common, after taking Mr. Pitt's mask, he observed to Mr. Gahagan, pointing to it on the opposite seat of the coach, 'There, I would not take fifty guineas for that mask, I can tell ye.' He would have done wrong if he had; for from this mask and Hoppner's picture, which was lent him by Lord Mulgrave, he was enabled to produce the statue erected in the Senate-house of Cambridge, for which he received three thousand guineas.[1]

Mr. George Lupton, the Statuary, of Keppel-row, New-road, informed me that he went to Cambridge with his men to put up Mr. Pitt's monument; and

[1] Mr. Gahagan carved this statue of Pitt, for which Mr. Nollekens paid him, I am sorry to say, a miserably small sum; and I really think, those who now bask in the sunshine of Mr. Nollekens's immense wealth, should take into consideration, the letter which he addressed to the Executors shortly after the death of his old master.

when he had erected the pedestal upon which it was to stand, he wrote to Mr. Nollekens and informed him of its being ready; but as he did not come immediately, Mr. Lupton placed the figure upon it. Soon after this, Mr. Nollekens arrived, and exclaimed, 'Thank God! it is up.' He went to Cambridge in a very shabby coat, notwithstanding he intended to accept the invitation of the heads of the University, and to feed upon what Lupton called 'The fat of the land'; the Rev. Thomas Kerrich being one of his feeders. It is said that Nollekens charged one thousand pounds for Pitt's pedestal; but Lupton assured me that he had only twelve pounds for the working expenses, and that Nollekens bought the stone remarkably cheap at Mr. Deval's sale, he thinks at about nine shillings the cube foot. He also farther observed that Chantrey was nothing to Nollekens, with respect to his charges.

The erection of this effigy was thus noticed by Prince Hoare, Esq. in his Academic Annals of 1809. 'Statue of the Right Hon. William Pitt; to be placed in the Senate-house in the University of Cambridge: by general subscription of the Members of the University. (Executed by Joseph Nollekens, R.A.) This great statesman and orator is represented in the act of speaking, holding a roll of paper in his left hand. The attitude is designed to convey an idea of that commanding energy and decision, with which he was accustomed to address the House of Commons. He is habited in the gown worn by the Masters of Arts in the University. The statue is to be erected in the Senate-house, at the eastern end of the room, in the place where the figure of *Glory* at present stands.'

The 'Guide through the University of Cambridge', published in 1814, after describing the statue of the Duke of Somerset, by Rysbrack, states, 'that on the right is a statue of the Right Hon. W. Pitt, erected at the expense of different Members of the University; upwards of 7000*l.* being subscribed for that purpose.

This statue was executed by Nollekens, and is considered by many good judges to be his *chef-d'œuvre.*'

Mr. Knight, one of the principal superintendents of the works at the New London Bridge, informed me that when Mrs. Siddons arrived to look at this statue, Mr. Nollekens was touching up the drapery; and that he heard that lady remark to the Sculptor, that in her opinion, he was frittering the folds. Nollekens at first replied only by a kind of a double grunt; but when that lady left the studio, he declared that he was glad she was gone, for she knew nothing about the matter. Now, in the opinion of several artists of eminence, Mrs. Siddons, who has very fine taste, and a considerable share of talent as a modeller, was perfectly correct.[1]

When Mr. Nollekens had finished the monument of the three Captains, ordered by Government to be erected in Westminster Abbey, it remained in his studio for nearly fourteen years, waiting for the inscription; and he being at last out of all patience, petitioned the late King, then at Weymouth, to take it into his royal consideration. The late Mr. Pitt was so highly displeased at his interference, that he never would sit to Mr. Nollekens for his bust, nor recommend him in any way whatever; and yet it is a fact, that after the decease of that great statesman, Mr. Nollekens made no less a sum by him than 15,000*l.*, according to the following calculation. The statue and pedestal for Trinity College, Cambridge, four thousand pounds. He also executed at least seventy-four busts in marble, for almost every one of which he had one hundred and twenty guineas; and there were upwards of six hundred casts taken at six guineas each. The marble for the figure did not ultimately cost him more than twenty pounds; for he had so cunningly

[1] Many of my readers may remember the head of Adam, which Mrs. Siddons exhibited at the Royal Academy, some years back; but very few can recollect that performance with more pleasure than myself.

economized the block, that he cut out from the corners several pieces for various busts: and even farther than this, the block not being long enough by the depth of Mr. Pitt's head, he contrived to drill out a lump from between the legs large enough for the head, which he put on the shoulders of the block. The arm was also carved from a single *piece;* and yet for this figure, *pieced* in a manner which the sculptors of Italy would have been ashamed of, he received the unheard-of-price of three thousand guineas, and one thousand for the pedestal; giving the Sculptor who carved it, only the odd three hundred pounds for his trouble. For the busts in marble, he paid Gahagan, Goblet, and another Sculptor of inferior merit, twenty-four pounds each, upon the average.

When the late Marquis of Londonderry was sitting for his bust, coals were at an enormous price; and the noble Lord, who had been for some time shivering in his seat, took the opportunity, when the Sculptor went out for more clay, of throwing some coals upon the fire. 'Oh! my good Lord, I don't know what Mr. Nollekens will say!' exclaimed Mrs. Nollekens, who was bolstered up and bound to an old night-chair by the fire-side: 'Never mind, my good lady,' answered his Lordship; 'tell him to put them into my bill.'—Lonsdale, the Portrait-painter, who found him one severe winter's evening starving himself before a handful of fire, requested to be permitted to throw a few coals on; and before Mr. Nollekens could reply, on they were. Lonsdale, strongly suspecting that they would be taken off as soon as he was gone, was determined to be convinced; and when he had reached the street-door, pretended to have forgotten something, re-ascended to the room, and found him, as he suspected, taking them off with the fire-feeder, so strongly recommended to him by the Bishop of St. Asaph; at the same time muttering to himself, '*Shameful!* shameful extravagance!' He never left the kind-hearted Lonsdale a legacy; at least, I know of none; though it was his intention to have put him down in a former Will for 1000*l.*

John Knowles, Esq. the friend, and for many years the constant companion, of Fuseli, communicated to me the remarks which that artist made to him respecting the talents of Nollekens.

'Mr. Coutts said to me yesterday,' observed Fuseli, '"My family have urged me to sit for a bust to be executed in marble. Now, as you know, Fuseli, that the price is not an object, pray tell me who you think will execute it best?" I had no difficulty in doing this; for although Nollekens is superannuated in many particulars, yet in a bust he stands unrivalled. If Mr. Coutts had required a group of figures, I should have recommended Flaxman; but for a bust, give me Nollekens.'

This bust of Mr. Coutts, the Banker, was one of Nollekens's last productions, and one in which he appeared to take much pleasure: but I must say that, as to likeness, it is certainly ridiculously severe. In my mind, it displays the distorted features of a distressed person labouring under the heavy pangs of poverty, penury, or peevishness, neither of which cheerless characteristics did Mr. Coutts at any period of his life possess. Indeed, it is what I deem a Cruikshank-caricature countenance. Chantrey has succeeded much better, and, indeed, completely, in his statue of him.[1] Mrs. Nollekens assured me that during the numerous sittings which that wealthy man gave Mr. Nollekens, no one could be more attentive to him than Mrs. Coutts, who never failed to bring with her in her carriage some of the most delicious and comforting soups or refreshments that could possibly be made; which she herself warmed in a saucepan over the parlour fire: 'and I declare, my good Sir,' con-

[1] This statue is placed in the Duchess of St. Alban's drawing-room, in her Grace's town-house, Piccadilly.

tinued Mrs. Nollekens, 'I believe it did me as much good to see old Mr. Coutts enjoy every spoonful of it, as it would have done had it passed through my own mouth.'

These savoury-soup scenes must have been comically curious, as well as truly melancholy; for at that time Mrs. Nollekens was in her last stage of existence, with her spine nearly bent double. A wry neck had much twisted her head, which, in the best possible position, reclined upon a wing of a nurse's old-fashioned high-backed night-chair,[1] covered with a broad chequered red and white stuff; and her swollen legs, which were almost useless, were placed upon a stool for the day, by her 'flesh-brush rubber', a woman who regularly attended her for an hour every morning. Then Mr. Coutts was blowing his broth, attended by Mrs. Coutts, a lively woman, most fashionably dressed; whilst Nollekens, to use the commonest of all similes, nearly as deaf as a post, was prosecuting his bust, and at the same time, repeating his loud interrogations as to the price of stocks to his sitter; who had twice most good-temperedly stayed the spoon, when it was considerably more than half-way to his mouth, and turned his head to answer him. As for the old conversation upon his early amusement of bell-tolling, that was a pleasure our Artist had given up, ever since he became a patient of the celebrated Aurist, Mr. Maule, who advised him by all means to keep his ears well stuffed with cotton.

[1] In the latter part of Mrs. Nollekens's life, her husband would frequently make drawings of her, either in her chair, or as her maid was leading her up or down stairs: these sketches he showed to Mr. Jackson; observing to him, even in her presence, 'Only see how much she has altered in a short time! That drawing I made in July, and this in August.'—'Ay, Sir,' observed Mrs. Nollekens, who was almost bent double in the great arm-chair, 'you never would make a drawing of me when I was fit to be seen.'

Mr. Henning, the Sculptor, when employed by Lady Moira to make a model in wax from Lord Moira's bust by Nollekens, was under the necessity of going to the artist's house to take the likeness; and he was in hope, from a man's standing so high in his profession, that he should derive considerable benefit from his conversation; but in this expectation he was, after repeatedly trying to bring him into discourse, most grievously disappointed.[1]

Fiamingo's models of boys were great favourites with Mr. Nollekens: he had several originals in clay, which he procured from Antwerp; and upon which he placed so high a value, that, though frequent and considerable offers were made, he would not part with them. Indeed he would not even listen to his flattering friend Angelica Kauffmann, who practised her wheedlings to the fullest extent of her fascinating powers, to become mistress of only one of the most inferior of his collection. He laid out little money in England in plaster casts, for most of those he possessed he brought from Rome; unless Papera, who, in the commencement of his career, carried the new things round to the artists in baskets, brought him a Fiamingo child which he had never seen. I recollect a basso-relievo of boys, which he admired very much, until Papera named John Deare as the modeller: when his admiration, I am sorry to say, decreased into the following remarks:—'Yes, it is; he is a clever fel-

[1] Mr. Henning had been previously introduced to Mr. Nollekens by his old friend, James Dawkins, Esq. who would now and then joke him as to his Venuses. Mr. Henning informed me, that Mr. Dawkins assured him, that his uncle's work of Palmyra and Balbeck had cost him no less a sum than fifty thousand pounds; his attendants in the Deserts being so numerous, that he seldom had fewer than three hundred men to protect him and assist in his discoveries. Surely this noble enterprise demands the most liberal notice of the future biographer of Mr. Dawkins.

low, certainly; but I don't see the wonderful merit in his Marine Venus that Sir Richard Worsley talks so much about; and there's Mr. Penn, with his Landing of Julius Cæsar: it's a clever thing, and so I have always told him.'

Nollekens, whenever he could contrive it, avoided a representation of flowing hair in marble, particularly in curled wigs; though in his bust of Lord Chancellor Bathurst, he was obliged to attend strictly to costume. The manner in which the wig of that bust is modelled, proves what I firmly believe to be the fact, that such profusion of hair either perplexed him, or was too expensive in the workmanship. Indeed, his master, Scheemakers, never shone in the art of wig-making, as his bust of Sir Hans Sloane, in the British Museum, sufficiently proves. His predecessor, Bird, in the wig of Sir Cloudesley Shovel, in Westminster Abbey, bad as it is, was more successful in its tooling. That of Doctor Lockyer, in Saint Mary Overjes, and those on the statues of Sir John Cutler, in the College of Physicians, and Grocers' Hall, are very little superior. Roubiliac's statue of Sir John Cass, at Saint Botolph's, Aldgate, exhibits a particularly tasteful wig;[1] but, notwithstanding his skill displayed in that instance, he was not fond of introducing it, and endeavoured to persuade his sitters to take their wigs off. His busts of Pope, Lord Bolingbroke, Martin Folkes, Doctors Mead and Frewin, and numerous others of men of literature, are without wigs. Jonathan Richardson has etched his own portrait and that of Lord Somers in flowing wigs; and these two prints exhibit more flow of curl and spirit of needle than any I can instance. Indeed, they are complete specimens of tasteful flowing hair; and yet Richardson has also etched

[1] This fine statue has lately been most villainously painted of various colours, in order to make it appear as *natural as life*, or like the *Westminster Abbey* wax-work.

his own head, and many more of Lord Bolingbroke and Pope, without wigs; which proves that he preferred the natural shape of the head.

Nollekens's bust of Doctor Johnson is without his wig, but with very thick and heavy locks, which much displeased the Doctor, who insisted upon it that all persons should be pourtrayed as they are seen in company; adding, that though a man for ease may wear a night-cap in his own chamber, he ought not to look like one who had taken physic. I recollect that Wilkie, the Academician, once observed to an artist who was about to paint his own portrait without his cravat, with his shirt-collar thrown open to exhibit his neck, 'Oh don't do that; you'll look as if you were going to be shaved.'

In the representation of hair, the spirited Painter has a decided superiority over the most exquisite and dexterous Sculptor; not only in colour and texture, but also as to time. The former is enabled to produce in one hour with his elastic and oily pencil, as much as would take the latter six weeks with his chisel and drill; as may be seen in the beautifully flowing hair of Vandyke, Dobson, Lely, and Kneller, and the laboured works of the best Sculptors. The difference in a Lely wig from that of a Kneller, is, that the former generally falls down the shoulders in front, and the latter is thrown over the shoulders behind.

It must, however, be understood, that though Kneller and Lely thus differed, they did not paint all their sitters according to their own fashion of wearing their wigs. On the contrary, we find by Blooteling's print of Thomas Earl of Danby, that his wig was peculiar. At the bottom of the sides of the wig, which falls over the front of the shoulders, there are three regularly distinct curls stiffly rolled up. But of all the wig-dandies of those days, the Duke of Ormond appears to have been the most fanciful; and I am supported in this conjecture by the four different portraits of that nobleman, engraven by Faithorne, Loggan, Williams, and White; which, though they all have large and flowing wigs, conspicuously vary in their modes of curling.

It may possibly be within the recollection of some few of my readers, when gentlemen indulged in an immensely expensive purchase of deep and flowing curled wigs, such as Wycherley and 'Beau Fielding' wore; and I have been credibly informed, that the enormous sum of fifty guineas was given by the best-dressing men of the time for a truly fashionable wig of the above description. Such wigs continued to be worn by many men of the old school during the latter part of the profession of Zincke, the Enamel-painter, whose portraits exhibit many of them. Sir James Thornhill and Jonathan Richardson wore flowing wigs, and so likewise did Sir James's son-in-law Hogarth, in the early part of his professional career. In the latter years of his life, he wore a Busby-wig when dressed; though, whilst painting, he preferred a velvet cap. There are persons now living, who recollect seeing the father of the late Mr. Prime, of Witton,[1] wearing a flowing wig, or what is better known in the Burletta of Tom Thumb, a Doodle and a Noodle. Mrs. Nollekens has frequently been heard to relate, that during the early part of Mr. Welch's magistracy, gentlemen were continually annoyed, and frequently robbed of their wigs in the open street and in mid-day. She stated that this method of wig-stealing was singularly daring, as well as laughably curious. A man dressed like a baker, bending beneath a large loaded bread-basket, which he had hoisted upon his shoulders, waited until the first gentleman wearing a costly wig was about to turn the corner of a street in a

[1] This gentleman resided in the house which had been the mansion of Sir Godfrey Kneller; the staircase of which, painted by that artist, remains perfectly in its original state.

crowded thoroughfare; and then, just as an accomplice ran forcibly against him, a boy concealed in the baker's basket, knocked off the gentleman's gold-laced hat, and instantly snatched his wig. Whilst the gentleman was stooping to pick up his hat, the fictitious baker made off, with his dexterous assistant, till he came to the first convenient turning, where he released the boy, who walked away with his booty neatly folded up in a school-boy's satchel, which he threw carelessly over his shoulder, as if slowly going to school, with his round, 'shining, morning face'; leaving the baker with a loaf or two in his basket, pretending to be waiting at a customers's door, at which it was supposed he had knocked. After numerous depredations of this kind, the bakers' men, who were avoided by the Wycherleys,[1] were determined not to be mistaken; and no longer carried their baskets hoisted on their shoulders, but swung them over the arm, and have ever since carried them at their backs; so that the wearers of wigs might see the contents of their bread-baskets.

But to return to our Sculptor: in my opinion, Mr. Nollekens trusted more to the eyes, nose, and mouth, for a likeness, than to the bones of the head; and in this belief I am supported most powerfully by the

[1] From Smith's portrait of Wycherley, engraven in 1703, we may conclude that he was, as reported, a very handsome man; and by the sleekness of the curls of his wig, that he took great pains with it; indeed, so much was it the fashion to attend to the easy grace of the curls, that it was his custom, while standing in the pit of the theatre conversing with ladies in the boxes, to comb and adjust his discomposed locks. Wig-combs, which were made of most beautiful specimens of tortoise-shell, and most fancifully engraven with representations of flowers and birds, and indeed sometimes inlaid with mother-of-pearl with their owners' names, were contained in a side-pocket case of the size of a thin octavo volume, for the purpose of having them always about their persons.

mask taken from Mr. Fox after his death. In his busts of that statesman,[1] the foreheads are low and rugged; whilst that of the mask is even, high, and prominent, full of dignified grandeur, and more so, perhaps, with the exception of Lord Bacon, than that of any other statesman of equal celebrity. The reader may be convinced of the correctness of this remark, by visiting Mr. Deville's Gallery in the Strand, where there are casts taken from both examples.

[1] Mr. Nollekens modelled and carved two different busts of Mr. Fox. The first was with a toupet and curls above the ears, as that gentleman wore his hair about 1783, just as Sir Joshua Reynolds has painted him; of which bust there are several engravings, the carving being by T. Gaugain. The second bust is with his hair cut close; and of this there are two plates; one by Skelton, for the small edition of Fox's Life of King James the Second, and the other by Evans, from a beautiful drawing by Mr. Howard, for the large edition of the same work. Of the mask taken by Nollekens after death, I am not aware of there being any engraving; ghastly as it is, and totally unlike as the features are to those of Mr. Fox when living, still the shape of the forehead is truly remarkable and interesting.

CHAPTER XVII

Sale of Mr. Nollekens's collection of Sculpture.—Mending antiques.—Sale of his prints. &c.—Account of his seated female figure.—Patrons of modern English Sculptors.—Antique foot.—Sir Joshua Reynolds's throne-chair.—List of busts, monuments, and statues, executed by Nollekens.—Chronological list of all his sculptures exhibited at the Royal Academy, from 1771 to 1816.—Conclusion.

THE sale of Mr. Nollekens's unsold works, and collection of antique and modern sculptures, took place under the hammer of Mr. Christie, on the premises in Mortimer-street, on Thursday, July 3d, 1823, and at the Auctioneer's room in Pall-Mall, on the two days following. The collection consisted of many of Mr. Nollekens's original models, carvings in marble, and works by Italian and other artists, particularly Michel Angelo and Fiamingo.

Mr. Nollekens's statue of a standing Venus in marble, pouring ambrosia on her hair, was purchased by Mrs. Palmer for 231*l*;[1] and his model of a sitting Venus, was bought by the Earl of Egremont. The antique marbles consisted of a statue of Minerva; a noble bust of Commodus, in perfect condition, and several other Imperial busts; one of Mercury; and a very spirited head of a Faun; chiefly purchased at the sales of the late B. Bond Hopkins, Esq. at Pain's Hill; and at the Earl of Besborough's, at Roehampton. These antiques, which were mostly purchased by the Duke of Newcastle, brought full thirty times the money they had cost Mr. Nollekens. His method of mending antiques was rather curious: he would mix the dust of the sort of stone he was mending, with his

[1] This figure is by no means so good as the one of Venus chiding Cupid, executed by the same artist for his liberal patron Lord Yarborough.

plaster; so that when dry, if the antiques were of Pentallic marble, the sparkling of the stone-dust in a great measure disguised the joining or mended parts. Mr. Roubiliac, when he had to mend a broken antique, would mix grated Gloucester cheese with his plaster, adding the grounds of porter and the yolk of an egg; which mixture, when dry, forms a very hard cement.

Mr. Nollekens's prints, drawings, and books of prints, were sold by M. Evans, in Pall Mall, on Thursday, December 4th, 1823. They principally consisted of nearly the entire works of Nicolas Poussin; a fine collection of the engravings after Sir Joshua Reynolds's pictures; several sketch-books filled by Mr. Nollekens when at Rome, and numerous drawings also by him, made upon the backs of letters.

Nollekens's figure with the sandal, carved for Lord Yarborough, was considerably the greatest favourite with the public of all his female figures; but that which he himself took the greatest delight in showing, was seated with her arms round her legs, Lot 21, purchased at his sale at Mr. Christie's, by the Earl of Egremont, for the sum of eighty-four pounds; his Lordship giving it the preference to others by the same artist. He engaged Mr. Rossi, the Academician, to execute it in marble, with strict injunctions that no alterations whatever, not even an improvement upon the model, should be attempted. In giving this order, his Lordship was, in my humble opinion, perfectly correct; for, if improvements had been made, it could no longer have been esteemed as a production of Nollekens's mind; though I am perfectly convinced, that had the figure been carved under his own eye, it would in many instances have been benefited by those corrections which most Sculptors are induced to make whilst they are executing finished carvings from their models. Mr. Williams, who carved this figure under the superintendence of Mr. Rossi, assured me, that in no instance could he have been engaged upon a more difficult task, especially in carving parts that were so intricately undercut; as the right hand of the figure placed before the right leg, was within a quarter of an inch of the shin-bone, and he had to invent tools of the most singular shapes to enable him to cut and file away the stone. It was the opinion of most artists, that many parts of this figure could have been much improved: they thought the ankles unquestionably too thick; and that, to have given it an air of the antique, the right thigh wanted flesh to fill up the ill-formed nature which Nollekens had strictly copied. The abdomen was far from good; and the face was too old, and of a common character; but the back was considered extremely beautiful. The attitude was a natural one, and acquired by mere chance, as good attitudes often are.

The woman from whom it was modelled, after standing for some time to Mr. Nollekens for parts of a figure for which he was then engaged, was desired to dress; and, upon her seating herself on the ground, to put on her stockings, her posture so pleased the Sculptor, that he immediately cried, 'Stop, don't move; I must model you as you now sit:' and it is a curious fact, that he, being at that time Visitor of the Royal Academy, placed the woman, who sat as the model there, precisely in the same position. It is also rather singular, that the above-mentioned Mr. Williams, who carved the figure for Mr. Rossi, is in possession of a drawing made by his father at the Academy, from the female who was so placed.

When Mr. Nollekens had completed this model, the late Earl of Carlisle purchased it, with an intention of having it carved in marble, and placed with the numerous other works of Art at Castle Howard; but upon some family objections being made, his Lordship gave the artist a portion of the purchase-money to resign his bargain, and it actually remained unsold for many years previous to the death of our Sculptor. It is now, however, honoured with a pedestal at Petworth, amidst numerous specimens of modern Art, of which Lord Egremont, to his eternal honour be it spoken, is a most liberal encourager. This Nobleman is not only in possession of Mr. Rossi's beautiful group of Celadon and Amelia; but, I am happy to state, has also commissioned the same artist to execute another figure for him. His Lordship will likewise have the good fortune to possess the group of the Angel Michael and Satan, one of the grandest works of the late Professor Flaxman, and perhaps equal to the productions of this, or any age of former times. The modern Sculptors, however, are not only indebted to the patronage of the above Nobleman, but also to that of their Graces the Dukes of Devonshire, Bedford, and Newcastle, who are in possession of some of the finest specimens of their abilities. Indeed our Sculptors of talent have so glorious a Patron in his Most Gracious Sovereign, that the greatest part of the Nobility and persons of opulence endeavour to vie with each other in the decoration of their halls and galleries; and in a few years, it may reasonably be expected, the mansions of wealthy Englishmen will exhibit such a display of native talent, that it will at once astonish and confound most of our Continental visitors and rivals.

Sir Thomas Lawrence is the fortunate possessor of an antique foot, valued by Nollekens as highly as any specimen in his collection; of which precious relique he has been heard to tell the following story. When he was at Rome, he often endeavoured to persuade Cardinal Albani, to whom it belonged, to part with it, but without success. At last, when Nollekens was about to come to England, the Cardinal, who knew no other way of getting possession of a female Torso, which Nollekens possessed, gave him the foot for it.

It has also been stated, that the Cardinal stole the foot in order to give it to Nollekens; and some, who stick at nothing, have said that Nollekens stole it from the Cardinal. This, however, I do not believe, as I never will encourage the thought of his being dishonest, or even in the slightest degree dishonourable. It is now kept by Sir Thomas Lawrence, under a glass shade; and it must have measured one foot five inches and a quarter from the heel to the great toe, before the tip of that member was mutilated. Sir Thomas Lawrence, when first he acquired it, was inclined to consider it as belonging to the famous Torso; the marble being the same, and the proportions agreeing most perfectly: but, upon a little reflection, the President gave up that pleasing idea, perfectly satisfied that it never could have belonged to that fragment, as the foot treads flat upon the ground, and is unquestionably in the action of a standing figure about to walk, which does not accord with the action of the thighs of the Torso, which, the reader will recollect, is seated.

I was the means of Sir Thomas acquiring another interesting relique of art, as will appear by the following statement.

Twelve months after the death of Dr. Fryer, I found, by a catalogue of his household property, that Sir Joshua Reynolds's throne-chair was inserted for sale by auction; and though I had many friends who were ignorant of that circumstance, and whose love for the Arts would have induced them to have gone to a high price for it, particularly one gentleman of rank and fortune, from whom I and my family have received repeated instances of kindness,—I considered it my duty, as an artist, to apprise Sir Thomas Lawrence of its approaching exposition; and, for that proper attention, I had the honour of receiving his warmest thanks. However, on the day of the sale, the President had nearly lost it; as the lot was actually about to be knocked down for the paltry sum of ten shillings and sixpence, just as the rescuing bidder entered the room;

which enabled him, after a slight contest of biddings, to place the treasure on that very day by Sir Thomas's fireside in Russell-square. Last year, in the ever-memorable sale of the Leicester Gallery of Pictures, consisting entirely of the productions of British artists, a comparatively diminutive chair of French character was conspicuously advertised as the throne-chair of Sir Joshua Reynolds. Sir Thomas Lawrence, as soon as possible, personally acquainted Mr. Christie with the absurd mistake; who, upon coming to the lot, with his usual manly fairness, acknowledged the error to the whole company, informing them that the real unostentatious chair was in the possession of the President of the Royal Academy.

Some time before Doctor Fryer's death, I requested him to give me a specimen of Barry's hand-writing, to insert in Boswell's Life of Dr. Johnson, which my wife has for several years been engaged in illustrating; when he most liberally gave me that artist's first sketch of the letter which he addressed to Lord and Lady Inchiquin, upon their honouring him with the presentation of the above-mentioned chair. And as many of my readers may not be in possession of Dr. Fryer's Life of Barry, where the perfect letter is inserted, I here give a copy of the first confused draught which now adorns my wife's book.

'Mr. Barry presents his respectful compliments to Lord and Lady Inchiquin, with every acknowledgment and thanks for their inestimable favour conferred on him this morning, in the gift of Sir Joshua's chair.

'Alas! this chair, that has had such a glorious career of fortune, instrumental as it has been in giving the most advantageous stability to the otherwise fleeting, perishable graces of a Lady Sarah Bunbury, or a Waldegrave, or in perpetuating the negligent, honest exterior of the authors of the Rambler, the Traveller, and of almost every one whom the public admiration gave a currency for abilities, beauty, rank, or fashion: the very chair that is immortalized in Mrs. Siddons' tragic muse, where is will have as much celebrity as the chair of Pindar, which for so many ages was shown in the Porch at Olympia.

'This chair, then, of Sir Joshua Reynolds may rest, very well satisfied with the reputation it has gained; and although its present possessor may not be enabled to grace it with any new ornament, yet it can surely count upon finding a most affectionate, reverential conservator, whilst God shall permit it to remain under his care.'

'Jan. 30, 1794.

No. 36, Castle-street, Oxford-market.'

The next record which I shall insert concerning Mr. Nollekens, is, a list of his principal performances, which I have arranged alphabetically, in order that the reader may readily find the bust, statue, or monument of any particular individual.

BUSTS

A.

Aberdeen, Lord
Ackland, Miss
Adam, Mr.
Alban's, Duchess of St.
Andover, Lady
*Anson,[1] Hon. Thomas
Argyle, Duchess of
Arkwright, Mr.
Arkwright, Mrs.
Asaph, Bishop of
Aubyn, Sir John St.
Aubyn, Lady St.
Auckland, Miss
Aufrere, Mr.
Aylesford, Lady

B.

Baillie, Doctor
Banks, Sir Joseph
Bathurst,[2] Lord Chancellor
Beaufort, Duchess of
*Bedford, Duke of

[1] Mr. Deville, of the Strand, having purchased of Mr. Goblet, Mr. Nollekens's principal assistant, the moulds of those Busts marked with a (*), the reader will be gratified by knowing, that casts of them may now be had as above, at a very reasonable rate.

[2] This bust is in the Registrar's-room of the Six Clerks' Office, Chancery-lane. In the Committee-room, under the same roof, is a whole-length portrait of the same Chancellor in his robes, by Dance; which has been severely cut at the lower part of the picture.

Bedford, John Duke of
Bedford, Duchess of
Barrington, Lord
Berwick, Lady
*Besborough, Lord
Bolton, Duke of
Borrows, Master
*Bradell, Mrs.
Brook, Lord
Brownlow, Lord
Brownlow, Lady
Brownlow, Lady
*Burney, Admiral
Burney, M.D.
*Burney, Rev. Doctor

C.

*Canning, Hon. George
Carlisle, Lord
Carr, Mr. John
Castlereagh, Lord
Cavendish, Lord Frederic
*Cavendish, Lord George
Chambers, Doctor
Charles II. King of England
Chatham, Lord
*Charlemont, Lord
Charlemont,[1] Lady
Clair, Miss Le
Coke, Mr.
Colpoys, Admiral
Coote, Sir Eyre
Cornelli, Mrs.
Coutts, Mr.
*Cowper, Lord
Cromwell, Oliver
Cumberland, His R. H. William Duke of

D.

Darnley, Lord
*Darnley, Lady
Dashwood, Mr. Bateman
Denison, Mr.
Devonshire, Duke of
Dillon, Lord
Donegal, Marquis
Dorset, Duke of
Drummond, Provost[2]
Dunning, Mr.
Dysart, Lady

E.

Ellis, Mrs.
*Erskine, Lord

F.

Farr, Hon. Edward
Finch, Mr. Thomas

---

[1] I have heard Northcote declare, that, in his opinion, the bust of Lady Charlemont is the finest of Nollekens's productions; and, indeed, that he considered it equal to any antique.

[2] George Drummond, so often Provost of Edinburgh, ranks very high among the benefactors of the Royal Infirmary in that city. In memory of its obligations, a bust of him has been placed in the Hall. It was done by Nollekens, and bears the highly complimentary inscription, of 'George Drummond, to whom his country is indebted for all the benefits which it derives from the Royal infirmary.' —*History of Edinburgh*.

*Fitzpatrick, General
Fitzwilliam, Lord
Foley, Mr.
Folkes, Lady
Fox, Hon. Charles James[1]
Fraine, Mr.
Fraser, Simon

G.

*George III. King of England
*Gainsborough, Lord
Garrick, Mr. David
Gower, Lord
Gower, Lord G. L.
*Gower, Lady
Gordon, Duke of[2]
Goldsmith, Oliver
Grafton, Duke of
*Granby, Marquis
*Grenville, Lord
*Grenville, Hon. Thomas
Grey, Lord
Gregory, Mr.
*Gwydir, Lord

H.

Hamilton, Mr.
Harringdon, Mr.
Hawkesbury, Lady
Heartley, Lady Louisa
*Helen's, Lord St.
Hillesbury, Lord
Holford, Mr. Robert
*Holland, Lord
Howard, the Hon. Mrs.
Howard, Mrs.

J.

Johnson, Bishop
*Johnson, Doctor[3]
Jersey, Lord

[1] It is said that the Empress Catherine of Russia placed Fox's bust by Nollekens between those of Cicero and Demosthenes. She had no fewer than *twelve* busts of Mr. Fox in marble, all executed by Nollekens, to give as presents.

'To the memory of Charles James Fox,' written by Mr. Roscoe, under a bust of him by Nollekens, in a Temple erected to his memory, upon the banks of the Clyde, by Mr. Todd, of Glasgow.

Champion of Freedom! whose exalted mind
Grasp'd at the general good of human kind!
Patriot! whose view could stretch from pole to pole,
And, whilst he bless'd his country, loved the whole!'

[2] This bust of the Duke of Gordon is considered one of Nollekens's finest works.

[3] At Nollekens's sale, Mr. Chantry requested me to bid for the first cast of this head of Dr. Johnson. Upon my asking him how far he would go for it, he observed, 'You buy it, for I shall think it cheap at any price; as it is, in my opinion, by far the finest head our friend ever produced;' and, indeed, it seemed to be considered so by another bidder, who made me pay ten guineas for it, almost four times the money Nollekens charged for the common casts.

K.

Keate, George
Keith, Lord
Key, Rev. Mr.
Keebel, Mr.
King, Admiral
Kirby, Mrs.

L.

Lake, Lord
Lauderdale, Lord
Levi, Moses
Lee, Mr.
*Liverpool, Lord
Liverpool, Lady
Lucan, the Daughter of Lord

M.

Madox, Mr.
Malone, Anthony
*Mansfield, Lord
Mansolini, Anna, at Bologna
Manners, Lady
Mathias, Mr.
Marchant, Master
Maud, Mr.
Maud, Mrs.
Meath, Bishop
*Milton, Lord
Mitford, Master
Moira, Lord
Monck, Lady Elizabeth
Montagu, Mr.
Mulgrave, Lord

N.

Neal, General
*Newcastle, Duke of
Newborough, Lord
Newborough, Lady
North, Hon. Dudley

O.

Orme, Robert

P.

Paoli, General
Parr, Count
Peranesi, J. B.
Pelham, Hon. Mr.
Pelham, Hon. Mrs.
*Perceval, Hon. Spencer [1]
Percy, Lord
Petre, Lord
*Pitt, Hon. William [2]
Popham, Mr.
Pringle, Sir John

R.

Richards, Mr.
Richards, Mr. John
Roberts, Doctor

---

[1] In a letter by Nollekens, dated November 27th, 1812, with which I have lately been favoured by the Rev. Henry Crowe, of Bath, to whom it is addressed, it is stated that his price for a bust in marble was then one hundred and fifty guineas; to which he adds that he had at that time orders for fifteen busts of Mr. Perceval at that price.

[2] The busts of Pitt and Fox, according to the theatrical phrase, were called 'Nollekens's *stock* pieces', for they were always in requisition.

Robinson, Sir William
Robinson, Sir Sept.
Rockingham, Marquis of
Roos, Lord
Rutland, Duke of
Rutland, Duchess of
Rutland, Duchess of, Isabella
Russia, Empress of

S.

Salesbury, Lady
Saville, Sir George
Simmonds, Daughter of Mr.
Somerset, Duke of
Spencer, Lord
Spencer, Lord Robert
Stanhope, Sir William
Stafford, Marquis of
*Sterne, Rev. Laurence
Stonor, Mr.
Stroonlof, General
Stuart, Lord Henry
Stuart, Sir John
Sykes, Sir Christopher

T.

*Taylor, Mr.
Townley, Mr. Charles
Townley, Mr. John
Trevor, Bishop
Tulmarsh, Mr.

W.

*Wales, His Royal Highness Prince of
*Wales, Her Royal Highness Princess of
Waddell, Mr. William
*Warwick, Lord
Welch, Mr. Saunders
Welch, Mrs. wife to the above
Wellesley, Marquis
*Wellesley, Hon. Pole
*Wellesley, Hon. William
*Wellington, Duke of
West, B. P. R. A.
*Whitbread, Samuel
Woodburne, Colonel
Woodhouse, Mr.
*Wyndham, Hon. William
*Wynne, Sir W. W.
William III. King of England

Y.

*York, His Royal Highness Duke of
York, Her Royal Highness Duchess of

MONUMENTS EXECUTED BY MR. NOLLEKENS

A.

Ashburton, Lord

B.

Bathurst, Lord
Barwell, Henry
Bateman, Lord
Baring, John
Besborough, Lord
Boston, Lord
Boscawen, Mr.
Birch, Taylor
Bodwell, Mr.
Booth, Sir Charles

Boyn, Lady
Boyde, Lady
Buckworth, Mr.

C.

Coke, Mrs.[1]
Champion, Major
Chase, Mr.
Cunliffe, Sir Foster

D.

Darby, Mrs.
Dashwood, Sir John
Davenport,
Dorset, Duke of
Dysart, Lord

E.

Earl, Mrs.
Elwes, Mr.

F.

Finch, Rev. Dr.
Fuller, John

G.

Goldsmith, Oliver

H.

Howard, Mrs.[2]
Hill, Joseph

I.

Irwin, Lady
Irby, Mrs.

J.

Jervoise, Mrs.

K.

Keate, George
Kent, H. R. H. Duke of

L.

Leigh, Lord
Long, Charles[3]
Lovaine, Lord

M.

Mackenzie, Stewart
Manners, Lord Robert
Mitford, Mrs.
Mordant, Sir J.
Mortman, Mr.
Mynell,

N.

Noel, General

P.

Pinfold, Sir Thomas
Pringle, Sir John

[1] This monument cost about 2000*l*. The whole of the figures were carved by Goblet.

[2] It has been roundly asserted, that Nollekens took the composition of this monument from that erected to the Cardinal Richelieu. Be this as it may, the figure of the child alone is equal to any thing ancient or modern, and the praise bestowed on that, Nollekens is unequivocally entitled to. The figure of Religion, in this monument, was carved by Goblet.

[3] This monument, consisting of a boy with an inverted torch, was erected at Saxmundham: for a notice and drawing of which I have been obliged to the Rev. John Mitford, Editor of an edition of Gray's Works, published in 1814.

R.

Robinson, Sir Sept.

S.

Salesbury, Sir Thomas
Sand, Lord
Standish, Mr.
Sayer, Admiral
Southell, Edward
Seymour, Lady Anne
Spencer, Earl
Shipley, Mrs.[1]
Stuart, Sir Charles

T.

Talbot, Lady
Trevers, Lord
Tyrell, Sir J.

W.

Willis, Dr. Robert
Wyndham, William
Wyndham, Family
Worcester, Bishop
Wynn, Lady

STATUES EXECUTED BY MR. NOLLEKENS IN MARBLE

Denison, Robert ...	For a Mausoleum.
Denison, William ...	
Diana	Marquis of Rockingham.
Juno	Ditto.
Mercury	Lord Yarborough.
Pitt, Hon. William ...	Senate-house, Cambridge.
Rockingham, Marquis of	Earl Fitzwilliam.
Venus[2]	Marquis of Rockingham.
Venus chiding Cupid[3] ...	Lord Yarborough.
Venus	Mr. Chamberlayne, Hampshire.
Venus anointing her hair	Bought at Mr. Nollekens's auction by Mrs. Palmer.

[1] The wife of the late Bishop of St. Asaph, who was a brother of Shipley, the drawing-master, of the Strand, where Nollekens went to draw of an evening when a boy.

[2] A noble Lord when viewing Mr. Nollekens's statue of Venus perfuming her hair, asked the artist from whence he took the idea of thus employing her. Surely it must have been from Homer? Nollekens made no reply; in fact, he knew very little of Homer.

[3] Nollekens was so provoked by an accident which happened to one of his figures during the exhibition at Somerset House, that he threatened F. M. Newton, the Secretary, who made light of the affair, should this Venus be in any way injured, to break every bone in his skin.

Among the few chimney-pieces executed by Mr. Nollekens, one of a superior kind was sent to Edinburgh for Mr. Scott.

Mr. Nollekens also executed five masks upon keystones for Somerset House, after drawings made purposely by Mr. Cipriani. He likewise executed orders of a very inferior kind, by putting them out to be done by the masons of the New-road; the profits of which were not inconsiderable, as he never gave them more than a quarter of what he charged himself.

As the manner in which every man of talent advances in his art is interesting to the enquiring mind, I have extracted, from a set of the Royal Academy Exhibition Catalogues, the subjects produced by Mr. Nollekens as they stand chronologically.

No. 1771.

139 A bust of a nobleman, in marble.
140 A model of Bacchus.
141 A ditto, Pætus and Arria, a group.

1772.

168 A bust of a gentleman, in marble.
169 A statue of Bacchus, ditto.[1]

1773.

211 A statue in marble, representing Venus taking off her sandal.
212 Cupid and Psyche, in basso-relievo.
213 Hope leaning on an urn.
214 Portrait of a young lady.

1774.

190 A bust of his Majesty, in marble.

1775.

208 A bust of a nobleman, in marble.
209 Venus chiding Cupid, a model.
210 A bust, ditto.

---

[1] The original beautiful little model from which this statue was carved, is in the possession of my friend John Gawler Bridge, Esq.

1776.

199 A statue of Juno, in marble.
200 A bust, ditto.
201 A bust, in marble.
202 A ditto.

1777.

249 A bust of a nobleman, in marble.
250 Ditto of a gentleman, ditto.
251 Ditto ditto ditto.
252 A bust of a gentleman, in marble.
253 Ditto of a lady, a model.
254 Ditto of a gentleman, ditto.

1778.

216 A marble group of Venus chiding Cupid.
217 A statue of Diana.
218 A model of two children, designed for a monument.
219 A bust of a gentleman.

1779.

217 A bust of a nobleman, in marble.
218 Ditto of a general.
219 A model of a monumental figure.

1782.

529 A monumental bas-relievo.
535 A figure of Adonis.
556 A Cupid sharpening his arrow.

1783.

464 Figure of Mercury, in marble.

1784.

497 Bust of a lady.
498 Bust of a nobleman.
520 Bust of a lady.

1785.

635 Busto of a gentleman.

1788.

597 A monumental figure.
605 A monumental figure.
647 Figure of Britannia.

1789.

605 Bust of a gentleman.

1790.

660 Lord Robert Manners expiring in the arms of Victory, intended by the late Duke of Rutland for a monument to be placed in the chapel at Belvoir Castle.

1791.

632 Bust of a gentleman.
633 Bust of a lady.

1792.

498 A bust of a lady.

1793.

585 Bust of a lady.
652 Bust of a gentleman.

1799.

622 Bust of a lady of quality.
933 Bust of a nobleman.
940 Bust of a lady.
951 Bust of a nobleman.
961 Bust of a nobleman.
972 A Venus.

1800.

988 Bust of a gentleman.
989 Bust of a nobleman.
1031 Venus anointing her hair.
1082 A monumental group, to the memory of a lady who died in child-bed, supported by Religion.

1801.

999 Portrait of Mr. John Townley, in the form of a Terminus.
1001 Bust of his Grace the Duke of Bedford.
1002 Bust of a young gentleman.
1007 A bust of Lady Hawkesbury.
1008 Bust of a young gentleman.
1009 Bust of Lord Petre.
1024 A sepulchral bas-relief to the memory of the late Duke of Dorset.

1802.

1059 Bust of Dr. Burney.
1063 A design for a monument to the memory of a late celebrated general, supported by Wisdom and Justice.
1064 A sketch: the Graces.
1065 Bust of the late Duke of Bedford.
1066 A sketch: Adam and Eve.
1067 A sketch of a monument for a naval officer expiring in the arms of Victory.
1073 Bust of the Hon. C. J. Fox.
1074 A sketch; the Slaughter of the Innocents.

1803.

924 Pudicity: a sketch.
925 Bust of Mr. Stonor.
930 Lot and his two Daughters: a sketch.
931 Dædalus and Icarus: a sketch.
932 The Judgment of Paris: a sketch.
1024 Bust of Lord Moira.

1804.

947 Portrait of the Hon. C. Grey.
948 Portrait of Miss C. Symmons.
949 Portrait of the Right Hon. General Fitzpatrick.
950 Portrait of the Earl of Lauderdale.
951 Portrait of Lord R. Spencer.

1805.

689 A sketch of an Hercules.
690 A sketch of a Faun playing.
693 A medallion of the late Miss Ackland, daughter of J. Ackland, Esq.
694 A sketch of Laocoon and his Sons.
695 A bust of the Marquis of Stafford.
711 A design of a monument, intended for Westminster Abbey, to the memory of two naval officers.
783 A bust of the late C. Townley, Esq.
789 A bust of T. W. Coke, Esq.

1808.

969 Bust of the Hon. Mr. Pelham.
970 Bust of the Earl of Darnley.
971 Bust of the Marquis Wellesley.
972 Bust of His Grace the Duke of Bedford.
978 Bust of His Royal Highness the Prince of Wales.
979 Bust of Sir W. W. Wynne, Bart.

1810.

753 His Grace the Duke of Rutland.
766 Bust of the Right Hon. Lord Brownlow.
874 Bust of the Hon. Mrs. Pelham.
875 Bust of the Right Hon. Lord Grenville.
876 Bust of her Grace the Duchess of Rutland.
885 Bust of the Countess of Charlemont.
886 Bust of the Right Hon. Lord Mulgrave.

1811.

926 A model of a monument of the late Mrs. Coke of Holkham.
938 Bust of the Right Hon. Lord Castlereagh.
940 Bust of the Right Hon. Earl of Chatham.
941 Bust of the Right Hon. Lord Grenville Leveson Gower.
948 Bust of the Right Hon. W. Wellesley Pole.
949 Bust of the Right Hon. Lord Roos.
951 Bust of the Right Hon. George Canning.
952 Bust of Admiral Sir J. Colpoys, K.B.

1812.

933 Bust of the Countess of Charlemont.[1]
934 Bust of Benjamin West, Esq. President of the Royal Academy.
936 Bust of the Right Hon. Lord Brooke.
937 Bust of Lord Gwydir.

[1] In order to account for the recurrence of the same bust, it may be proper to remark that Mr. Nollekens in many instances exhibited the model one year, and a carving from it in marble in the next.

1813.

919 Bust of the Right Hon. Spencer Perceval.
925 Bust of the Right Hon. Lord G. Cavendish.
926 Bust of H. R. H. the Duke of York.
935 Bust of the Marquis of Wellington.

1814.

781 Bust of S. Whitbread, Esq. M.P.
789 Bust of the Earl of Charlemont.
792 Bust of his Grace the Duke of Grafton.
800 Bust of Earl Cowper.
801 Bust of the Earl of Aberdeen.

1815.

888 Bust of Lord Erskine.
889 Bust of the Rev. C. Burney, D.D.
895 Bust of the Earl of Egremont.

1816.

932 Bust of Lord St. Helen's.
950 Bust of T. Coutts, Esq.
951 Bust of the Earl of Liverpool.
961 Bust of his Grace the Duke of Newcastle.

Such, and so numerous, are the works of Nollekens, who will long be remembered, not only as having held a conspicuous rank among contemporary Artists, in an era abounding in men of genius; but as having, by assiduity rarely surpassed, and parsimony seldom equalled, amassed a princely fortune; from which, however, his avaricious spirit forbade him to derive any comfort or dignity, excepting the poor consolation of being surrounded, in his dotage, by parasites who administered to his unintellectual enjoyments, and flattered even his infirmities, in the hope of sharing the vast property which Death would force him to resign.

INDEX

'In order to render this little work a book of reference to the London topographer as well as to the historian' (see p. 139), all the references to London topography are arranged alphabetically under the heading 'London'.